Britain Best Holidays 2002

including sections for
Channel Tunnel • Ferries • Airports • plus Golfing & Activity section

with
Hotels • Guesthouses • Farms • Inns Caravans & Camping • Self-catering

For Contents see Page 31
For Index of towns/counties see back of book

FHG Publications Paisley

Part of IPC Country and Leisure Media

LONDON

YORKSHIRE DALES to SCOTTISH HIGHLANDS

Almost 600 superb, personally inspected, self catering holiday properties in beautiful rural and coastal locations. From Yorkshire's Dales and Moors, the Lakes and Cumbria, through Northumbria and the Borders to Scotland's Highlands and Islands. Cosy cottages to country houses, many welcome pets and most are open all year.

Dales Holiday Cottages

01756 799821 & 790919
Skipton, North Yorkshire, BD23 2AA.
www.dalesholcot.com
on-line booking, with secure server.

SELF-CATERING

BED AND BREAKFAST IN LONDON
Stay with us or one of our selected families.

Comfortable, centrally located quiet Edwardian home. Great base for sightseeing, close to the river, traditional pubs, lots of local restaurants and antique shops. Excellent transport facilities – easy access to West End, Theatreland, shopping, Harrods, museums, Albert Hall, Earls Court and Olympia Exhibition centres. Direct lines to Eurostar (Waterloo), Airports: Heathrow, Gatwick (Victoria), Stansted (Liverpool Street). Bed and Continental Breakfast Prices: Double/Twin/Triple £24 pppn; Single £34.00; Children's reductions. Smoking only in garden.

Sohel and Anne Armanios
67 Rannoch Road, Hammersmith, London W6 9SS
Tel: 020 7385 4904 • Fax: 020 7610 3235
IDEAL LONDON LOCATIONS

BOARD

- Central London
- ★★ B&B Hotel
- Family friendly • Est. 30 years
- Tranquil position
- Set in a garden square
- 2 mins Paddington Station
- Airlines check-in 15 mins Heathrow on Express Link

E-mail: info@aafalcon.co.uk
• Website: www.aafalcon.co.uk
• Tel: +44 (0) 20 7723 8368
• Fax: +44 (0) 20 7402 7009
11 Norfolk Sq., Hyde Park North, London W2

Our guests first and always
Affordable prices from: Singles £35, Doubles £55
For latest seasonal prices please call

- En-suite facilities
- Very clean and comfortable
- Close to tourist attractions and shops
- Triple and Family rooms
- Full freshly cooked English breakfasts

FALCON HOTEL

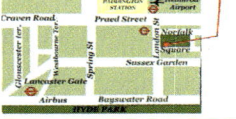

BOARD

Please mention Britain's Best Holidays when enquiring

LONDON

DALMACIA HOTEL
71 Shepherds Bush Road, Hammersmith, London W6 7LS

Tel 020 7603 2887 **Fax: 020 7602 9226**

www.dalmacia-hotel.co.uk

- All rooms en suite
- Prices include breakfast & VAT
- Tea & Coffee facilities
- Hairdryers & Euro electrics
- Satellite TV & remote
- Direct-Dial Telephones
- Underground 800 metres
- Visa, Mastercard & Switch accepted

Single £49

Double £60

Triple £81

LONDON
Tourist Board and Convention Bureau

Bring this voucher for 10% off

Please mention Britain's Best Holidays when enquiring

CORNWALL/CUMBRIA

SELF-CATERING

POLZEATH
Overlooking golden sands –
Flats, Chalets and Cottages.

Many guests, their children and pets return regularly to relax in two-and-a-half acres of Pinewood grounds.

The 12 self-contained units all have colour television. Table tennis, a launderette and baby-sitting are available (cots and highchairs too). Own path to beach (surfing and rock pools), shops, tennis, crazy golf and children's playground (four-five minutes' walk). Sea-fishing trips, golf, riding, sailing and wind-surfing are within three-four miles. Superb coastal walks start right at the door so a car is not essential. Spring and Autumn are kindest for your pets.

Interested? Please phone or write for colour brochure to:
**LEN SHARPE, PINEWOOD FLATS, POLZEATH, WADEBRIDGE, CORNWALL PL27 6TQ
or Tel: 0120 886 2269 for availability**

BOARD

Penryn House

Situated in the tranquil heart of the beautiful fishing village of Polperro, we pride ourselves on providing comfort and excellent service in an informal atmosphere.

Relax in our fireside lounge bar or guest lounge; enjoy the restaurant with fresh home cooking using local produce.

Our comfortable en suite bedrooms have TV, telephones, clock/radios, hairdryers and well-stocked courtesy trays.

Easy access to the coastal paths and a short journey to the Eden Project, National Trust properties and Dartmoor and Bodmin Moor. Also close to golf, riding, fishing and sailing.

The Coombes, Polperro PL13 2RQ
Tel: 01503 272157

A good value, worry-free getaway.

BOARD

A warm, friendly welcome awaits you at Lakeside Guest House, at the northern tip of Bassenthwaite Lake. We have eight bedrooms (seven en suite) with TV, radio/alarm, hairdryer, shoe cleaning and tea/coffee facilities. Delicious home-cooked breakfast, or relax in our residents' lounge.

The Lake District National Park, Hadrian's Wall and Scottish Borders are easily accessible for a day visit or take advantage of sailing, rowing, fishing, walking and golf available nearby.

Lakeside is a non-smoking establishment. Sorry, no pets.

Self-catering lodge also available (sleeps 3/4)
PLEASE CALL FOR OUR COLOUR BROCHURE

Lakeside Guesthouse
Dubwath, Bassenthwaite Lake, Cumbria CA13 9YD
Tel: 01768 776358 • Fax: 01768 776163

RAC
♦♦♦♦

SELF-CATERING

No. 1 Cuddy's Hall

A self-catering holiday cottage situated on a smallholding in a rural area of North Cumbria. Surrounded by Kershope Forest (part of Kielder Forest Park). Excellent walks and cycle routes. Cosy and spotlessly clean. Sleeping five (one double, one twin and one single bedroom).

• Open all year • Short Breaks available •Central touring area for Cumbria, Northumberland and Scotland • See also advertisement in main section of book under Cumbria.
Full details from: Mrs Joanna Furness, 2 Cuddy's Hall, Bailey, Newcastleton, Roxburghshire TD9 0TP • Tel: 016977 48160

Please mention Britain's Best Holidays when enquiring

CUMBRIA/DEVON

Elder Grove — Lake Road, Ambleside, Cumbria

Enjoy quality accommodation and service in our Victorian house, conveniently situated for walking or sightseeing and close to Ambleside with many shops and restaurants. We offer 10 comfortable bedrooms, all with private bathrooms, also colour televisions, kettle tray, hair dryers and radios. Start the day with a choice of breakfast from a full Cumbrian breakfast to a lighter bite served in our unique Lakeland dining room, and in the evenings relax in our bar or lounge. We have parking, central heating and ask for no smoking please.

ETC ♦♦♦♦

*Contact Paul and Vicky McDougall for brochure and tariff on 015394 32504
e-mail: info@eldergrove.co.uk Website: www.eldergrove.co.uk*

Greenhowe Caravan Park
Great Langdale, English Lakeland.

**Greenhowe Caravan Park
Great Langdale, Ambleside,
Cumbria LA22 9JU**

Greenhowe is a permanent Caravan Park with Self Contained Holiday Accommodation. Subject to availability Holiday Homes may be rented for short or long periods from 1st March until mid-November. The Park is situated in the Lake District half-a-mile from Dungeon Ghyll at the foot of the Langdale Pikes. It is an ideal centre for Climbing, Fell Walking, Riding, Swimming, Water-Skiing. Please ask about Short Breaks.

*Winners of the Rose Award 1983-2000. ETC Grading "Very Good".
For free colour brochure*
Telephone: (015394) 37231   Fax: (015394) 37464   Freephone: 0800 0717231

PETS WELCOME
Fishing, Walking, Pure Escapism

Tranquil quality cottages overlooking two fishing lakes amidst Lakeland's beautiful Eden Valley countryside, only 30 minutes' drive **equidistant** from Ullswater, North Pennines, Hadrian's Wall and Scottish Borders. Beds freshly made for you. Peace and freedom in your surroundings. Exclusive residents' coarse and fly fishing on your doorstep. Good golf courses nearby. Cottages are clean, well maintained and equipped. Laundry area. **PETS VERY WELCOME.** Exceptional wildlife and walking area. Relax and escape to your home in the country.
Tel/Fax: 01768 898711   6 - 10pm for availability and bookings. Or SAE to -
Crossfield Cottages, Kirkoswald, Penrith CA10 1EU.   **24 hour Brochure Line: 01768 898711**

ETC ★★★

THE AVONCOURT HOTEL
TORRS WALK AVENUE, ILFRACOMBE TEL: 01271 862543

Chris and Tony welcome you to their friendly family-run hotel. The hotel is situated in a quiet private road adjacent to National Trust land. It faces south with panoramic views of town and countryside. All bedrooms are on first or ground floor and the excellent food and relaxed atmosphere will make your holiday a memorable one. The heated rooms are en suite with tea/coffee making facilities and colour TV. There is also a cosy licensed bar and a TV lounge. Ample parking.

Please mention Britain's Best Holidays when enquiring

"Easily the best choice of cottages in Devon..."

...and comfortably the best value

Contact us now for a **free** colour guide and unbiased recommendation service to the 400 best value cottages around Devon's unspoilt National Trust Coast

North Devon Holiday Homes

Barnstaple, Devon EX31 1BD
Tel: 01271 376322 Fax: 01271 346544
e-mail:info@northdevonholidays.co.uk/ website: northdevonholidays.co.uk/

DEVON

BOARD

CHILDREN STAY FREE

Sandy Cove Hotel

ETC ★★★

Sandy Cove Hotel stands in 20 acres of cliff, coast and garden. The hotel restaurant overlooks the sea and cliffs with spectacular views of the bay. You will probably wonder how we can do it for the price when we offer a FIVE COURSE MEAL including seafood platters with lobster; smoked salmon and steak. Every Saturday a Swedish Smorgasbord and Carvery carved by the chef and followed by dancing till late. All bedrooms have colour TV, telephone, teamaking and are en suite. The cocktail bar overlooks the bay and you have the use of the hotel's 80° heated indoor pool and recreation centre with sauna, sunbed, gym equipment and whirlpool. ALL FREE OF CHARGE.

Enquire from the Hotel for details of Special Offers throughout the Year!

Prices include 5 Course Evening Meal and Coffee.
CHILDREN FREE ACCOMMODATION
Children under 5 – completely FREE incl. meals
PLEASE RING FOR FREE COLOUR BROCHURE

Sandy Cove Hotel
**COMBE MARTIN BAY
DEVON EX34 9SR
TEL: (01271) 882243 AND 882888**
FAX: (01271) 883830   E-mail: RGI4003483@aol.com

**INDOOR POOL
HEATED TO 80°
WITH ROLLING SIDES
TO ENJOY THE SUN**

Please mention Britain's Best Holidays when enquiring

DEVON

SELF-CATERING

Self-catering you can trust

There's no better way to experience the charms of North Devon than from the comfort and luxury of a Marsdens holiday cottage.

Our full colour brochure includes properties each inspected by our staff, as well as graded by the English Tourism Council, and most are commended for quality.

Romantic whitewashed cottages, nestling in the heart of North Devon's idyllic countryside and Exmoor or secluded beach houses, just a stone's throw away from some of Britain's most spectacular and unspoilt coastlines...whatever your idea of a perfect holiday, we can help make it a reality. Little wonder, then, that so many of our customers come back for more.

For more details, call today for your free brochure, or see our cottages on our website.

01271 813777 for free colour brochure

www.marsdens.co.uk
email: holidays@marsdens.co.uk

24 HOUR ON LINE BOOKING AVAILABLE

MARSDENS
COTTAGE HOLIDAYS
**2 The Square, Braunton,
North Devon EX33 2JB**

Please mention Britain's Best Holidays when enquiring

DEVON/DORSET

SELF-CATERING

Rosewood

Rosewood is a delightful opportunity to enjoy one of the prettiest areas in Devon. Relax on the "suntrap" patio amidst a garden full of colour! Clovelly, Rosemoor Gardens, Milky Way, Tarka Trail, coastal walks, swimming, golf, surfing, canoeing and fishing nearby. Shops and pubs 1½ miles. Beaches within 3 miles. On the perimeter of a 45 acre stock farm Rosewood offers – attractive entrance hall leading to a large, well equipped kitchen/diningroom with electric cooker and microwave. Tastefully furnished sittingroom, TV, stereo, woodburner. Downstairs bathroom. Three bedrooms, one double, one double and single, one single. Private parking. Children Welcome. Sorry, no pets. Terms from £250.

Knotty Corner, Bideford, North Devon EX39 5BT
Telephone: Mrs Christine Thompson 01237 451514
E-mail: christhompson81@hotmail.com

BOARD

Spacious and comfortable, Start House is situated in a quiet hamlet, one mile from Slapton. All the bedrooms overlook a beautiful valley running south-east to Slapton Ley and the sea. The delicious breakfasts, traditional or vegetarian, are cooked to order using local produce. Evening meals are available by arrangement. We are an ideal base for walkers and wildlife enthusiasts, and garden lovers will find much of interest in our large garden. Open all year for Bed and Breakfast from £23, we also have a self-catering flat for two people. Non-smokers only. Full details on request.

START HOUSE

Start House, Start, Slapton, Kingsbridge TQ7 2QD (01548 580254)

SELF-CATERING

Rediscover Paradise

Parkfield Holiday Apartments have 1, 2 or 3 bedrooms, each fully equipped with TV and video, own lovely views.
Parkfield's landscaped grounds accommodate a children's play area, ample parking and kennels for dogs which are welcome.
The tranquil setting is a short drive to beaches, coastal walks, traditional pubs, steam railways and other family attractions.
For more information please phone/fax or write to June or Roy at:
Parkfield Apartments, Claddon lane,
Maidencombe, Torquay TQ1 4TB Tel: 01803 328952
website: www.parkfieldapartments.co.uk

Parkfield Holiday Apartments

BOARD

THE POACHERS INN

Piddletrenthide, Near Dorchester DT2 7QX
01300 348358; Fax: 01300 348153

Country Inn set in the heart of lovely Piddle Valley. Within easy reach of all Dorset's attractions. All rooms en suite with colour TV, tea and coffee, telephone; swimming pool (May-September). Riverside garden, restaurant where Half Board guests choose from à la carte menu at no extra cost.

Bed and Breakfast – £30 per person per night.
Dinner, Bed and Breakfast – £42 per person per night. 10% discount for seven nights.

Low Season Breaks – two nights Dinner, Bed and Breakfast – £84 per person.
Third night Dinner, Bed and Breakfast – FREE. (Oct - April) Send for brochure.

ETC ◆◆◆◆
AA ◆◆◆◆

Please mention Britain's Best Holidays when enquiring

DORSET/GLOUCESTERSHIRE/HAMPSHIRE

BOARD

Nethercroft
Winterbourne Abbas, Dorchester DT2 9LU
Tel: 01305 889337

This country house with its friendly and homely atmosphere welcomes you to the heart of Hardy's Wessex. Central for touring the many places of interest that Dorset has to offer, including Corfe Castle, Lyme Regis, Dorchester, Weymouth, Lulworth Cove, etc. Lovely country walks and many local attractions. Two double rooms, one single, washbasins or en suite. Separate bathroom, shower and toilets. TV lounge, dining room. Large garden. Open all year. Central heating. Car essential, ample parking. Bed and Breakfast from £18.
Take A35 from Dorchester, we are the last house at the western edge of the village.

BOARD

THE FOUNTAIN INN & LODGE
Parkend, Royal Forest of Dean, Gloucestershire GL15 4JD.

Traditional village inn, well known locally for its excellent meals and real ales. A Forest Fayre menu offers such delicious main courses as Lamb Steak In Woodland Berry Sauce and Gloucester Sausage in Onion Gravy, together with a large selection of curries, vegetarian dishes, and other daily specials. Centrally situated in one of England's foremost wooded areas, the inn makes an ideal base for sightseeing, or for exploring some of the many peaceful forest walks nearby. All bedrooms (including one specially adapted for the less able) are en suite, decorated and furnished to an excellent standard, and have television and tea/coffee making facilities. Various half-board breaks are available throughout the year.

Tel: 01594 562189 • Fax: 01594 564438 • E-mail: TheFountainInn@aol.com
Website: www.SmoothHound.co.uk/hotels/fount.html

CARAVANS

One visit
is never enough

For the perfect camping and touring holiday, nothing compares to Sandy Balls.

For a FREE brochure call now on
01425 653042
quoting ref: FHG CC02

Sandy Balls Holiday Centre, Godshill, Fordingbridge, Hants, SP6 2JZ. England. Fax: +44 (0)1425 653067
e.mail: post@sandy-balls.co.uk www.sandy-balls.co.uk

OPEN ALL YEAR ROUND

NORFOLK/SOMERSET

PETERSFIELD HOUSE HOTEL

Horning, Norfolk NR12 8PF • Tel: 01692 630741 • Fax: 01692 630845
e-mail: reception@petersfieldhotel.co.uk • website: www.petersfieldhotel.co.uk

The Petersfield House Hotel is a family owned Country House Hotel situated in a peaceful location in the heart of the beautiful Norfolk Broads, within easy reach of the North Norfolk Coast. Our landscaped gardens and moorings are an ideal setting to relax and enjoy our beautiful Broadland surroundings. The restaurant offers light lunches, Table d'Hote and an extensive à la Carte menu. Saturday night dinner dances and themed evenings are held regularly. Bargain breaks are available from £55.00 per person. Open throughout the year.

For further information and a brochure please call us on the above number or visit our website.

Court Farm

Exford, Exmoor, Somerset TA24 7LY   ETC ★★★
Tel/Fax: 01643 831207 e-mail: beth@courtfarm.co.uk

For B&B our cosy farmhouse, reached down a quiet lane, has much character with inglenook fireplaces and exposed beams. Our two 2-bedroom cottages each take 5 people. They have large kitchen/diners, sitting room, 2 bedrooms (double with Gothic 4-poster and twin bunk beds). Snowdrop Cottage sleeps two people. There is a sitting/dining room and well-equipped kitchen. The double bedroom has en suite bathroom and the garden has rustic furniture.

We provide all electricity, full oil central heating and all bed linen in the price. Cottages are open 52 weeks and we have ample parking. For more details visit our website: www.courtfarm.co.uk
Horses, pets: We have stabling and grazing available. Well behaved pets are welcome in the cottages.

'LANA'

Hollow Farm, Westbury-sub-Mendip,
Near Wells, Somerset BA5 1HH
Tel: 01749 870635
Mrs Sheila Stott

Modern farmhouse accommodation on working farm. Gently elevated site offering beautiful views over the moors and Somerset Levels, Glastonbury Tor in the distance and the Mendip Hills. En suite rooms including fridge, hair dryer, tea/coffee making facilities, shaver point, colour TV and central heating. Non-smoking. Terms from £20 pppn (reduced rates 3 nights or more, children under 12 years old £15.

Ralegh's Cross Inn

Brendon Hill, Exmoor, Somerset TA23 0LN
Tel: (01984) 640343 Fax: (01643) 851227

Perched high in the beautiful Brendon Hills, Exmoor National Park, Ralegh's Cross Inn offers comfortable and tastefully refurbished en suite rooms, all non-smoking with colour TV and hospitality tray. A full à la carte menu with freshly prepared starters, home-cooked main courses and home-made desserts is available daily. We're also famous locally for our tasty Farmer's Carvery. A walker's, rider's and fisherman's paradise with many nearby places of interest for the tourist too.

Open all year. Colour brochure available.

Please mention Britain's Best Holidays when enquiring

SOMERSET/SUFFOLK/EAST SUSSEX/NORTH YORKSHIRE

CARAVANS

S^T AUDRIES BAY *Holiday Club*

West Quantoxhead, Nr. Minehead, Somerset TA4 4DY
Tel: 01984 632515 Fax: 01984 632785

The family holiday centre on the Somerset coast. Facilities include indoor heated pool, family entertainment programme, wide range of sports and leisure facilities, licensed bar and restaurant and an all day snack bar. Situated only 15 miles from the M5, near Exmoor at the foot of the Quantock Hills. Well maintained level site with sea views. On site shop. Family owned and managed. Half board holidays available in comfortable chalets, selfcatering in luxury caravans. Touring caravans and tents welcome. Luxury holiday homes for sale. No hidden extras, children FREE most weeks.

website: www.staudriesbay.co.uk

BOARD

BROADLANDS HOTEL & LEISURE

BRIDGE ROAD, OULTON BROAD LOWESTOFT SUFFOLK NR32 3LN

The Broadlands Hotel is located within walking distance of Lake Lothing in the area known as the Norfolk Broads. We have 52 rooms, all en suite, with hospitality tray, hairdryer, TV and telephone. We also have an indoor swimming pool, steam room and spa bath. Restaurant and residents' bar. Car park available.

Tel: 01502 516031 • Fax: 01502 501454

BOARD

FAIRLIGHT COTTAGE

Warren Road (via Coastguard Lane), Fairlight, East Sussex TN35 4AG

Peace, tranquillity and a warm welcome await you at our comfortable country house, adjoining 650 acres of country park in an area of outstanding natural beauty. Close to ancient towns of Rye, Battle, Winchelsea and Hastings. Panoramic sea views from large balcony. Centrally heated en suite bedrooms with beverage trays and colour TV. Comfortable guest lounge. Delicious breakfasts; dinner by arrangement – bring your own drinks. No smoking. Ample parking. Pets welcome.

B&B from £25 pppn. • Single supplement • Dinner £15.00
Janet & Ray Adams • 01424 812545 • e-mail: fairlightcottage@supanet.com

---

BOARD

The Fox & Hounds Inn

Residential 16th Century Coaching Inn set amidst the beautiful North York Moors.
Freshly prepared dishes served every lunchtime and evening.
Superb en suite accommodation available, with all rooms having glorious views.
Open all year. Special Breaks available October to May.
Situated between Castleton and Danby on the Fryup Road.

ETC ♦♦♦♦ *For bookings please*
Tel: 01287 660218 or Fax: 01287 660030
Ainthorpe, Danby, Yorkshire YO21 2LD

Please mention Britain's Best Holidays when enquiring

ANGLESEY & GWYNEDD/POWYS/BORDERS/DUMFRIES & GALLOWAY

BRYN BRAS CASTLE

LLANRUG, Nr. CAERNARFON, NORTH WALES LL55 4RE
Tel & Fax: Llanberis (01286) 870210

This romantic neo-Romanesque Castle is set in the gentle Snowdonian foothills near North Wales' mountains, beaches, resorts and heritage. Built in 1830, on an earlier structure, the Regency castle reflects peace not war - it stands in 32 acres of tranquil gardens, with views. Bryn Bras offers distinctive and individual Apartments, for 2-4 persons, within the castle, each having spacious rooms radiating comfort, warmth and tranquillity and providing freedom and independence. All highest grade.

Many inns and restaurants nearby. This welcoming castle, still a family home, particularly appeals to romantic couples.

Open all year including for Short Breaks.
e-mail: holidays@brynbrascastle.co.uk
website: www.brynbrascastle.co.uk
BROCHURE SENT WITH PLEASURE.

SELF-CATERING

THE BEACONS

In the heart of the magnificent Brecon Beacons National Park, an elegant Georgian townhouse with beautifully appointed standard, en suite and luxury period rooms. The candlelit restaurant offers fine food and wines (5 nights). Cosy cellar bar and comfortable lounge, private parking and secure bike store. Excellently situated for Brecon's historic centre and National Park exploration. A lovely house with a welcoming atmosphere.
Two nights DB&B from £65.90 to £88.90 per person.

AA ♦♦♦ • RAC ♦♦♦
Ring Stephen & Melanie Dale for more information.
16 Bridge Street, Brecon LD3 8AH
Telephone & Fax: 01874 623339
E-mail: beacons@brecon.co.uk
Website: www.beacons.brecon.co.uk

WTB ★★★ *Guest House*

BOARD

BAILEY MILL COURTYARD

Bailey Mill, Newcastleton, Roxburghshire TD9 0TR
Tel 016977 48617 • Fax: 016977 48074

A warm welcome awaits you from Pam and Ian on this small farm holiday complex, nestling on the Roxburghshire/Cumbrian border. The rural self-contained apartments create a courtyard setting or enjoy Bed and Breakfast or Full Board riding holidays in the farmhouse. Colour TV and Sky link; heating (oil), electricity and linen included in the rent. On site sauna, toning table, jacuzzi, games room, laundry, babysitting, fully licensed bar and meal service. Enjoy walking or trekking through surrounding forests. Eight horses and six mountain bikes available. Central touring area for Lake District, Hadrian's Wall and Scotland. Colour brochure available

Self catering £78 – £498 weekly • B&B from £20 per person   ETC ★★/★★★ Self Catering

BOARD/SELF-CATERING

THE Urr Valley HOTEL

A privately owned hotel set in 14 acres of mature woodland and gardens within walking distance of Castle Douglas. Galloway is one of the most beautiful and diverse areas of countryside in Britain - offering everything from golden sandy beaches to grouse moors, and picturesque harbour villages to forest walks. Panelled walls, log fires and a cosy Sportsman's bar with over 50 whiskies to offer. 17 en suite rooms, with colour TV, Tea & Coffee making facilities, hair dryers, trouser press and direct dial telephones.

The Urr Valley Hotel is delighted to welcome dogs and the intimate atmosphere of the building is increased by the presence of two 'in house' golden retrievers. We allow dogs into all areas except those where food is served and we have excellent outdoor watering facilities. The grounds are perfect for exercising pets and their owners, and we look forward to welcoming you in the near future. AA ★★

The Urr Valley Hotel,
Ernespie Road, Castle Douglas,
Dumfries & Galloway, Scotland DG7 3JG
Tel: 01556 502188   Fax: 01556 504055
e-mail:info@urrvalleyhotel.co.uk website: www.urrvalleyhotel.co.uk

BOARD

Please mention Britain's Best Holidays when enquiring

HIGHLANDS/PERTH & KINROSS

SELF-CATERING

Crubenbeg Holiday Cottages

Rural self-catering cottages in the central Highlands where one can relax and stroll from the doorstep or take part in the choice of many sporting activities in the area. We have a children's play area, a Games Room, Pond stocked with trout for fishing and a barbecue. Pets welcome.

Newtonmore, Inverness-shire. PH20 1BE
Tel: 01540 673566 • Fax: 01540 673509
E-mail: enquiry@crubenbeg.com • Website: www.crubenbeg.com

BOARD

Newmill Farm
STB ★★★ B&B

Mrs Ann Guthrie, Newmill Farm, Stanley, Perthshire PH1 4QD
Telephone: (01738) 828281 e-mail: guthrienewmill@sol.co.uk
website: www.newmillfarm.co.uk

Newmill Farm is situated only six miles from Perth, in 330 acres of lovely farmland. Accommodation comprises twin & double en suite rooms and a family room with private bathroom; lounge, sittingroom, diningroom; bathroom, shower room and toilet. The many castles and historic ruins around Perth are testimony to Scotland's turbulent past. Situated at the "Gateway to the Highlands" the farm is ideally placed for those seeking some of the loveliest unspoilt scenery in Western Europe. Many golf courses and trout rivers nearby. Bed and breakfast from £18, Evening meal on request. Reductions and facilities for children. Pets welcome.

SELF-CATERING

VALE OF ATHOLL COUNTRY COTTAGES

Rather nice Country Cottages converted from former barns, set around a delightfully landscaped garden courtyard, each with private patio & furniture. One to three bedrooms sleeping 2-6 all beautifully appointed to STB 3 STAR. The award-winning loft restaurant is only across the courtyard only minutes from Blair Castle & the House of Bruar. Sorry no pets, full colour brochure available.

INDOOR: LUXURY POOL, PADDLING POOL, JACUZZI, STEAM, SAUNA, GYM, STANDING TAN.
OUTDOOR: TENNIS, PRIVATE FISHING, NEXT TO GOLF COURSE.

Vale of Atholl Country Cottages, Blair Atholl, by Pitlochry, Perthshire PH18 5TE
Tel: 01796 481567 Fax: 01796 481511

Publisher's Note

While every effort is made to ensure accuracy, we regret that FHG Publications cannot accept responsibility for errors, omissions or misrepresentations in our entries or any consequences thereof. Prices in particular should be checked because we go to press early. We will follow up complaints but cannot act as arbiters or agents for either party.

The Association of Scotland's Self Caterers

Selected Self-Catering Holidays in Scotland

Members of the ASSC are committed to high and consistant standards in self catering. Contact your choice direct and be assured of an excellent holiday.

Brochures: 0990 168 571 • Web site: www.assc.co.uk

Owner-Operators ready to match our standards and interested in joining are requested to contact our Secretary for information – 0990 168 571

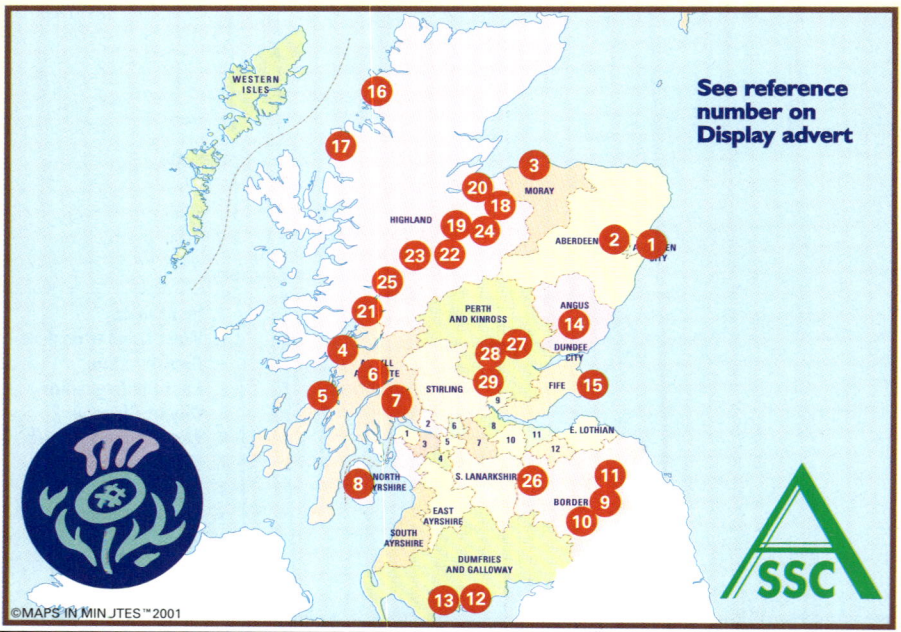

ABERDEEN, BANFF & MORAY/ ARGYLL & BUTE

THE ROBERT GORDON UNIVERSITY   TEL: 01224 262134 FAX: 01224 262144

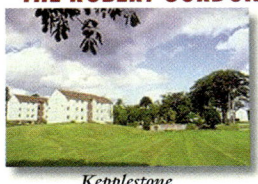
Kepplestone

King Street

The Robert Gordon University in the heart of Aberdeen offers a wide variety of accommodation to visitors from June through to August. Aberdeen is ideal for visiting Royal Deeside, Castles and historical buildings, playing golf or touring the Malt Whisky Trail. The city itself is a place to discover, and Aberdonians are friendly and welcoming people. We offer self-catering accommodation for individuals or for groups of people at superb rates. Each of our flats is self-contained, centrally heated, fully furnished and suitable for children and disabled guests. All flats have colour TV and some have microwave facilities. Bed linen and cooking utensils are all provided as is a complimentary 'welcome pack' of basic groceries. Towels available on request. Each residence has laundry and telephone facilities as well as ample car parking.

Contact: The Robert Gordon University, Business and Vacation Accommodation, Customer Services Dept, Schoolhill, Aberdeen. AB10 1FR
e-mail: accommodation@rgu.ac.uk • website: www.scotland2000.com/rgu

---

THE GREENKNOWE

A comfortable, detached, renovated cottage in a quiet location at the southern edge of the village of Kintore. Ideally situated for touring castles and pre-historic sites or for walking, fishing and golfing. The cottage is on one level with large sittingroom facing south and the garden. Sleeps four.
•Walkers Welcome Scheme•

Terms £225–£350 per week including electricity and linen.
Mr & Mrs P. A. Lumsden, Kingsfield House, Kingsfield Road, Kintore, Aberdeenshire AB51 0UD
Tel: 01467 632366 • Fax 01467 632399 • e-mail: kfield@clara.net

---

North East Farm Chalet *Near Elgin*

One 'A' frame chalet on working farm. 'Habitat' furnished, fully equipped for two – six people, colour TV, bed linen, duvets. Beautiful rural location in Moray – famous for flowers – district of lowlands, highlands, rivers, forests, lovely beaches, historic towns, welcoming people. Excellent local facilities. Moray golf tickets available. *From £180–£300 (January-December)*
Contact: Mrs. J. M. Shaw, Sheriffston, Elgin, Moray IV30 8LA
Tel & Fax: 01343 842695 • e-mail: jennifer.shaw@moray.gov.uk

Cologin
Country Chalets
Oban
All Scottish Glens have their secrets: let us share ours with you – and your pets !

Call now for our colour brochure and find out more
Open all year round. Rates from £150 to £475 per week. Autumn Gold breaks and mid-week deals also available
MRS LINDA BATTISON, COLOGIN FARMHOUSE, LERAGS GLEN, BY OBAN, ARGYLL PA34 4SE Tel: (01631) 564501 • Fax: (01631) 566925
E-mail: cologin@west-highland-holidays.co.uk
Web: www.west-highland-holidays.co.uk

STB
★★
★★★
and
★★★★
Self
Catering

APPIN HOLIDAY HOMES
Midway between Oban and Fort William
. . . in the Scottish Highlands

Fine hill and shoreline walks amid natural beauty. Warm welcoming lodges and lochside caravan, set apart within landscaped park. Fishing (FREE), boating, cycling, pony trekking, Sealife Centre, Castle Stalker, licensed inn, all nearby. Lots to do and see. Price guide £165 to £395 per unit weekly. Sleeps two to five. Free colour brochure.

MR & MRS I. F. WEIR, APPIN HOLIDAY HOMES, APPIN, ARGYLL PA38 4BQ
TEL: 01631 730287 –   WEB: www.appinholidayhomes.co.uk • E-MAIL: info@appinholidayhomes.co.uk

Please mention Britain's Best Holidays when enquiring

ARGYLL & BUTE/AYRSHIRE & ARRAN/BORDERS

6. Mr & Mrs E. Crawford
Blarghour Farm
Loch Awe-side, by Dalmally, Argyll PA33 1BW
Tel: 01866 833246   Fax: 01866 833338
e-mail: blarghour@aol.com • web: www.blarghour.com

At Blarghour Farm one may choose from four centrally heated and double glazed holiday homes sleeping from two to eight people, all enjoying splendid views of lovely Loch Awe. Kitchens are well appointed, lounges tastefully decorated and furnished with payphone, TV and gas fire, beds are made up and towels supplied while the two larger houses have shower rooms in addition to bathrooms, all with shaver point. The two larger houses are suitable for children and have cots and high chairs. No pets are allowed.
Open all year. Centrally situated for touring. Illustrated brochure on request.

7. WEST LOCH TARBERT, ARGYLL – DUNMORE COURT

Four cottages in architect design conversion of home farm on the estate of Dunmore House. Spacious accommodation for 5-7 persons. All have stone fireplaces for log fires. Bird-watching, fishing and walking. Easy access to island ferries. Pets welcome. Open all year. Colour brochure.
From £165-£425. STB ★★

Telephone: 01880 820654
e-mail: dunmorecourtsc@cs.com

Contact: Mrs Amanda Minshall,
Dunmore Court, Kilberry Road,
Near Tarbert, Argyll PA29 6XZ

8. ARRAN HOLIDAY PROPERTIES
Isle of Arran Booking Agents for Self Catering Accommodation

Properties throughout the Island
All villages – all dates • STB Quality Assured*
Short Breaks Available • Major Credit Cards accepted

Please ask for our brochure, One Call Does It All:
Weekdays/Office hours 01770 302303/302310
Evenings & weekends 01770 860 556
www.arranproperties.co.uk

Invercloy House, Brodick, Isle of Arran KA27 8AJ
* All our properties have applied for grading under the STB Quality Assurance Scheme

9. Plum Braes Barn & Edmonston, Ednam, Near Kelso

Plumbraes Barn has been converted into 3 cottages (Cockle Kitty Cottage, Garden Bank and Plum Tree Cottage), all with private gardens, wood burners, central heating, king-size Austrian sleigh beds and kitchens including dishwashers. Laundry. Private parking. **Edmonston** is a large chalet-style farmhouse with 5 bedrooms (one ground level). Central heating, log fire, lounge with panoramic views, kitchen, paddocks, free fishing and wildflower meadow.
Details from: Mrs M. Stewart, Cliftonhill Farm, Ednam, Kelso TD5 7QE
• Tel: 01573 225028 • e-mail: archie@sol.co.uk
websites: www.plumbraesbarn.freeserve.co.uk • www.edinburghholidaycottages.com

10. Mill House, Letterbox & Stockman's Cottages
– Three recently renovated, quality Cottages, each sleeping four, on a working farm three miles from Jedburgh. All ideal centres for exploring, sporting holidays or getting away from it all. Each cottage has two public rooms (ground floor available). Minimum let two days. Terms £190-£330. Open all year. Bus three miles, airport 54 miles.
Green Tourism Business Award – SILVER.
Mrs A. Fraser, Overwells, Jedburgh, Roxburghshire TD8 6LT
Telephone: 01835 863020 • Fax: 01835 864334

BORDERS/DUMFRIES & GALLOWAY/DUNDEE & ANGUS/FIFE/HIGHLANDS

QUIXWOOD

Abbey St Bathans, Duns TD11 3RS • 01361 840233

Come and enjoy a comfortable break in our spacious semi-detached farm cottage. It is conveniently situated on a quiet road with all round views of beautiful rolling farmland, yet only 2.5 miles from the A1, giving easy access to North and South and all parts of the Scottish Borders. Edinburgh is less than one hour away by car.

The cottage sleeps 6 people and has a cot and highchair. There are 2 single bedrooms, one twin and one double bedroom, bathroom with shower, a dining kitchen and a large lounge with TV and video. All rooms are on ground floor level. Linen and towels are provided and central heating is included. There is a large garden to relax in or for children to play. For people who enjoy walking, the Southern Upland Way is just a mile away, or a 15 minute drive takes you to the coast.

Prices range from £170-£250 per week with short break terms available.

BAREND HOLIDAY VILLAGE SANDYHILLS, DALBEATTIE

Scandinavian style log chalets, centrally heated for all year round use, with TV and video. On site launderette, bar, restaurant, sauna and indoor heated pool. The chalets accommodate up to eight people, from £240-£640 p.w. including linen, heating and swimming. Pets welcome.

Tel: 01387 780663; Fax: 01387 780283
website: www.barendholidayvillage.co.uk

STB ★★★ Self Catering

Rusko Holidays Rusko, Gatehouse of Fleet, Castle Douglas DG7 2BS
Tel: 01557 814215 • Fax: 01557 814679 • www.ruskoholidays.co.uk

Lovely, spacious farmhouse and cosy comfortable cottages on beautiful private estate near beaches, hills, forests and golf course. Use of tennis court, loch and river fishing with tuition given, wonderful area for walking, riding and sailing. Sleeps 2-10. Rates £150-£680. Pets, including horses, welcome. TV, telephone, washing machine, enclosed garden.
STB ★★ to ★★★ Self Catering, Walkers & Cyclists Welcome, Disabled Cat 3, Welcome Host

---

THE WELTON OF KINGOLDRUM by Kirriemuir, Angus DD8 5HY

Three luxurious self-catering properties on a secluded working farm, in a spectacular setting with superb panoramic views. Ideal for hillwalking and bird-watching. An excellent base for golf, fishing, riding, skiing, shooting etc. and touring the glens, coast and castles.

Detached Cottage – STB ★★★★ Disabled category 3. Sleeps 4
Semi-detached Bungalow – STB ★★★ Bedrooms en suite. Sleeps 4
Studio flat – STB ★★★ en suite. Sleeps 2

For further information and brochure contact Jenny Scott.
Telephone / Fax: 01575 574743
e-mail: weltonholidays@btinternet.com
website: http://www.cottageguide.co.uk/thewelton
Open all year. Short breaks available. Prices £165 - £350

The Old Bank House Restaurant and Apartments

In an enviable position overlooking its own beach just west of the harbour in Anstruther. Four letting apartments, sleeping 2-8 persons, all en suite, with telephone, central heating and fully equipped kitchens. Double occupancy rate from £20 pppn. Ricardo Sparrow, Old Bank House, 23-25 High St, Anstruther, FIFE KY10 3DQ • Tel: 01333 310189
• E-mail:ricardosrest@hotmail.com • www.undiscoveredscotland.co.uk/anstruther/oldbank/

Clashmore Holiday Cottages
Our three croft cottages at Clashmore, are the ideal base for a holiday in the Highlands. They are cosy and fully equipped, with linen provided. Nearby there are sandy beaches, mountains and lochs for wild brown trout fishing. Children welcome but sorry no pets. Open all year, sleeping two-five £160-£330 per week.

Contact Mr and Mrs Mackenzie, Lochview,
216 Clashmore, Stoer, Lochinver, Sutherland IV27 4JQ
Tel & Fax: 01571 855226 e-mail: clashcotts@supanet.com

Please mention Britain's Best Holidays when enquiring

HIGHLANDS

17 **Innes Maree Bungalows, Poolewe IV22 2JU**
Only a few minutes walk from the world-famous Inverewe Gardens in magnificent Wester Ross. A purpose built complex of six superb modern bungalows, all equipped to the highest standards of luxury and comfort. Each bungalow sleeps six with main bedroom en suite. Children and pets welcome. Terms from £185 to £425 inclusive of bed linen and electricity. Brochure available. **Tel & Fax 01445 781454** STB ★★★★
E-mail: innes-maree@lineone.net • Website: www.poolewebungalows.com

18 **BLACKPARK FARM** Westhill, Inverness IV2 5BP
This newly built holiday home is located one mile from Culloden Battlefield with panoramic views over Inverness and beyond. Fully equipped with many extras to make your holiday special, including oil fired central heating to ensure warmth on the coldest of winter days. Ideally based for touring the Highlands including Loch Ness, Skye etc. Extensive information is available on our website. A Highland welcome awaits you.
Tel: 01463 790200 • Fax: 01463 794342 • e-mail: i.alexander@blackpark.co.uk • website: www.blackpark.co.uk

19 **ALVIE HOLIDAY COTTAGES**
A secluded and beautiful Highland Estate with breathtaking views over the Spey Valley and the Cairngorm Mountains beyond. Woodland walks, fishing on the River Spey plus many other family activities available nearby. Three traditional farm cottages or two flats in the Estate's Edwardian shooting lodge. All furnished to the most comfortable standards.
For further details e-mail: info@alvie-estate.co.uk or visit our website: www.alvie-estate.co.uk
Or contact: Alvie Estate Office, Kingcraig, Kingussie PH21 1NE • Tel: 01540 651255 • Fax: 01540 651380

20 *Balblair Cottages*
Croy, Inverness IV2 5PH • Tel: 01667 493407

Three Cottages, imaginatively created from a stone farm steading on a small livestock holding, 10 miles east of Inverness. Each cottage has its own south facing garden with patio furniture, double glazing, electric central heating and wood burning stove, making Balblair an ideal all year round base for a Highland Holiday. Cawdor Castle, Fort George, Clava Cairns, Inverness and Nairn are all within ten miles, while Loch Ness, the Cairngorms, the Isle of Skye and even John O' Groats can be visited in a day by car. Bed linen and towels are provided. Telephone. Children and Pets welcome.
E-Mail: FHG@Balblaircottages.co.uk • Website: www.balblaircottages.co.uk

21 ## Cuilcheanna Cottages
Onich, Fort William PH33 6SD

A small peaceful site for self catering with three cottages and eight caravans. Situated in the village of Onich, 400 yards off the main road. An excellent centre for touring and hill walking in the West Highlands.

For further details please phone
01855 821526 or 01855 821310

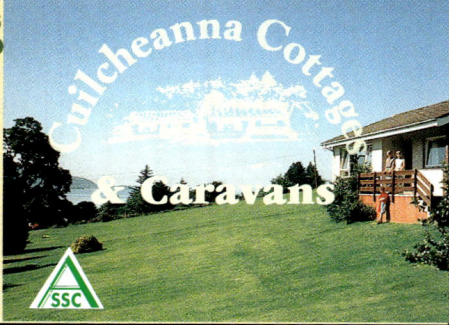

22 **Croft Holidays,** Newtonmore PH20 1BA (01540 673504) STB ★★★ SELF-CATERING
Thoughtfully renovated cottages in quiet, picturesque surroundings, on outskirts of lovely Highland village in "Monarch of the Glen" country. Central heating, open fire, TV, fridge/freezer, microwave, washer, drying room, downstairs en suite bedroom, disabled access. Waymarked trails, golf course, restaurants, pubs, shops, museums in village. Central for touring, many tourist attractions, great area for walking (guided walk included), birdwatching, cycling, pony trekking, water sports. Short breaks or long stays welcome all year. Cottages sleeping 4- £140 to £290 per week, sleeping 6- £180 to £460 per week, incl. heating. Well behaved pets welcome.
Brochure/special offers. e-mail: fhg@croftholidays.co.uk   website: www.croftholidays.co.uk

Please mention Britain's Best Holidays when enquiring

HIGHLANDS/LANARKSHIRE

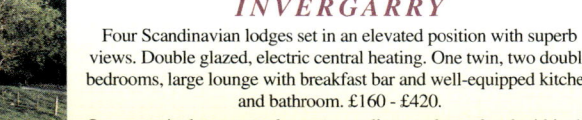

HIGH GARRY LODGES
INVERGARRY

Four Scandinavian lodges set in an elevated position with superb views. Double glazed, electric central heating. One twin, two double bedrooms, large lounge with breakfast bar and well-equipped kitchen and bathroom. £160 - £420.

One attractively converted cottage nestling at a lower level within the confines of this small working farm. One double, one twin bedroom. Tastefully renovated to a high standard. £190 - £475.

Mr & Mrs Wilson, High Garry Lodges,
Ardgarry Farm, Faichem, Invergarry,
Inverness-shire. PH35 4HG

Tel: 01809 501226
Fax: 01809 501307

Visitors may participate at feeding times
Ideal for touring West Highlands. Fishing,
Golf and Bird-watching.
Brochure available.

SUMMER WATERSPORTS AND WINTER SKIING

Loch Insh Log Chalets, Kincraig,
Inverness-shire PH21 1NU
Tel: 01540 651272 Fax: 01540 651208
e-mail: office@lochinsh.com
website: www.lochinsh.com

Just six miles south of Aviemore these superb log chalets are set in 14 acres of woodland in the magnificent Spey Valley, surrounded on three sides by forest and rolling fields with the fourth side being half a mile of beach frontage. Free watersports hire for guests, 8.30-10am/4-5.30pm daily. Watersports, salmon fishing, archery, dry ski slope skiing. Hire/instruction available by the hour, day or week mid April to end October. Boathouse Restaurant on the shore of Loch Insh offers coffees, bar meals, children's meals and evening à la carte. Large gift shop and bar. Children's adventure area, interpretation trail, ski slope, mountain bike hire and stocked trout lochan are open all year round. Ski and snowboard hire, instruction available December-April.

Pets Welcome! Free Fishing!

RIVERSIDE LODGES
INVERGLOY, SPEAN BRIDGE, INVERNESS-SHIRE PH34 4DY
TEL: 01397 712684
e-mail: enquiries@riversidelodge.org.uk
website: www.riversidelodge.org.uk

Peace and quiet are synonymous with Riverside, where our three identical lodges each sleep up to six people. Accessible from the A82 but totally hidden from it, our 12 acres of woodland garden front on Loch Lochy. Cots, linen, boat, fishing tackle, barbecue, all for hire. Pets welcome. Easy access and assistance to launch boats from our own beach. Fishing from the Gorge, Loch or private Lochan.
Brochures provided on request.

CARMICHAEL COUNTRY COTTAGES
Westmains, Carmichael, Biggar ML12 6PG • Tel: 01899 308336 • Fax: 01899 308481

200 year old stone cottages in this 700 year old family estate. We guarantee comfort, warmth and a friendly welcome in an accessible, unique, rural and historic time capsule. We farm deer, cattle and sheep and sell meats and tartan - Carmichael of course. Open all year. Terms from £180 to £480.

15 cottages with a total of 32 bedrooms. Private tennis court and fishing loch, cafe, farm shop and visitor centre
e-mail: chiefcarm@aol.com • website: www.carmichael.co.uk/cottages

---

When making postal enquiries, remember that a stamped, addressed envelope is always appreciated

Please mention Britain's Best Holidays when enquiring

PERTH & KINROSS

LAIGHWOOD HOLIDAYS
NEAR DUNKELD
For your comfort and enjoyment

We can provide properties from a large de luxe house for eight to well-equipped cottages and apartments for two - four, some open all year. All are accessible by tarmac farm roads. Laighwood is centrally located for sightseeing and for all country pursuits, including golf, fishing and squash. Sorry, no pets. Brochure (state which size of property), on request from Laighwood Holidays, Laighwood, Dunkeld PH8 0HB.

Telephone: 01350 724241   Fax: 01350 724212
e-mail: holidays@laighwood.co.uk • website: www.laighwood.co.uk

---

Mains of Murthly
Aberfeldy PH15 2EA

Two beautifully situated stone built holiday cottages on a working farm, overlooking Aberfeldy, distance 1¼ miles
- Fully equipped for three to five persons.
- Log fires • Children welcome.
- Pets accepted • Ample parking.

Fishing available on private stretch of River Tay. Golf courses nearby and excellent recreation centre with swimming pool in Aberfeldy.
Available all year, with terms from £180.

Further details contact Mrs Pamela McDiarmid, Tel & Fax 01887 820427

RIVERSIDE LOG CABINS

Dunira, Comrie, Perthshire PH6 2JZ
Tel & Fax: 01764 654048 • e-mail: riverside@logcabins.demon.co.uk

Sitting on the bank of the River Earn, in an Area of Outstanding Natural Beauty, these three bedroom cabins are ideally situated to explore most of Scotland. Oban and the West Coast (via Glencoe), St Andrews, Stirling and the shopping and cultural Meccas of Glasgow and Edinburgh are all within a 90 minute drive. Many local golf courses, beautiful walks, fishing, sailing, water skiing, riding and country sports nearby. Inverness and Loch Ness (including the monster?) provide an excellent day trip.
Colour brochure available on request.

NOTE

All the information in this guide is given in good faith in the belief that it is correct. However, the publishers cannot guarantee the facts given in these pages, neither are they responsible for changes in ownership or facilities that may take place after the date of going to press.
Readers should always satisfy themselves that the facilities they require are available and that the terms, if quoted, still apply.

Britain's Best Holidays 2002
Golf & Activity Holidays

Dungannon Golf Club, Co.Tyrone — Painting by Seamus Keenan

Available from most bookshops, the year 2002 edition of
The GOLF GUIDE, where to play, where to stay
covers details of every UK golf course – well over 2800 entries – for holiday or business golf.
Hundreds of hotel entries offer convenient accommodation, accompanying details of the courses – the 'pro', par score, length etc.
Holiday Golf in Ireland, France, Portugal, Spain, The USA and Thailand.   In association with GOLF MONTHLY

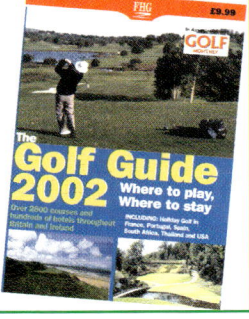

£9.99 from bookshops or larger newsagents
FHG Publications,
Abbey Mill Business Centre, Paisley PA1 1TJ

Please mention Britain's Best Holidays Golf and Activity Section when enquiring

CORNWALL/DEVON/MERSEYSIDE

SELF-CATERING

LANGFIELD MANOR   Broadclose, Bude, Cornwall EX23 8DP

Treat yourself to a special holiday amidst the magnificent splendours of the North Cornwall coastline. Seven quality apartments in this fine Edwardian house with its lovely games room situated in one-and-a-half acres of delightful, sheltered, south facing gardens. Come and enjoy the conservatory and the sun terrace set around the 36ft swimming pool. A superb centre for any holiday, out in the country yet only three minutes' walk to the shops and 10 minutes' walk to Bude's sandy beaches. Here we are just across the lane from the Bude and North Cornwall Golf Club. Children welcome. Sorry, no pets

Tel: 01288 352415 • Fax: 01288 353416
E-mail: info@langfieldmanor.co.uk
website: www.langfieldmanor.co.uk

BOARD

WHITSAND BAY HOTEL   Portwrinkle, By Torpoint, Plymouth, Cornwall PL11 3BU
Tel: 01503 230276 • Fax: 01503 230329
website: www.cornish-golf-hotels.co.uk
e-mail: earlehotels@btconnect.com

★ Spectacularly sited with 100 miles of sea views
★ Sandy beach easily accessible ★ Fully licensed
★ Children of all ages especially welcome ★ Facilities include **indoor heated swimming pool**, leisure/fitness complex, **own 18-hole golf course**, clay pigeon shooting; shark/sea/freshwater fishing and horse riding nearby. **Self-catering accommodation** in grounds with full hotel facilities. Near the Eden Project and The Lost Gardens of Heligan. **AA/RAC Merit Award, Recommended by Quality Hotel Guides.**

SELF-CATERING

HOPE BARTON BARNS
Tel: 01548 561393
★★★★ Open All Year

Nestling in its own valley close to the sandy cove, Hope Barton Barns is an exclusive group of 17 stone barns in two courtyards and three luxury apartments in the converted farmhouse. Superbly furnished and fully equipped, accommodation ranges from a studio to four bedrooms, sleeping two to 10. Heated indoor pool, sauna, gym, lounge bar, tennis court, trout lake and a children's play barn. We have 35 acres of pastures and streams. Farmhouse meals. Ample parking. Golf, sailing and coastal walking nearby. A perfect setting for family summer holidays, walking in Spring/Autumn or just a "get away from it all" break. Free range children and well behaved dogs welcome. For full colour brochure please contact: **Mike or Judy Tromans.**

Hope Cove – Near Salcombe – South Devon – TQ7 3HT

BOARD

The Golf Links Hotel
85 The Promenade, Southport PR9 0JN
Tel: 01704 530405

Privately owned and personally managed. An elegant Victorian house standing in its own grounds, ideally situated on the promenade overlooking the golf course and beach. Easy walking distance to town, theatre, marine lake, park and beach. The hotel has a comfortable public bar which offers excellent bar meals, a sun patio overlooking 18 hole golf course.
Open all year. Families welcome. Pets welcome.
Excellent value for money and a friendly service.
Terms from £19.50 to £23.50

ESSEX

Stoke by Nayland

Set in the heart of Dedham Vale, an area captured in the paintings of Gainsborough and Constable, Stoke by Nayland offers some of the finest golfing facilities in East Anglia. Each of the two courses, named after the aforementioned artists, provides an outstanding and enjoyable experience for all standards of golfers. Both are par 72. The Gainsborough was the first to be constructed and runs for 6515 yards of the 300-acre complex. It features undulating fairways and many water hazards, including two of the four lakes which form an integral part of both courses. The 10th hole was voted one of the best in East Anglia by the PGA Eastern Region.

Trees are a feature of both courses, numbering around 60,000 altogether, so finding the fairway is essential. The Constable, slightly longer at 6544 yards, offers splendid views of Stoke by Nayland Church and quickly presents an early challenge, with approach shots over water needed to hit the third and fourth greens. The final holes on both courses provide a testing finish, requiring a drive from tee to green over the largest of the lakes. The substantial multi-purpose clubhouse offers restaurant and bar facilities, along with a spike bar, new leisure facility including gym, pool, sauna and spa now open with a 30 bedroomed hotel.

Useful Information

Society Packages for 12 or more: 36 holes. Lunch and dinner from £47.50. Various others on application.

Green Fees:
Weekdays £25 per round, £40 per day, weekends £35 per round

Restrictions:
Handicap certificates required at weekends (am).

How to get there:
Leave the M25 at Junction 28 onto the A12 to Colchester. Take the A134 to Sudbury, Stoke-by-Nayland Golf Club is on the B1068, signposted from the A134 at Leavenheath.

Accommodation:
30 Bedroomed Hotel opened early 2000. All rooms overlook the courses and lake.

Other Facilities:
Leisure complex including gym, indoor pool, sauna and spa, health and beauty treatments. 20 bay covered driving range. 300 seater banqueting facility

The Stoke-by-Nayland Club Ltd
Keepers Lane, Leavenheath, Colchester, Essex. CO6 4PZ
Tel: 01206 262836   Fax: 01206 263356
e-mail: info@golfclub.co.uk   web: www.stokebynaylandclub.co.uk

ARGYLL & BUTE/DUNDEE & ANGUS/FIFE

GIGHA HOTEL

Spend a relaxing holiday on the Isle of Gigha (pronounced Gee-a). Meaning "God's Isle", it is surely a little piece of heaven. Explore the sandy bays, lochs, easy walks, cycling, golf, birds and wildlife. But for the jewel in the crown visit Achamore Gardens, with rhododendrons, azaleas and semi-exotic plants. Grass airstrip, 9-hole golf course and a regular ferry service. Holiday Cottages also available.

Gigha Hotel, Isle of Gigha, Argyll PA41 7AA
Tel: 01583 505254   Fax: 01583 505244
Website: www.isle-of-gigha.co.uk
STB ★★★ Hotel

GLENESK HOTEL & COUNTRY CLUB

High Street, Edzell,
Tayside. DD6 7TF
Tel: 01356 648319
Fax: 01356 647333

Close your eyes and think of a hotel that's set in some of Scotland's loveliest countryside. A hotel which offers traditional three star luxury and that vital ingredient of owner attention. Then picture a hotel that's only a short wedge away from a championship golf course, and is within a short drive of such courses as Carnoustie and St Andrews. Visualise a hotel that offers hunting, shooting, fishing and hill walking breaks, and a luxurious country club with beautiful indoor pool and leisure facilities to relax in after a long day in the outdoors. Finally imagine a hotel which boasts cuisine from traditional Scottish breakfasts to delicious à la carte dinners.
A hotel with a reputation that's second to none.
Now turn these images into reality by visiting the Glenesk Hotel!

The Pitfirrane Arms Hotel

Crossford hotels (Dunfermline) Ltd.

The hotel is conveniently situated for touring, within easy access of Edinburgh, Glasgow and the M90 motorway. We have 38 comfortable bedrooms - 16 twin, 12 double and 10 single-bedded rooms. All rooms have private en suite facilities, colour television, tea/coffee maker, telephone and radio. We have 10 golf courses within 10 miles !

Crossford, Dunfermline, Fife KY12 8NJ
Tel: 01383 736132   Fax: 01383 621760
Website: www.scothotels.com   E-mail: info@scothotels.com

Visit the FHG website
www.holidayguides.com
for details of the wide choice of accommodation featured in the full range of FHG titles

BRITAIN'S BEST HOLIDAYS 2002

Hotels, guesthouses, farmhouses for food and accommodation. Cottages, flats, caravans, campsites for self-catering. Golfing and activity holidays.

Other FHG Publications

Recommended Country Hotels of Britain
Recommended Wayside & Country Inns of Britain
Recommended Short Break Holidays in Britain
Pets Welcome!
The Golf Guide: Where to Play/Where to Stay
Farm Holiday Guide England/Scotland/Wales/Ireland and the Channel Islands
Self-Catering Holidays in Britain
Bed and Breakfast Stops
Guide to Caravan and Camping Holidays
B&B in Britain
Children Welcome! Family Holiday and Attractions Guide

ISBN 185055 333 5

© IPC Media Ltd 2002
Cover photographs Mike Guy and Langland Bay Golf Club.
Cover design: Focus Network

No part of this publication may be reproduced by any means or
transmitted without the permission of the Publishers.

Maps: ©MAPS IN MINUTES™ 2001. ©Crown Copyright, Ordnance Survey 2001.

Typeset by FHG Publications Ltd. Paisley.
Printed and bound in Great Britain by William Clowes, Beccles, Suffolk.

Distribution. Book Trade: WLM, Unit 11, Newmarket Court, Newmarket Drive, Derby DE24 8NW
(Tel: 01332 573737. Fax: 01332 573399).
News Trade: Market Force (UK) Ltd, 247 Tottenham Court Road, London W1P 0AU
(Tel: 020 7261 6809; Fax: 020 7261 7227).

Published by FHG Publications Ltd., Abbey Mill Business Centre,
Seedhill, Paisley PA1 ITJ (Tel: 0141-887 0428 Fax: 0141-889 7204).
e-mail: fhg@ipcmedia.com

Britain's Best Holidays is an FHG publication, published by
IPC Country & Leisure Media Ltd, part of IPC Media Group of Companies.

CONTENTS

COLOUR SECTION 1-28
TOURIST BOARD RATINGS 33
READERS OFFER VOUCHERS 35-54

Board Accommodation
England 55
Scotland 93
Wales 109

SELF-CATERING Accommodation
England 113
Scotland 135
Wales 155

CARAVANS AND CAMPING
England 161
Scotland 170

GOLF & ACTIVITY HOLIDAYS
(including Narrowboat Holidays 171
CHANNEL TUNNEL, AIRPORTS & FERRIES SUPPLEMENT 177
DIRECTORY OF WEBSITE & E-MAIL ADDRESSES 182
INDEX OF TOWNS & COUNTIES 217
OTHER FHG TITLES – ORDER FORM 219

BRITAIN'S BEST HOLIDAYS 2002

Everyone has their own idea of what is the 'best' type of holiday for them with some opting for a 'meals included' holiday at one of the many small hotels, guest houses or B&B establishments to be found throughout Britain, while others prefer the freedom and economy of self-catering.

In **Britain's Best Holidays 2002** you will find a choice of all types of accommodation - Board, Self-catering and Caravan and Camping Holidays, and for those who feel that no holiday is complete without a round of golf, we have a section on Golf and Activity Holidays where you will also find a selection of Narrowboat Holidays. Most of the entries feature our unique easy-reference symbols and an explanation of these can be found at regular intervals throughout the book.

Anne Cuthbertson, Editor

HOW TO USE THIS GUIDE

The entries in **Britain's Best Holidays** are split into four main sections: **Board** (hotels, guesthouses, farms, bed and breakfast, etc.), **Self-catering**, **Caravans** (including Camping) and **Activity Holidays**. Counties are classified under each section and the headline on each page indicates this. Display advertisers also have an entry in the appropriate county section. Every advertiser therefore has a descriptive review and this is always preceded by a row of symbols, largely self explanatory. A key is given below and regularly throughout the book. Within each section the **same** symbols appear in the **same** position so that you can run your eye down each page and tell at a glance whether or not a particular service or amenity is available. You can identify very quickly those entries which do, or do not, meet your needs. You can then read the detailed review for further information and how to book.

The symbols are as follows:

Common Symbols

1-12	Months open	Car essential	Within two miles of the coast
	Pets Welcome	Sporting or special interest activities included	
	Suitable for the disabled		

BOARD
- Baby sitting available
- Children welcome
- Central heating
- Licensed

SELF-CATERING
- Linen supplied
- 2/10 Min/Max accommodated in one unit
- Shops on site or nearby
- Children welcome

CARAVANS/CAMPING
- HTC Caravans for Hire (H)
- Site for Touring Vans (T)
- Camping Site (C)
- Shops on site or nearby
- Hot water and/or showers
- Licensed

Ratings You Can Trust

  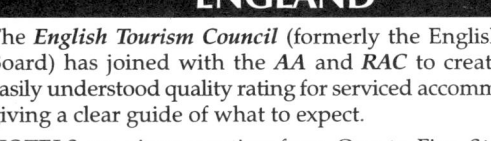

The *English Tourism Council* (formerly the English Tourist Board) has joined with the *AA* and *RAC* to create a new, easily understood quality rating for serviced accommodation, giving a clear guide of what to expect.

HOTELS are given a rating from One to Five *Stars* – the more Stars, the higher the quality and the greater the range of facilities and level of services provided.

GUEST ACCOMMODATION, which includes guest houses, bed and breakfasts, inns and farmhouses, is rated from One to Five *Diamonds*. Progressively higher levels of quality and customer care must be provided for each one of the One to Five Diamond ratings.

HOLIDAY PARKS, TOURING PARKS and CAMPING PARKS are now also assessed using *Stars*. Standards of quality range from a One Star (acceptable) to a Five Star (exceptional) park.

Look out also for the new *SELF-CATERING* Star ratings. The more *Stars* (from One to Five) awarded to an establishment, the higher the levels of quality you can expect. Establishments at higher rating levels also have to meet some additional requirements for facilities.

NB Some self-catering properties had not been assessed at the time of going to press and in these cases the old-style KEY symbols will still be shown.

SCOTLAND

Star Quality Grades will reflect the most important aspects of a visit, such as the warmth of welcome, efficiency and friendliness of service, the quality of the food and the cleanliness and condition of the furnishings, fittings and decor.

THE MORE STARS,
THE HIGHER THE STANDARDS.

The description, such as Hotel, Guest House, Bed and Breakfast, Lodge, Holiday Park, Self-catering etc tells you the type of property and style of operation.

WALES

Places which score highly will have an especially welcoming atmosphere and pleasing ambience, high levels of comfort and guest care, and attractive surroundings enhanced by thoughtful design and attention to detail

STAR QUALITY GUIDE FOR

HOTELS, GUEST HOUSES AND FARMHOUSES
SELF-CATERING ACCOMMODATION
(Cottages, Apartments, Houses)
CARAVAN HOLIDAY HOME PARKS
(Holiday Parks, Touring Parks, Camping Parks)

★★★★★★ *Exceptional quality*
★★★★ *Excellent quality*
★★★ *Very good quality*
★★ *Good quality*
★ *Fair to good quality*

In England, Scotland and Wales, all graded properties are inspected annually by Tourist Authority trained Assessors.

FHG Diploma Winners 2001

Each year we award a small number of diplomas to holiday proprietors whose services have been specially commended by our readers. The following were our FHG Diploma Winners for 2001.

England

CUMBRIA
- Mr & Mrs Haskell, Borwick Lodge, Outgate, Hawkshead, Cumbria LA22 0PU (015394 36332).
- Mrs Sue Coleman, Rockside Guest House, Ambleside Road, Windermere, Cumbria LA23 1AQ (015394 45343).

DEVON
- Mr & Mrs Menzies, Beachdown Chalet, Challaborough Bay, Kingsbridge, Devon TQ7 4JB (01548 810089).

KENT
- Mrs Pateman, Pine Lodge Touring Park, Near Bearsted, Maidstone, Kent ME17 1XH (016227 30018).

NORTHUMBERLAND
- Mr & Mrs Fearns, Bounder House, Belsay, Newcastle-upon-Tyne, Northumberland NE20 0JR (01661 881267)

SOMERSET
- Pat & Sue Weir, Slipper Cottage, 41 Bishopston, Montacute, Somerset TA15 6UX (01935 823073)

Scotland

DUMFRIES & GALLOWAY
- Mr Tweedie, Annandale Arms, High Street, Moffat, Dumfriesshire DG10 9HF (01683 220013)

HIGHLANDS
- Mrs Morrison, Nether Lochaber Hotel, Onich, Near Fort William, Inverness-shire PH33 6SE (01855 821235)

PERTH & KINROSS
- Mrs J. MacLaren, Blackcraig Castle, Bridge of Cally, Perthshire PH10 7PX (01250 886251)

HELP IMPROVE BRITISH TOURISM STANDARDS

Why not write and tell us about the holiday accommodation you have chosen from one of our popular publications? Complete a nomination form giving details of why you think YOUR host or hostess should win one of our attractive framed diplomas and send it to:
FHG Publications, Abbey Mill Business Centre, Seedhill, Paisley PA1 1TJ

Visit the FHG website
www.holidayguides.com
for details of the wide choice of accommodation featured in the full range of FHG titles

FHG READERS' OFFER 2002

Leighton Buzzard Railway
Page's Park Station, Billington Road,
Leighton Buzzard, Bedfordshire LU7 4TN
Tel: 01525 373888 • e-mail: info@buzzrail.co.uk
website: www.buzzrail.co.uk
One FREE adult/child with full-fare adult ticket

valid from 10/3/02 – 27/10/02

NOT TO BE USED IN CONJUNCTION WITH ANY OTHER OFFER

FHG READERS' OFFER 2002

Bekonscot Model Village
Warwick Road, Beaconsfield, Buckinghamshire HP9 2PL
Tel: 01494 672919 • e-mail: Bekonscot@dial.pipex.com
website: www.bekonscot.org.uk
One child FREE when accompanied by full-paying adult

valid February to October 2002

NOT TO BE USED IN CONJUNCTION WITH ANY OTHER OFFER

FHG READERS' OFFER 2002

CLAYMOORE NAVIGATION
The Wharf, Preston Brook, Warrington, Cheshire WA4 4BA
Tel Lo-Cost: 08450 900 1800
website: www.virtual-canals.com
£10 OFF a wonderful family day out on our dayboat

valid during 2002

NOT TO BE USED IN CONJUNCTION WITH ANY OTHER OFFER

FHG READERS' OFFER 2002

Cars of the Stars Motor Museum
Standish Street, Keswick, Cumbria CA12 5HH
Tel: 017687 73757 • e-mail: cotsmm@aol.com
website: www.carsofthestars.com
One child FREE with two paying adults

Valid 2002

NOT TO BE USED IN CONJUNCTION WITH ANY OTHER OFFER

FHG READERS' OFFER 2002

Windermere Steamboat Museum
Rayrigg Road, Windermere, Cumbria LA23 1BN
Tel: 015394 45565
TWO for the price of ONE (adults) OR 25% off family ticket

valid March to October 2002

NOT TO BE USED IN CONJUNCTION WITH ANY OTHER OFFER

A 65-minute journey into the lost world of the English narrow gauge light railway. Features historic steam locomotives from many countries.

PETS MUST BE KEPT UNDER CONTROL AND NOT ALLOWED ON TRACKS

Open: Sundays and Bank Holiday weekends 10 March to 27 October. Additional days in summer.

Directions: On A4146 towards Hemel Hempstead, close to roundabout junction with A505.

FHG PUBLICATIONS, ABBEY MILL BUSINESS CENTRE, PAISLEY PA1 1TJ

Be a giant in a magical miniature world of make-believe depicting rural England in the 1930's. "A little piece of history that is forever England."

Open: 10am to 5pm daily 9th February to 27th October.

Directions: Junction 16 M25, Junction 2 M40.

FHG PUBLICATIONS, ABBEY MILL BUSINESS CENTRE, PAISLEY PA1 1TJ

Claymoore Navigation, established 28 years, has 13 quality narrowboats from 2 to 10 berths for holiday hire. Short Breaks available plus: • 12-seat day boat • 50-seat restaurant/function boat • Maintenance facilities for private boats • Excellent service

Open: 8.30am to 5.30pm seven days all year. Please phone for free brochure and information

Directions: quarter-of-a-mile downhill from Junction 11 M56

FHG PUBLICATIONS, ABBEY MILL BUSINESS CENTRE, PAISLEY PA1 1TJ

A collection of cars from film and TV, including Chitty Chitty Bang Bang, James Bond cars, Del Boy's van, Fab1 and many more.

PETS MUST BE KEPT ON LEAD

Open: Daily 10am-5pm. Closed February half term. Weekends only in December.

Directions: In centre of Keswick close to car park

FHG PUBLICATIONS, ABBEY MILL BUSINESS CENTRE, PAISLEY PA1 1TJ

World's finest steamboat collection and premier all-weather attraction. Swallows and Amazons exhibition, model boat pond, tea shop, souvenir shop. Free guided tours. Model boat exhibition.

Open: 10am to 5pm 3rd weekend in March to last weekend October

Directions: on A592 between Windermere and Bowness-on-Windermere

FHG PUBLICATIONS, ABBEY MILL BUSINESS CENTRE, PAISLEY PA1 1TJ

FHG READERS' OFFER 2002

Blue-John Cavern
Castleton, Hope Valley, Derbyshire S30 2WP
Tel: 01433 620642
One child FREE with every paying adult

Valid until end 2002

NOT TO BE USED IN CONJUNCTION WITH ANY OTHER OFFER

FHG READERS' OFFER 2002

Treak Cliff Cavern
HOME OF BLUE JOHN STONE
Castleton, Hope Valley, Derbyshire S33 8WP
Tel: 01433 620571
10% discount (not valid on Special Events days)

valid during 2002

NOT TO BE USED IN CONJUNCTION WITH ANY OTHER OFFER

FHG READERS' OFFER 2002

The Big Sheep
Bideford, Devon EX39 5AP
Tel: 01237 472366
Admit one child FREE with each paying adult

valid during 2002

NOT TO BE USED IN CONJUNCTION WITH ANY OTHER OFFER

FHG READERS' OFFER 2002

Coldharbour Mill Working Wool Museum
Coldharbour Mill, Uffculme, Cullompton, Devon EX15 3EE
Tel: 01884 840960 • e-mail: info@coldharbourmill.org.uk
website: www.coldharbourmill.org.uk
TWO adult tickets for the price of ONE

valid during 2002

NOT TO BE USED IN CONJUNCTION WITH ANY OTHER OFFER

FHG READERS' OFFER 2002

The Gnome Reserve & Wild Flower Garden
West Putford, Near Bradworthy, Devon EX22 7XE
Tel: 01409 241435 • e-mail: info@gnomereserve.co.uk
website: www.gnomereserve.co.uk
One FREE child with full paying adult

Valid during 2002

NOT TO BE USED IN CONJUNCTION WITH ANY OTHER OFFER

Large range of natural water worn caverns featuring mining equipment, stalactites and stalagmites, and fine deposits of Blue-John stone, Britain's rarest semi-precious stone.

DOGS MUST BE KEPT ON LEAD

Open: 9.30am to 5.30pm

Directions: Situated 2 miles west of Castleton; follow brown tourist signs

FHG PUBLICATIONS, ABBEY MILL BUSINESS CENTRE, PAISLEY PA1 1TJ

An underground wonderland of stalactites, stalagmites, rocks, minerals and fossils. Home of the unique Blue John stone – see the largest single piece ever found. Suitable for all ages.

Open: Opens 10am. Enquire for last tour of day and closed days.

Directions: ½ mile west of Castleton on A6187 (old A625)

FHG PUBLICATIONS, ABBEY MILL BUSINESS CENTRE, PAISLEY PA1 1TJ

"England for Excellence" award-winning rural attraction combining traditional rural crafts with hilarious novelties such as sheep racing and duck trialling, Indoor adventure zone for adults and children.

Open: daily, 10am to 6pm April - Oct Phone for Winter opening times and details

Directions: on A39 North Devon link road, two miles west of Bideford Bridge

FHG PUBLICATIONS, ABBEY MILL BUSINESS CENTRE, PAISLEY PA1 1TJ

An exciting working wool museum with machinery that spins yarn and weaves cloth, including the Devon tartan. Mill machinery, restaurant, gardens in a waterside setting. Home of the giant New World tapestry.

Open: April to October: daily 10.30am to 5pm; November to March: Monday to Friday 10.30am to 5pm

Directions: Two miles from Junction 27 M5; follow signs to Willand (B3181) then brown tourist signs to Museum

FHG PUBLICATIONS, ABBEY MILL BUSINESS CENTRE, PAISLEY PA1 1TJ

Visit 1000+ gnomes and pixies in two acre beech wood. Gnome hats are loaned free of charge - so the gnomes think you are one of them - don't forget your camera! Also 2-acre wild flower garden with 250 labelled species.

Open: daily 10am to 6pm 21st March to 31st October

Directions: Between Bideford and Bude; follow brown tourist signs from A39/A388/A386

FHG PUBLICATIONS, ABBEY MILL BUSINESS CENTRE, PAISLEY PA1 1TJ

FHG READERS' OFFER 2002

Killhope Lead Mining Museum
Cowshill, Upper Weardale, Co. Durham DL13 1AR
Tel: 01388 537505
website: www.durham.gov.uk/killhope
One child FREE with full-paying adult (not valid for Park Level Mine)

valid April to October 2002

NOT TO BE USED IN CONJUNCTION WITH ANY OTHER OFFER

FHG READERS' OFFER 2002

Barleylands Farm
Barleylands Road, Billericay, Essex CM11 2UD
Tel: 01268 290229 • e-mail: barleyfarm@aol.com
FREE adult ticket when accompanied by one child

Valid 1st March to 31st October. Not special event days

NOT TO BE USED IN CONJUNCTION WITH ANY OTHER OFFER

FHG READERS' OFFER 2002

NATIONAL WATERWAYS MUSEUM
Llanthony Warehouse, Gloucester Docks, Gloucester GL1 2EH
Tel: 01452 318054 • e-mail: info@nwm.demon.co.uk
website: www.nwm.org.uk
25% OFF museum admission (excludes combination tickets)

valid during 2002

NOT TO BE USED IN CONJUNCTION WITH ANY OTHER OFFER

FHG READERS' OFFER 2002

Verulamium Museum
St Michael's, St Albans, Herts AL3 4SW
Tel: 01727 751810
"Two for One"

valid from 1/8/02 until 31/12/02

NOT TO BE USED IN CONJUNCTION WITH ANY OTHER OFFER

FHG READERS' OFFER 2002

DONINGTON GRAND PRIX COLLECTION
DONINGTON PARK
Castle Donington, Near Derby, Leics DE74 2RP
Tel: 01332 811027
One child FREE with each full-paying adult

valid until 01/01/03

NOT TO BE USED IN CONJUNCTION WITH ANY OTHER OFFER

Britain's best preserved lead mining site – and a great day out for all the family, with lots to see and do. Underground Experience – Park Level Mine now open.

Open: April 1st to October 31st 10.30am to 5pm daily

Directions: alongside A689, midway between Stanhope and Alston in the heart of the North Pennines.

FHG PUBLICATIONS, ABBEY MILL BUSINESS CENTRE, PAISLEY PA1 1TJ

Farm Centre with animals, museum, blacksmith, glassblowing, miniature railway (Sundays and August), craft shops, tea room and licensed restaurant.

DOGS MUST BE KEPT ON LEAD

Open: 1st March to 31st October

Directions: M25, A127 towards Southend. Take A176 junction off A127, 3rd exit Wash Road, 2nd left Barleylands Road.

FHG PUBLICATIONS, ABBEY MILL BUSINESS CENTRE, PAISLEY PA1 1TJ

On three floors of a Listed Victorian warehouse charting 200 years of inland waterway history. • *Historic boats* • *Painted boat gallery* • *Blacksmith* • *Archive film* • *Interactive displays* • *Family room*
"A great day out"

Open: every day 10am to 5pm (excluding Christmas Day)

Directions: Junction 11A or 12 off M5 – follow brown signs for Historic Docks. Railway and bus station 10 minute walk. Free coach parking.

FHG PUBLICATIONS, ABBEY MILL BUSINESS CENTRE, PAISLEY PA1 1TJ

The museum of everyday life in Roman Britain. An award-winning museum with re-created Roman rooms, hands-on discovery areas, and some of the best mosaics outside the Mediterranean

Open: Monday to Saturday 10am-5.30pm
Sunday 2pm-5.30pm

Directions: St Alban's

FHG PUBLICATIONS, ABBEY MILL BUSINESS CENTRE, PAISLEY PA1 1TJ

The world's largest collection of Grand Prix racing cars – over 130 exhibits within five halls, including McLaren Formula One cars.

Open: daily 10am to 5pm (last admission 4pm). Closed Christmas/New Year.

Directions: 2 miles from M1 (J23a/24) and M42/A42; to north-west via A50.

FHG PUBLICATIONS, ABBEY MILL BUSINESS CENTRE, PAISLEY PA1 1TJ

FHG READERS' OFFER 2002

Butterfly & Wildlife Park
Long Sutton, Spalding, Lincs PE12 9LE
Tel: 01406 363833
One FREE child with one full-paying adult

valid April to October 2002 (Not Bank Holiday weekends)

NOT TO BE USED IN CONJUNCTION WITH ANY OTHER OFFER

FHG READERS' OFFER 2002

Cleethorpes Humber Estuary Discovery Centre
Lakeside, King's Road, Cleethorpes, N.E. Lincolnshire DN35 8LN
Tel: 01472 323232 • e-mail: discovery.centre@nelincs.gov.uk
website: www.time-discoverycentre.co.uk
One child free with every full-paying adult/senior citizen

Valid during 2002 (exhibition only, not special events)

NOT TO BE USED IN CONJUNCTION WITH ANY OTHER OFFER

FHG READERS' OFFER 2002

Skegness Natureland Seal Sanctuary
North Parade, Skegness, Lincolnshire PE25 1DB
Tel: 01754 764345 • e-mail: natureland@fsbdial.co.uk
website: www.skegnessnatureland.co.uk
FREE entry for one child when accompanied by full-paying adult.

Valid during 2002

NOT TO BE USED IN CONJUNCTION WITH ANY OTHER OFFER

FHG READERS' OFFER 2002

Southport Zoo and Conservation Trust
Princes Park, Southport, Merseyside PR8 1RX
Tel: 01704 538102
FREE Zoo Pack per family

valid during 2002 except Bank Holidays

NOT TO BE USED IN CONJUNCTION WITH ANY OTHER OFFER

FHG READERS' OFFER 2002

The Caves of Nottingham
Drury Walk, Broadmarsh Centre, Nottingham NG1 7LS
Tel: 0115 924 1424 • e-mail: info@cavesofnottingham.co.uk
One child FREE when accompanied by two full paying adults

Valid during 2002 except Bank Holidays and August.

NOT TO BE USED IN CONJUNCTION WITH ANY OTHER OFFER

Large wildlife park with Reptile Land, Tropical House, Insectarium, Birds of Prey Centre, farm animals, wallaby enclosure, llamas; adventure playground, tea room and gift shop.	**Open:** daily from 10am April to 28th October 2002 **Directions:** off A17 at Long Sutton

FHG PUBLICATIONS, ABBEY MILL BUSINESS CENTRE, PAISLEY PA1 1TJ

Delve into Cleethorpes' hidden past with our exciting hands-on displays. Learn more about the wildlife on the Lincolnshire coast and discover the ancient forest found buried along the beach. Fun for all the family	**Open:** Open daily 10am to 5pm (Please check for seasonal variations), except Christmas/Boxing/New Year's Days **Directions:** Follow Lakeside signs from Cleethorpes seafront, A180 or A15 through Grimsby

FHG PUBLICATIONS, ABBEY MILL BUSINESS CENTRE, PAISLEY PA1 1TJ

Well known for rescuing and rehabilitating orphaned and injured seal pups found washed ashore on Lincolnshire beaches. Also: penguins, aquarium, pets' corner, reptiles, Floral Palace (tropical birds and butterflies etc).	**Open:** Daily from 10am. Closed Christmas/Boxing/New Year's Days. **Directions:** At the north end of Skegness seafront

FHG PUBLICATIONS, ABBEY MILL BUSINESS CENTRE, PAISLEY PA1 1TJ

Lions, snow leopards, chimpanzees, monkeys, reptiles, aquarium and lots more, set amidst landscaped gardens. Gift shop, cafe and picnic areas.	**Open:** all year round from 10am **Directions:** on the coast 16 miles north of Liverpool; follow the brown and white tourist signs

FHG PUBLICATIONS, ABBEY MILL BUSINESS CENTRE, PAISLEY PA1 1TJ

750-year old man-made cave system beneath a modern day shopping centre. Discover how the caves were used with a unique 40-minute audio tour.	**Open:** daily Mon-Sat 10am to 4.15pm, Sundays 11am to 4pm **Directions:** In Nottingham city centre, within Broadmarsh Shopping Centre

FHG PUBLICATIONS, ABBEY MILL BUSINESS CENTRE, PAISLEY PA1 1TJ

FHG READERS' OFFER 2002

Newark Air Museum

The Airfield, Winthorpe, Newark, Nottinghamshire NG24 2NY
Tel: 01636 707170 • e-mail: newarkair@lineone.net
Party rate DISCOUNT for every voucher
(50p per person off normal admission).

Valid during 2002

NOT TO BE USED IN CONJUNCTION WITH ANY OTHER OFFER

FHG READERS' OFFER 2002

Cogges Manor Farm Museum

Church Lane, Witney, Oxfordshire OX28 3LA
Tel: 01993 772602
TWO for the price of ONE

Valid April to end of October 2002

NOT TO BE USED IN CONJUNCTION WITH ANY OTHER OFFER

FHG READERS' OFFER 2002

Avon Valley Railway

Bitton Station, Bath Road, Bitton, Bristol, BS30 6HD
Tel: 0117 932 5538 • website: www.avonvalleyrailway.co.uk
Up to two FREE child tickets with every fare-paying adult
(Not valid for "Day out with Thomas Events")

valid from May to September 2002

NOT TO BE USED IN CONJUNCTION WITH ANY OTHER OFFER

FHG READERS' OFFER 2002

Wookey Hole Caves & Papermill

Wookey Hole, Wells, Somerset BA5 1BB
Tel: 01749 672243 • e-mail: witch@wookey.co.uk
£1 per person OFF full admission price (up to max. 5 persons)

valid during 2002

NOT TO BE USED IN CONJUNCTION WITH ANY OTHER OFFER

FHG READERS' OFFER 2002

Royal Doulton Visitor Centre

Nile Street, Burslem, Stoke-on-Trent, Staffs ST6 2AJ
Tel: 01782 292434
Two admissions for the price of one – does not apply to factory tours

valid during 2002

NOT TO BE USED IN CONJUNCTION WITH ANY OTHER OFFER

A collection of 55 aircraft and cockpit sections from across the history of aviation. Extensive aero engine and artefact displays.

Open: daily from 10am (closed Christmas period).

Directions: Follow brown and white signs from A1, A46, A17 and A1133

FHG PUBLICATIONS, ABBEY MILL BUSINESS CENTRE, PAISLEY PA1 1TJ

Historic manor house and farm with traditional animals. Baking in the Victorian kitchen every afternoon.

Open: April to 1st December: Tuesday to Friday 10.30am to 5.30pm. Saturday and Sunday 12-5.30pm

Directions: Just off A40 Oxford to Cheltenham road at Witney

FHG PUBLICATIONS, ABBEY MILL BUSINESS CENTRE, PAISLEY PA1 1TJ

The Avon Valley Railway is more than just a train ride, offering a whole new experience for some, or a nostalgic memory for others. Steam trains operate every Sunday May to September, plus Bank Holidays and Christmas.

PETS MUST BE KEPT ON LEADS AND OFF TRAIN SEATS

Open: Steam trains operate every Sunday May to Sept plus Bank Holidays and Christmas

Directions: On the A431 midway between Bristol and Bath at Bitton

FHG PUBLICATIONS, ABBEY MILL BUSINESS CENTRE, PAISLEY PA1 1TJ

---

* *Britain's most spectacular caves*
* *Traditional paper-making*
* *Penny Arcade*
* *Magical Mirror Maze*

Open: Summer 10am to 5pm; Winter 10.30am to 4.30pm. Closed 17-25 Dec.

Directions: from M5 J22 follow brown-and-white signs via A38 and A371. Two miles from Wells.

FHG PUBLICATIONS, ABBEY MILL BUSINESS CENTRE, PAISLEY PA1 1TJ

The world's largest display of Royal Doulton figures past and present. Video theatre, demonstration room, museum, restaurant and shop. Factory Tours by prior booking weekdays only.

Open: Monday to Saturday 9.30am to 5pm; Sundays 10.30am to 4.30pm Closed Christmas/New Year period.

Directions: from M6 Junction 15/16; follow A500 to junction with A527. Signposted.

FHG PUBLICATIONS, ABBEY MILL BUSINESS CENTRE, PAISLEY PA1 1TJ

FHG READERS' OFFER 2002

Easton Farm Park

Easton, Near Wickham Market, Ipswich, Suffolk IP13 0EQ
Tel: 01728 746475 • e-mail: easton@eastonfarmpark.co.uk
website: www.eastonfarmpark.co.uk

£1 per person OFF for up to 4 full paying admissions

NOT TO BE USED IN CONJUNCTION WITH ANY OTHER OFFER

Valid until end 2002

FHG READERS' OFFER 2002

PARADISE PARK

Avis Road, Newhaven, East Sussex BN9 0DH
Tel: 01273 512123 • Fax: 01273 616005
website: www.paradisepark.co.uk

Admit one FREE adult or child with one adult paying full entrance price

NOT TO BE USED IN CONJUNCTION WITH ANY OTHER OFFER

valid during 2002

FHG READERS' OFFER 2002

Buckleys Yesterday's World

High Street, Battle, East Sussex TN33 0AQ
Tel: 01424 775378 • e-mail: info@yesterdaysworld.co.uk
website: www.yesterdaysworld.co.uk

50p OFF each admission

NOT TO BE USED IN CONJUNCTION WITH ANY OTHER OFFER

Valid until end 2002

FHG READERS' OFFER 2002

Wildfowl & Wetlands Trust

District 15, Washington, Tyne & Wear NE38 8LE
Tel: 0191 416 5454

One FREE admission with full-paying adult

NOT TO BE USED IN CONJUNCTION WITH ANY OTHER OFFER

valid from 1st Jan 2002 to 30th Sep 2002

FHG READERS' OFFER 2002

Stratford Butterfly Farm

Swans Nest Lane, Stratford-upon-Avon, Warwickshire CV37 7LS
Tel: 01789 299288 • e-mail: sales@butterflyfarm.co.uk
website: www.butterflyfarm.co.uk

One child FREE with each paying adult

NOT TO BE USED IN CONJUNCTION WITH ANY OTHER OFFER

Valid during 2002

Lots of baby animals. FREE pony rides, face painting, green trail, 'pat-a-pet', indoor children's soft play area; gift shop, tearoom, pets' paddocks

DOGS MUST BE KEPT ON LEADS

Open: March to October 10.30am to 6pm

Directions: Follow brown tourist signs off A12 and other roads

FHG PUBLICATIONS, ABBEY MILL BUSINESS CENTRE, PAISLEY PA1 1TJ

A plant lover's paradise with outstanding themed gardens and extensive Museum of Natural History. Conservatory gardens contain a large and varied collection of the world's flora. Sussex History Trail. Dinosaur Museum. Rides and amusements.

Open: Open daily, except Christmas Day and Boxing Day.

Directions: signposted off A26 and A259

FHG PUBLICATIONS, ABBEY MILL BUSINESS CENTRE, PAISLEY PA1 1TJ

Experience history and nostalgia at its very best at one of the South of England's favourite attractions. Over 30 room and shop displays bring the park to life

PETS NOT ALLOWED IN CHILDREN'S PLAY AREA

Open: 9.30am to 6pm (last admission 4.45pm, one hour earlier in winter)

Directions: Just off A21 in Battle High Street opposite the Abbey

FHG PUBLICATIONS, ABBEY MILL BUSINESS CENTRE, PAISLEY PA1 1TJ

---

100 acres of parkland, home to hundreds of duck, geese, swans and flamingos. Discovery centre, cafe, gift shop; play area.

Open: every day except Christmas Day

Directions: signposted from A19, A195, A1231 and A182

FHG PUBLICATIONS, ABBEY MILL BUSINESS CENTRE, PAISLEY PA1 1TJ

Wander through a lush landscape of exotic foliage where a myriad of multi-coloured butterflies sip nectar from tropical blossoms. Stroll past bubbling streams and splashing waterfalls; view insects and spiders all safely behind glass.

Open: 10am to 6pm summer, 10am to dusk winter

FHG PUBLICATIONS, ABBEY MILL BUSINESS CENTRE, PAISLEY PA1 1TJ

Atwell-Wilson Motor Museum

Stockley Lane, Calne, Wiltshire SN11 0NF

Tel: 01249 813119

TWO admissions for the price of ONE

Valid during 2002

NOT TO BE USED IN CONJUNCTION WITH ANY OTHER OFFER

Embsay & Bolton Abbey Steam Railway

Bolton Abbey Station, Skipton, N. Yorkshire BD23 6AF

Tel: 01756 710614

One adult travels FREE when accompanied by a full fare paying adult
(does not include Special Event days)

valid during 2002

NOT TO BE USED IN CONJUNCTION WITH ANY OTHER OFFER

Yorkshire Dales Falconry and Conservation Centre

Crows Nest, Giggleswick, Settle, North Yorkshire LA2 8AS

Tel: 01729 822832

One FREE adult admission with every full-paying adult

valid 1/4 to 30/9/2002 (not Bank Holidays)

NOT TO BE USED IN CONJUNCTION WITH ANY OTHER OFFER

Museum of Rail Travel

Ingrow Railway Centre, Near Keighley, West Yorkshire BD22 8NJ

Tel: 01535 680425

"One for one" FREE admission

Valid during 2002 except during special events (ring to check)

NOT TO BE USED IN CONJUNCTION WITH ANY OTHER OFFER

Argyll Wildlife Park

By Inveraray, Argyll PA32 8XT

Tel: 01499 302264

ONE child (3-16) with two full paying adults

Valid Easter to 31/10/2002

NOT TO BE USED IN CONJUNCTION WITH ANY OTHER OFFER

Around 100 vintage and classic cars, motorbikes and commercials, with over 30 taxed. Superb view of Wiltshire Downs; children's play and picnic area	**Open:** Sunday to Thursday 11am to 5pm (1st April to 31st Oct); 11am to 4pm (1st Nov to 31st March) **Directions:** A4 from Calne to Marlborough, follow brown tourist signs

FHG PUBLICATIONS, ABBEY MILL BUSINESS CENTRE, PAISLEY PA1 1TJ

Steam trains operate over a 4½ mile line from Bolton Abbey Station to Embsay Station. Many family events including Thomas the Tank Engine take place during major Bank Holidays.	**Open:** steam trains run every Sunday throughout the year and up to 7 days a week in summer. 10.30am to 4.30pm **Directions:** Embsay Station signposted from the A59 Skipton by-pass; Bolton Abbey Station signposted from the A59 at Bolton Abbey.

FHG PUBLICATIONS, ABBEY MILL BUSINESS CENTRE, PAISLEY PA1 1TJ

Award-winning bird of prey centre featuring free-flying demonstrations daily. 30 species on permanent display including the largest bird of prey in the world – the Andean Condor. Children's adventure playground. Tea-room and gift shop.	**Open:** daily 10am to 5pm **Directions:** just outside Settle on the A65 Skipton to Kendal road.

FHG PUBLICATIONS, ABBEY MILL BUSINESS CENTRE, PAISLEY PA1 1TJ

A fascinating display of railway carriages and a wide range of railway items telling the story of rail travel over the years. ALL PETS MUST BE KEPT ON LEADS	**Open:** daily 11am to 4.30pm **Directions:** Approximately one mile from Keighley on A629 Halifax road. Follow brown tourist signs

FHG PUBLICATIONS, ABBEY MILL BUSINESS CENTRE, PAISLEY PA1 1TJ

45-acre natural wildlife park, with nature trails. On view are fallow deer, raccoons, wallabies, Scottish wild cats, foxes, monkeys, birds of prey, deer and much more. Small cafe and gift shop	**Open:** Easter weekend to October 31st. Open 10am, last admission 5pm **Directions:** A82 Glasgow-Tarbet, then A83 Campbeltown. One mile south of Inveraray village

FHG PUBLICATIONS, ABBEY MILL BUSINESS CENTRE, PAISLEY PA1 1TJ

Dunaskin Heritage Centre

Waterside, Patna, Ayrshire KA6 7JF
Tel: 01292 531144 • e-mail: dunaskin@btconnect.com
website: www.dunaskin.org

TWO for the price of ONE

READERS' OFFER 2002 — valid from 1st May to 31st October 2002

NOT TO BE USED IN CONJUNCTION WITH ANY OTHER OFFER

Kelburn Castle & Country Centre

Fairlie, Near Largs, Ayrshire KA29 0BE
Tel: 01475 568685 • e-mail: info@kelburncountrycentre.com
website: www.kelburncountrycentre.com

One child FREE for each full paying adult

READERS' OFFER 2002 — Valid until October 2002

NOT TO BE USED IN CONJUNCTION WITH ANY OTHER OFFER

CREETOWN GEM ROCK MUSEUM

Chain Road, Creetown, Near Newton Stewart, Kirkcudbrightshire DG8 7HJ
Tel: 01671 820357 • e-mail: gem.rock@btinternet.com
website: www.gemrock.net

10% OFF admission prices

READERS' OFFER 2002 — valid during 2002

NOT TO BE USED IN CONJUNCTION WITH ANY OTHER OFFER

Almond Valley Heritage Centre

Millfield, Livingston, West Lothian EH54 7AR
Tel: 01506 414957 • e-mail: info@almondvalley.co.uk

Free child with adult paying full admission

READERS' OFFER 2002 — Valid during 2002

NOT TO BE USED IN CONJUNCTION WITH ANY OTHER OFFER

MYRETON MOTOR MUSEUM

Aberlady, East Lothian EH32 0PZ
Tel: 01875 870288

One child FREE with each paying adult

READERS' OFFER 2002 — valid during 2002

NOT TO BE USED IN CONJUNCTION WITH ANY OTHER OFFER

Set in the rolling hills of Ayrshire, Europe's best preserved ironworks. Guided tours, audio-visuals, walks with electronic wands. Restaurant/coffee shop

Open: April to October daily 10am to 5pm

Directions: A713 Ayr to Castle Douglas road, 12 miles from Ayr, 3 miles from Dalmellington

FHG PUBLICATIONS, ABBEY MILL BUSINESS CENTRE, PAISLEY PA1 1TJ

The historic home of the Earls of Glasgow. Waterfalls, gardens, famous Glen, unusual trees. Riding school, stockade, play areas, exhibitions, shop, cafe and The Secret Forest.

PETS MUST BE KEPT ON LEAD

Open: daily 10am to 6pm Easter to October

Directions: On A78 between Largs and Fairlie, 45 mins drive from Glasgow

FHG PUBLICATIONS, ABBEY MILL BUSINESS CENTRE, PAISLEY PA1 1TJ

Worldwide collection of gems, minerals, crystals and fossils
• Erupting Volcano • Audio Visual •
• Crystal Cave • Unique Giftshop •
• Relax in our themed tea room •
• Internet Cafe •

Open: Open daily Easter to 30th November; Dec/Feb – weekends only.

Directions: 7 miles from Newton Stewart, 11 miles from Gatehouse of Fleet; just off A75 Carlisle to Stranraer road.

FHG PUBLICATIONS, ABBEY MILL BUSINESS CENTRE, PAISLEY PA1 1TJ

An innovative museum exploring the history and environment of West Lothian on a 200-acre site packed full of things to see and do, indoors and out.

Open: daily (except Christmas and New Year) 10am to 5pm

Directions: 15 miles from Edinburgh, follow "Heritage Centre" signs from A899

FHG PUBLICATIONS, ABBEY MILL BUSINESS CENTRE, PAISLEY PA1 1TJ

Motor cars from 1896, motorcycles from 1902, commercial vehicles from 1919, cycles from 1880, British WWII military vehicles, ephemera, period advertising etc

Open: daily Easter to September 10.30am to 4.30pm; October to Easter weekends only; Saturday 12pm to 3pm; Sunday 11am to 4pm.

Directions: off A198 near Aberlady. Two miles from A1

FHG PUBLICATIONS, ABBEY MILL BUSINESS CENTRE, PAISLEY PA1 1TJ

FHG READERS' OFFER 2002

Deep Sea World

North Queensferry, Fife KY11 1JR

Tel: 01383 41188

0906 941 0077 (24hr info line, calls cost 10p per minute)

One child FREE with a full-paying adult

valid until end 2002

NOT TO BE USED IN CONJUNCTION WITH ANY OTHER OFFER

FHG READERS' OFFER 2002

Oban Rare Breeds Farm Park

Glencruitten, Oban, Argyll PA34 4QB

Tel: 01631 770608

website: www.obanrarebreeds.com

10% DISCOUNT on all admissions

valid during 2002

NOT TO BE USED IN CONJUNCTION WITH ANY OTHER OFFER

FHG READERS' OFFER 2002

Landmark Forest Heritage Park

Carrbridge, Inverness-shire PH23 3AJ

Tel: 01479 841613 • Freephone 0800 731 3446

10% DISCOUNT for pet owners. Free admission for pets!
Maximum of 4 persons per voucher.

Valid during 2002

NOT TO BE USED IN CONJUNCTION WITH ANY OTHER OFFER

FHG READERS' OFFER 2002

Highland and Rare Breeds Farm

Elphin, Near Ullapool, Sutherland IV27 4HH

Tel: 01854 666204

One FREE adult or child with adult paying full entrance price

valid May to September 2002

NOT TO BE USED IN CONJUNCTION WITH ANY OTHER OFFER

FHG READERS' OFFER 2002

MUSEUM OF CHILDHOOD MEMORIES

1 Castle Street, Beaumaris, Anglesey LL58 8AP

Tel: 01248 712498 • website: www.nwi.co.uk/museumofchildhood

One child FREE with two adults

valid during 2002

NOT TO BE USED IN CONJUNCTION WITH ANY OTHER OFFER

Scotland's award-winning aquarium where you can enjoy a spectacular diver's eye view of our marine environment through the world's longest underwater safari. New 'Amazing Amphibians' display, behind the scenes tours. Aquamazing entertainment for all the family

Open: daily except Christmas Day.

Directions: from Edinburgh follow signs for Forth Road Bridge, then signs through North Queensferry. From North, follow signs through Inverkeithing and North Queensferry.

FHG PUBLICATIONS, ABBEY MILL BUSINESS CENTRE, PAISLEY PA1 1TJ

Rare breeds of farm animals, pets' corner, conservation groups, tea room, woodland walk in beautiful location

Open: 10am to 5.30pm mid March to end October

Directions: two-and-a-half miles from Oban along Glencruitten road

FHG PUBLICATIONS, ABBEY MILL BUSINESS CENTRE, PAISLEY PA1 1TJ

Great day out for all the family. Forest trails, Clydesdale Horse, Steam powered sawmill; Try a 2 man saw. Wild Water Coaster (April to Oct), Microworld - an expedition into inner space. Meals and snacks, shop.

DOGS MUST BE KEPT ON LEADS

Open: daily except Christmas Day

Directions: 20 miles south of Inverness at Carrbridge, just off the A9

FHG PUBLICATIONS, ABBEY MILL BUSINESS CENTRE, PAISLEY PA1 1TJ

Highland croft open to visitors for "hands-on" experience with over 30 different breeds of farm animals – "stroke the goats and scratch the pigs". Farm information centre and old farm implements. For all ages, cloud or shine!

Open: July and August 10am to 5pm

Directions: on A835 15 miles north of Ullapool

FHG PUBLICATIONS, ABBEY MILL BUSINESS CENTRE, PAISLEY PA1 1TJ

Nine rooms in a Georgian house filled with items illustrating the happier times of family life over the past 150 years. Joyful nostalgia unlimited.

Open: March to end October

Directions: opposite Beaumaris Castle

FHG PUBLICATIONS, ABBEY MILL BUSINESS CENTRE, PAISLEY PA1 1TJ

| FHG READERS' OFFER 2002 | **Llanberis Lake Railway**
Gilfach Ddu, Llanberis, Gwynedd LL55 4TY
Tel: 01286 870549 • e-mail: info@lake-railway.co.uk
website: www.lake-railway.co.uk
One pet travels FREE with each full fare paying adult | Valid Easter to October 2002 |

NOT TO BE USED IN CONJUNCTION WITH ANY OTHER OFFER

| FHG READERS' OFFER 2002 | *Alice in Wonderland Centre*
3/4 Trinity Square, Llandudno, Conwy, North Wales LL30 2PY
Tel: 01492 860082 • e-mail: alice@wonderland.co.uk
website: www.wonderland.co.uk
One child FREE with two paying adults. Guide Dogs welcome | valid during 2002 |

NOT TO BE USED IN CONJUNCTION WITH ANY OTHER OFFER

| FHG READERS' OFFER 2002 | **National Cycle Collection**
Automobile Palace, Temple Street, Llandrindod Wells, Powys LD1 5DL
Tel: 01597 825531
TWO for the price of ONE | Valid during 2002 except Special Event days |

NOT TO BE USED IN CONJUNCTION WITH ANY OTHER OFFER

| FHG READERS' OFFER 2002 | **Celtica**
Y Plas, Ffordd Aberystwyth, Machynlleth, Powys SY20 8ER
Tel: 01654 702702 • e-mail: info@celticawales.com
website: www.celticawales.com
Child FREE when accompanied by full-paying adult | valid during 2002 |

NOT TO BE USED IN CONJUNCTION WITH ANY OTHER OFFER

| FHG READERS' OFFER 2002 | **Rhondda Heritage Park**
Lewis Merthyr Colliery, Coed Cae Road, Trehafod, Near Pontypridd CF37 7NP
Tel: 01443 682036 e-mail: rhonpark@netwales.co.uk
website: www.netwales.co.uk/rhondda-heritage
Two adults or children for the price of one. | Valid until end 2002 for full tours only. Not valid on special event days. |

NOT TO BE USED IN CONJUNCTION WITH ANY OTHER OFFER

A 40-minute ride along the shores of beautiful Padarn Lake behind a quaint historic steam engine. Magnificent views of the mountains from lakeside picnic spots

DOGS MUST BE KEPT ON LEAD AT ALL TIMES ON TRAIN

Open: Most days Easter to October. Free timetable leaflet on request

Directions: just off A4086 Caernarfon to Capel Curig road at Llanberis; follow 'Country Park' signs

FHG PUBLICATIONS, ABBEY MILL BUSINESS CENTRE, PAISLEY PA1 1TJ

Walk through the Rabbit Hole to the colourful scenes of Lewis Carroll's classic story set in beautiful life-size displays. Recorded commentaries and transcripts available in several languages

Open: 10am to 5pm daily (closed Sundays Easter to November); closed Christmas/Boxing/New Year's Days.

Directions: situated just off the main street, 250 yards from coach and rail stations

FHG PUBLICATIONS, ABBEY MILL BUSINESS CENTRE, PAISLEY PA1 1TJ

Journey through the lanes of cycle history and see bicycles from Boneshakers and Penny Farthings up to modern Raleigh cycles. Over 200 machines on display

PETS MUST BE KEPT ON LEADS

Open: daily 10am onwards

Directions: AA signs to car park. Town centre attraction

FHG PUBLICATIONS, ABBEY MILL BUSINESS CENTRE, PAISLEY PA1 1TJ

Discover over 2000 years of Celtic influence on British and European history. A unique, informative and stimulating AV experience of Celtic heritage and culture. Tea room, gift shop and indoor play area.

Open: daily throughout the year (except Christmas and New Year).

Directions: in restored mansion just south of clock tower in town centre; car park just off Aberystwyth road

FHG PUBLICATIONS, ABBEY MILL BUSINESS CENTRE, PAISLEY PA1 1TJ

Make a pit stop whatever the weather! Join an ex-miner on a tour of discovery, ride the cage to pit bottom and take a thrilling ride back to the surface. AV presentations, period village street, children's adventure play area, restaurant and gift shop. Full disabled access.

Open: Open daily 10am to 6pm (last tour 4.30pm). Closed Mondays October to Easter, also Christmas/Boxing days

Directions: Exit Junction 32 M4, signposted from A470 Pontypridd. Trehafod is located between Pontypridd and Porth

FHG PUBLICATIONS, ABBEY MILL BUSINESS CENTRE, PAISLEY PA1 1TJ

ENGLAND BOARD

GREATER LONDON

BED AND BREAKFAST IN LONDON
Stay with us or one of our selected families.
Comfortable, centrally located quiet Edwardian home. Great base for sightseeing, close to the river, traditional pubs, lots of local restaurants and antique shops. Excellent transport facilities – easy access to West End, Theatreland, shopping, Harrods, museums, Albert Hall, Earls Court and Olympia Exhibition centres. Direct lines to Eurostar (Waterloo), Airports: Heathrow, Gatwick (Victoria), Stansted (Liverpool Street). Bed and Continental Breakfast Prices: Double/Twin/Triple £24 pppn; Single £34.00; Children's reductions. Smoking only in garden.

Sohel and Anne Armanios
67 Rannoch Road, Hammersmith, London W6 9SS
Tel: 020 7385 4904 • Fax: 020 7610 3235
IDEAL LONDON LOCATIONS

See also Colour Advertisement

FIVE KINGS GUEST HOUSE

Five Kings is a family-run guest house and member of the English Tourism Council with Two Diamonds awarded. 16 rooms, seven en suite. All rooms have colour TV.

Situated in a quiet area yet only 15 minutes to Central London. Oxford Street, Leicester Square, Camden Lock, London Zoo, Kings Cross and St Pancras Stations are only two miles away.

No parking restriction in Anson Road

Single £24-£30   Double/twin £36-£46,
Family 1x3 £52-£56   Family 1x4 £62-£66

All prices include English breakfast and VAT

Five Kings Guest House
59 Anson Road, Tufnell Park, London N7 0AR
Telephone: 020 7607 3996 Fax: 020 7609 5554

FREE or REDUCED RATE entry to Holiday Visits and Attractions — see our READERS' OFFER VOUCHERS on pages 35-54

Hotel

See also Colour Display Advertisement

LONDON. Falcon Hotel, 11 Norfolk Square, Hyde Park W2 1RU (020 7723 8603; Fax: 020 7402 7009). Situated in central London this 2 star B&B Hotel is family friendly. Established for 30 years and set in a tranquil position within a garden square. Two minutes from Paddington Station, 15 minutes from Heathrow on Express Link. En suite facilities, very clean and comfortable. Triple and Family rooms available. Close to tourist attractions and shops. Full freshly cooked English breakfasts. Affordable prices from: Singles £35, Doubles £55. **ETC** ★★
e-mail:info@aafalcon.co.uk
website: www.aafalcon.co.uk

Hotel 1-12

See also Colour Display Advertisement

LONDON. Anne and Sohel Armanios, 67 Rannoch Road, Hammmersmith, London W6 9SS (020 7385 4904; Fax: 020 7610 3235). Ideal London location. Comfortable, centrally located, quiet Edwardian family home. Great base for sightseeing. Close to river, traditional pubs, many local restaurants and antique shops. Excellent transport facilities, three minutes' walk to buses, 10 minutes' walk to Underground. Direct line to West End, theatres, shopping, Harrods, museums, galleries, Royal Albert Hall, Earl's Court and Olympia exhibition centres. Direct line to Eurostar (Waterloo), Heathrow, Victoria (Gatwick), Liverpool Street (Stansted) Airports. Stay with us or with one of our selected families. We have double/twin and triple rooms with central heating and TV. Smoking only in garden. Bed and Continental Breakfast £24 per person per night Double/TwinTriple. Reductions for children. Single occupancy £34 per night.

Hotel

LONDON. Five Kings Guest House, 59 Anson Road, Tufnell Park, London N7 0AR (020-7607 3996; Fax: 020-7609 5554). Five Kings is a family-run guest house and member of the English Tourism Council with two diamonds awarded. 16 rooms, seven en suite, all with colour TV. Situated in a quiet area yet only 15 minutes to central London, Oxford Street, Leicester Square, Camden Lock and London Zoo. Kings Cross and St Pancras Stations are only two miles away. No parking restriction in Anson Road. Single from £24 to £30; Double/twin from £36 to £46; triple room from £50 to £56, family (four) from £60 to £66. All prices include English breakfast and VAT. **ETC** ♦♦.

Hotel

See also Colour Advertisement

LONDON. Dalmacia Hotel, 71 Shepherds Bush Road, Hammersmith W6 7LS (020 7603 2887; Fax: 020 7602 9226) Conveniently located for visiting all of London's attractions, offering comfortable, value-for-money accommodation. All rooms en suite with remote-control satellite TV and direct-dial telephones. Underground 800 metres. Les Routiers and London Tourist Board Listed. Brochure available. Terms: single £49, double £60, triple £81. Visa, Mastercard and Switch accepted.
website: www.dalmacia-hotel.co.uk

VISITS & ATTRACTIONS

London Aquarium • *South Bank, London SE1* • *020 7967 8000*
Experience the array of tropical sharks, sting rays, deadly stonefish and piranhas.
Don't miss the new 2m Zebra Shark.

Bramah Museum of Tea & Coffee • *Butler's Wharf, London SE1* • *020 7378 0222*
Set amongst atmospheric warehouses, telling the story of 400 years of social and commercial history in ceramics, metal and graphic arts.

National Portrait Gallery • *St Martin's Place, London WC2* • *0870 0660597*
The largest collection of portraiture in the world, with over 10, 000 images of men and women who have shaped the history and culture of the nation. Varied programme of special exhibitions.

ATHENA HOTEL

110-114 SUSSEX GARDENS, HYDE PARK, LONDON W2 1UA
Tel: 0207 706 3866; Fax: 0207 262 6143
E-Mail: athena@stavrouhotels.co.uk   Website: www.stavrouhotels.co.uk

TREAT YOURSELVES TO A QUALITY HOTEL AT AFFORDABLE PRICES

The Athena is a newly completed family run hotel in a restored Victorian building. Professionally designed, including a lift to all floors and exquisitely decorated, we offer our clientele the ambience and warm hospitality necessary for a relaxing and enjoyable stay. Ideally located in a beautiful tree-lined avenue, extremely well-positioned for sightseeing London's famous sights and shops; Hyde Park, Madame Tussaud's, Oxford Street, Marble Arch, Knightsbridge, Buckingham Palace and many more are all within walking distance.

Travel connections to all over London are excellent, with Paddington and Lancaster Gate Stations, Heathrow Express, A2 Airbus and buses minutes away.
Our tastefully decorated bedrooms have en suite bath/shower rooms, satellite colour TV, bedside telephones, tea/coffee making facilities. Hairdryers, trouser press, laundry and ironing facilities available on request. Ample car parking.

All prices include a full traditional English Breakfast and VAT
CREDIT CARDS WELCOME

Single Rooms from £50-£65

Double/Twin Rooms from £60-£89

Triple & Family Rooms from £25 per person

WE LOOK FORWARD TO SEEING YOU

58   Greater London   BOARD

Hotel

See also Inside Back Cover   **LONDON. Gower Hotel, 129 Sussex Gardens, Hyde Park, London W2 2RX (020 7262 2262; Fax: 020 7262 2006).** The Gower is a small family-run hotel centrally located within two minutes of Paddington Station which benefits from the Heathrow Express train - "15 minutes to and from Heathrow Airport". Excellently located for sightseeing London's famous sights and shops, Hyde Park, Madame Tussauds, Harrods, Oxford Street, Marble Arch, Buckingham Palace and many more all nearby. All rooms have private shower and WC, radio, TV (satellite and video channels), direct dial telephones, tea/coffee making facilities. All are recently refurbished and fully centrally heated. 24 hour reception. Single rooms from £30 to £54, double/twin from £26 to £36, triple and family rooms from £20 to £30. All prices are per person and are inclusive of VAT and a large traditional English breakfast. Credit cards welcome. We look forward to seeing you. **ETC** ◆◆
e-mail: gower@stavrouhotels.co.uk
website: www.stavrouhotels.co.uk

Hotel   1-12

See also Inside Back Cover   **LONDON. Queens Hotel, 33 Anson Road, Tufnell Park, London N7 (020 7607 4725; Fax: 020 7697 9725).** Family-run hotel in large double fronted Victorian building close to underground; car parking available. London Zoo, Regent's Park, Hampstead and Highgate villages, the canals and much more of historic London easily reached. Most rooms have en suite facilities and are clean and well maintained. Central heating, TV lounge and facilities for tea/coffee. Garden at rear. Singles from £25 to £34, double/twin rooms from £20 to £27; triple and family rooms from £18 per person, depending on season. Includes full English breakfast and VAT. Children half-price. **ETC** ◆◆
e-mail: queens@stavrouhotels.co.uk
website: www.stavrouhotels.co.uk

Hotel

LONDON. Athena Hotel, 110-114 Sussex Gardens, Hyde Park, London W2 1UA (020 7706 3866; Fax: 020 7262 6143). Treat yourselves to a quality hotel at affordable prices. The Athena is a family run hotel which is newly completed in a restored Victorian building, professionally designed, including a lift to all floors and exquisitely decorated. We offer our clientele the ambience and warmth necessary for relaxing and an enjoyable stay with our warm hospitality. Ideally located in a beautiful tree-lined avenue, extremely well positioned for sightseeing London's finest sights. Our tastefully decorated bedrooms have en suite bath/shower rooms, satellite colour TV, bedside telephones, tea/coffee making facilities. Hairdryers, trouser press, laundry and ironing facilities available on request. Ample car space. Single room £50 - £65. Double /twin £60 - £89, triple/family room from £25 per person. All prices include a full traditional breakfast + VAT. **ETC** ◆◆◆
e-mail: athena@stavrouhotels.co.uk
website: www.stavrouhotels.co.uk

1-12 Months open	🐾 Pets welcome	♿ Suitable for disabled	🚗 Car essential
S Sporting/special interests provided	≈ Coast under two miles	🐎 Children welcome	
♀ Licensed	🍼 Babysitting available	▥ Central heating	

PLEASE NOTE

All the information in this book is given in good faith in the belief that it is correct. However, the publishers cannot guarantee the facts given in these pages, neither are they responsible for changes in policy, ownership or terms that may take place after the date of going to press. Readers should always satisfy themselves that the facilities they require are available and that the terms, if quoted, still apply.

CAMBRIDGESHIRE

Guesthouse

CAMBRIDGE. Cristina's Guest House, 47 St Andrews Road, Cambridge CB4 1DH (Tel & Fax: 01223 365855 or 327700). Guests are assured of a warm welcome here, quietly located in the beautiful city of Cambridge, only 15 minutes' walk from the city centre and colleges. All rooms have colour TV and tea/coffee making equipment, hair dryer and radio alarm clock. Most rooms have private shower and toilet. Centrally heated with comfortable TV lounge. Private car park, locked at night. A no smoking house. **ETC/AA ♦♦♦**.
e-mail: cristinasguesthouse@ntlworld.com
website: www.cristinasguesthouse.com

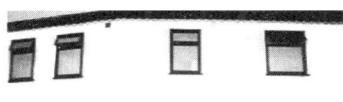

VISITS & ATTRACTIONS

Fitzwilliam Museum • *Cambridge, Cambridgeshire* • *01223 332904*
website: www.fitzmuseum.cam.ac.uk
One of the UK's finest collections of armour, antiquities, sculpture, furniture, pottery, paintings, prints, coins and much more.

The peaceful River Ouse at Hemingford Grey, Cambridgeshire

CORNWALL

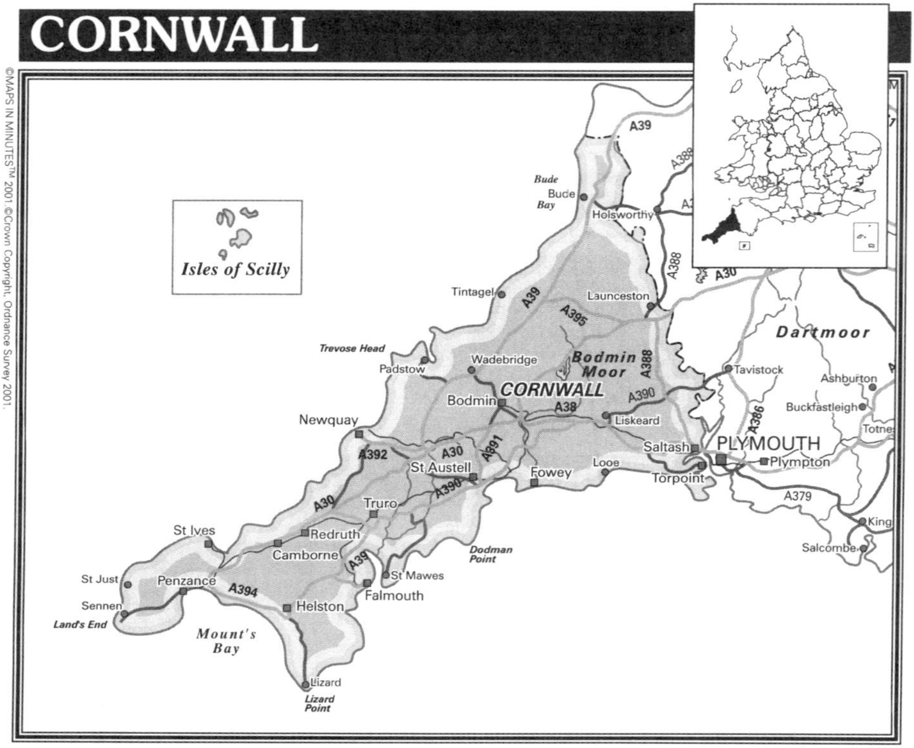

The FHG GOLF GUIDE
Where to Play Where to Stay
2002

Available from most bookshops, the 2002 edition of **THE GOLF GUIDE** covers details of every UK golf course – well over 2800 entries – for holiday or business golf. Hundreds of hotel entries offer convenient accommodation, accompanying details of the courses – the 'pro', par score, length etc.

In association with 'Golf Monthly' and including Holiday Golf in Ireland, France, Portugal, Spain, The USA, South Africa and Thailand.

£9.99 from bookshops or from the publishers (postage charged outside UK) • FHG Publications, Abbey Mill Business Centre, Paisley PA1 1TJ

FREE or REDUCED RATE entry to Holiday Visits and Attractions – see our READERS' OFFER VOUCHERS on pages 35-54

Hotel 1-12

FALMOUTH. Mrs E. Eddy, Trevu House Hotel, 45 Melvill Road, Falmouth TR11 4DG 01326 312852; Fax: 01326 318631). Trevu House is a small family-run hotel with a friendly home-from-home atmosphere, with special emphasis on comfort, cleanliness and personal service. The situation is ideal for a seaside holiday being only about two minutes' walk from Gyllyngvase Beach and within easy reach of the town, harbour and railway station. Spacious accommodation is tastefully furnished with bright modern decor. Large comfortable lounge. Bedrooms are en suite and have modern divan beds (some 6' wide), colour TVs, tea/coffee making facilities and central heating. We pride ourselves on our high standard of breakfast cuisine which is well presented and served at separate tables. Trevu House is a non-smoking establishment. Full fire certificate held. Small car park. Bed and Breakfast from £19.00. No single room supplement. Brochure available upon request.
e-mail: elaine.eddy@lineone.net
website: www.trevu-house-hotel.co.uk

Guesthouse 1-12

NEWQUAY. Gill & Brian Scott, Fairview House, 2 Fairview Terrace, Newquay TR7 1RJ (Tel & Fax: 01637 871179). Under new management for 2002. Fairview House offers a warm and friendly welcome where every effort is made to make your stay as relaxing and enjoyable as possible. Our comfortable bedrooms are mostly en suite with colour TV and tea/coffee making facilities. We endeavour to serve the best traditional English breakfast with evening meals by prior arrangement. Situated enviably close to the centre of town and sandy beaches but also within easy reach of all that Newquay has to offer, we are ideally placed to discover the charms of Cornwall. Cosy licensed bar, unrestricted parking, open all year.

Hotel

See also Colour Display Advertisement

POLPERRO. Penryn House, The Coombes, Polperro PL13 2RQ (01503 272157). Situated in the tranquil heart of the beautiful fishing village of Polperro, we pride ourselves on providing comfort and excellent service in an informal atmosphere. Relax in our fireside lounge bar or guest lounge; enjoy the restaurant with fresh home cooking using local produce. Our comfortable en suite bedrooms have TV, telephones, clock/radios, hairdryers and well-stocked courtesy trays. Easy access to the coastal paths and a short journey to the Eden Project, National Trust properties and Dartmoor and Bodmin Moor. Also close to golf, riding, fishing and sailing. **ETC/AA ★★★**

VISITS & ATTRACTIONS

The Eden Project • *Near St Austell, Cornwall* • *01726 811911*
website: www.edenproject.com
A gateway into the fascinating interaction of plants and people. Two gigantic geodesic conservatories - the Humid Tropics Biome and the Warm Temperate Biome - set amidst landscaped outdoor terraces.

Goonhilly Satellite Earth Station • *Helston, Cornwall* • *01326 221333*
website: www.goonhilly.bt.com
Explore the wonders of pioneering technology at one of the most important communication stations in the world. Scan the skies by operating an IV dish aerial yourself.

Hotel

TINTAGEL. Willapark Manor Hotel, Bossiney, Near Tintagel PL34 0BA (01840 770782). Willapark Manor is a lovely character house in a beautiful setting amidst 14 acres grounds, overlooking Bossiney Bay. Surrounded by woodland, it is secluded and has direct access to the coastal path and beach. It is a family-run hotel with a friendly and informal atmosphere, excellent cuisine and a well-stocked cocktail bar. Beautifully appointed bedrooms, all en suite and with colour TV and tea/coffee making facilities. Some four-posters. A warm welcome and a memorable holiday assured. ONE OF THE MOST BEAUTIFULLY SITUATED HOTELS IN ENGLAND. Dinner, bed and breakfast from £260 weekly, from £43 daily including VAT. Bed and breakfast from £28.50 daily. **ETC ★★**

Hotel

See also Inside Front Cover

TORPOINT. Whitsand Bay Hotel, Portwrinkle, By Torpoint, Plymouth PL11 3BU (01503 230276; Fax: 01503 230329). Whitsand Bay is spectacularly sited with 100 miles of sea views with a sandy beach easily accessible and also near the Eden Project and The Lost Gardens of Heligan. Facilities include an indoor heated swimming pool, leisure/fitness complex, our OWN 18-HOLE GOLF COURSE, clay pigeon shooting, shark/sea/freshwater fishing and horse-riding nearby. Children of all ages are welcome. Excellent ROSETTE-STANDARD RESTAURANT. **AA ★★★, RAC ★★** *MERIT AWARD.* Self-catering accommodation within grounds with full hotel facilities also available.
e-mail: earlehotels@btconnect.com
website: www.cornish-golf-hotels.co.uk

1-12 Months open	🐾 Pets welcome	♿ Suitable for disabled	🚗 Car essential
[S] Sporting/special interests provided		〰 Coast under two miles	🐴 Children welcome
♀ Licensed	🍼 Babysitting available		▥ Central heating

Other specialised

FHG PUBLICATIONS

Published annually: available in all good bookshops
or direct from the publisher.

- Recommended COUNTRY HOTELS OF BRITAIN   £5.25
- Recommended WAYSIDE & COUNTRY INNS OF BRITAIN   £5.25
- Recommended SHORT BREAK HOLIDAYS IN BRITAIN   £5.25
- PETS WELCOME!   £6.75 • B&B IN BRITAIN   £4.25
- THE GOLF GUIDE Where to Play / Where to Stay   £9.99

**FHG PUBLICATIONS LTD, Abbey Mill Business Centre,
Seedhill, Paisley, Renfrewshire PA1 1TJ**
Tel: 0141-887 0428 • Fax: 0141-889 7204
e-mail: fhg@ipcmedia.com • website: www.holidayguides.com

CUMBRIA

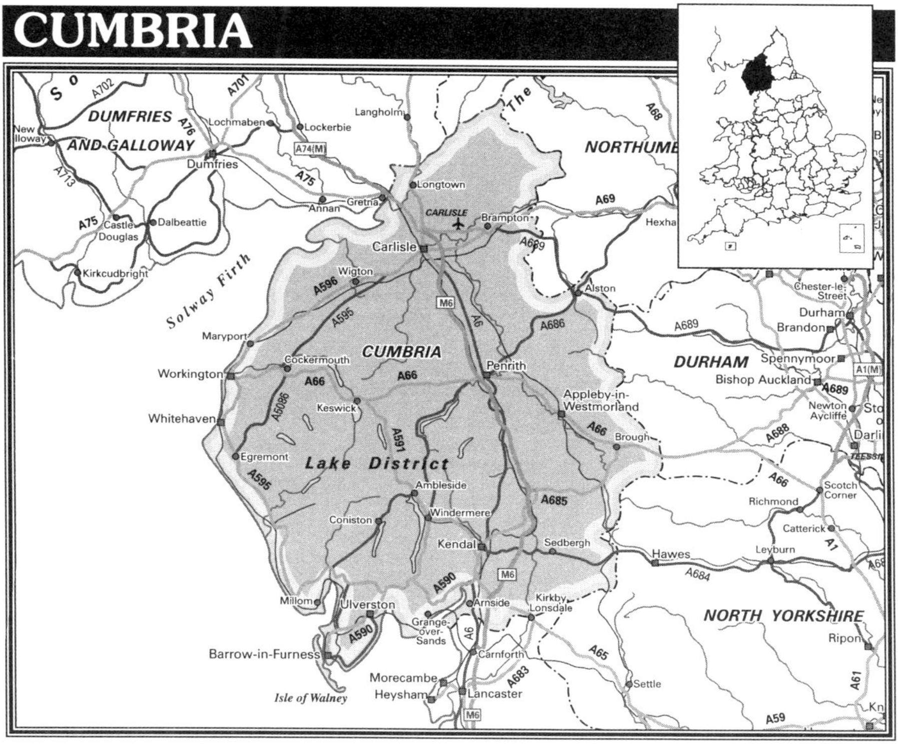

A warm, friendly welcome awaits you at Lakeside Guest House, at the northern tip of Bassenthwaite Lake. We have eight bedrooms (seven en suite) with TV, radio/alarm, hairdryer, shoe cleaning and tea/coffee facilities. Delicious home-cooked breakfast, or relax in our residents' lounge.

The Lake District National Park, Hadrian's Wall and Scottish Borders are easily accessible for a day visit or take advantage of sailing, rowing, fishing, walking and golf available nearby.

Lakeside is a non-smoking establishment. Sorry, no pets.

Self-catering lodge also available (sleeps 3/4)
PLEASE CALL FOR OUR COLOUR BROCHURE

Lakeside Guesthouse
Dubwath, Bassenthwaite Lake, Cumbria CA13 9YD
Tel: 01768 776358 • Fax: 01768 776163

See also Colour Advertisement

VISITS & ATTRACTIONS

Rheged Discovery Centre • *Off M6 Junction 40, A66* • *01768 868000* • *website: www.rheged.com*
The Lake District's most spectacular attraction. Six-storey high giant cinema screen takes you on a journey through 2000 years of Cumbria's history, myths and legends.
Set in Britain's largest grass-covered building.

The Dock Museum • *Barrow-in-Furness, Cumbria* • *01229 870871*
A fascinating modern museum telling how this tiny hamlet became the biggest iron and steel centre in the world, and then a major British ship-building force. Film show, galleries, shop, cafe.

Cumbria

Hotel   1-12

AMBLESIDE. Peter & Anne Hart, Bracken Fell, Outgate, Ambleside LA22 0NH (015394 36289).

A delightful country residence with two acres of gardens, situated in beautiful open countryside between Ambleside and Hawkshead in the picturesque hamlet of Outgate. This comfortable home with its lovely accommodation and friendly service is ideally located for exploring the Lake District. Each bedroom has its own private facilities, colour TV, hairdryer, complimentary tea and coffee and a superb view. There is a comfortable lounge, dining room and ample private parking. Two country inns where evening meals are available are within walking distance. Bed and Breakfast from £23. No pets or children under 12 years. Non-smoking. Self-catering accommodation also available. Write or phone for brochure. ETC ◆◆◆
e-mail: hart.brackenfell@virgin.net
website: www.brackenfell.com

Guesthouse

See also Colour Display Advertisement   **AMBLESIDE. Elder Grove, Lake Road, Ambleside LA22 0DB (015394 32504).** Enjoy quality accommodation and service in our Victorian house, conveniently situated for walking or sightseeing and close to Ambleside with many shops and restaurants. We offer 10 comfortable bedrooms, all with private bathroom, also colour television, kettle tray, hairdryer and radio. Start the day with a choice of breakfast from a full Cumbrian Breakfast to a lighter bite served in our unique Lakeland diningroom, and in the evenings relax in our bar or lounge. We have parking, central heating and ask for no smoking please. Contact Paul and Vicky McDougall for brochure and tariff. ETC ◆◆◆◆.
e-mail: info@eldergrove.co.uk
website: www.eldergrove.co.uk

Farmhouse   1-12

CARLISLE. Mrs G. Elwen, New Pallyards, Hethersgill, Carlisle CA6 6HZ (01228 577308). As filmed for BBC TV! We welcome you to our beef/sheep farm, nine miles north of Junction 44 on M6. A wonderful area to visit, and an ideal base for the Lakes, Scottish Borders and Hadrian's Wall. Local salmon and sea trout fishing. Good home cooking. B&B - two family rooms and two double rooms, all en suite. One single and one twin-bedded room, suitable for disabled guests. SELF-CATERING accommodation also available in our comfortable well-equipped bungalow with three/four bedrooms; two lovely cottages on working farm (ETC ★★★★). We are proud to have won a National Salon Culinaire Award for the Best Breakfast in Britain. Bed and Breakfast from £21; Dinner, Bed and Breakfast from £160 to £170 weekly. Self-catering units from £90 to £460 weekly. ETC ◆◆◆◆ GOLD AWARD WINNER, HWFH, FHB.
e-mail info@newpallyards.freeserve.co.uk
website: www.newpallyards.freeserve.co.uk

Farmhouse   1-12

CARLISLE. Mrs Dorothy Nicholson, Gill Farm, Blackford, Carlisle CA6 4EL (01228 675326; Mobile: 07808 571586). In a delightful setting on a beef and sheep farm, this Georgian style farmhouse dated 1740 offers a friendly welcome to all guests breaking journeys to or from Scotland or having a holiday in our beautiful countryside. Near Hadrian's Wall, Gretna Green and Lake District. Golf, fishing, swimming and large agricultural auction markets all nearby; also cycle path passes our entrance. Accommodation is in one double room en suite, one family and one twin/single bedrooms. All rooms have washbasins, shaver points and tea/coffee making facilities. Two bathrooms, shower; lounge with colour TV; separate diningroom. Open all year. Reductions for children; cot provided. Central heating. Car essential, good parking. Pets permitted. Bed and Breakfast from £18. Telephone for further details or directions.

Please mention Britain's Best Holidays when enquiring about accommodation

BOARD Cumbria 65

Guesthouse 1-12

COCKERMOUTH. Mr and Mrs J.F. Graham, Rose Cottage Guest House. Lorton Road, Cockermouth

CA13 9DX (Tel & Fax: 01900 822189). A well established 10 bedroomed guest house in residential area of Cockermouth, just 10 minutes' walk from the interesting town centre. An excellent base for touring, within easy reach of Coast, Lakes and Fells. Private parking for 10/12 cars. All comfortable bedrooms have en suite facilities, colour TV, tea/coffee making and full central heating. No smoking areas within the guest house. Open all year except Christmas and New Year. Pets accepted by arrangement; children welcome. Bed and full English Breakfast from £22.50 to £30. Write for brochure. **ETC ◆◆◆**
website: www.rosecottageguest.co.uk

Hotel 1-12

HAWKSHEAD. Peter & Anne Hart, Bracken Fell, Outgate, Ambleside LA22 0NH (015394 36289).

A delightful country residence with two acres of gardens, situated in beautiful open countryside between Ambleside and Hawkshead in the picturesque hamlet of Outgate. This comfortable home with its lovely accommodation and friendly service is ideally located for exploring the Lake District. Each bedroom has its own private facilities, colour TV, hairdryer, complimentary tea and coffee and a superb view. There is a comfortable lounge, dining room and ample private parking. Two country inns where evening meals are available are within walking distance. Bed and Breakfast from £23. No pets or children under 12 years. Non-smoking. Self-catering accommodation also available. Write or phone for brochure. **ETC ◆◆◆**
e-mail: hart.brackenfell@virgin.net
website: www.brackenfell.com

Guesthouse

KESWICK. Mrs S. Park, Langdale, 14 Leonard Street, Keswick CA12 4EL (017687 73977). Victorian town

house, quietly situated, yet close to town, park, lake and fells. All rooms furnished to a very high standard, having quality en suite facilities, central heating, colour TV, tea/coffee making facilities throughout. Family, double or twin rooms available. Enjoy a good home cooked English or vegetarian breakfast or our popular Continental breakfast. We have a non smoking policy throughout the house. We will ensure your stay is a pleasant one. Bed and Breakfast from £21; Theatre Breaks. Special three nights midweek/weekend breaks November to March.

Guesthouse ♀

See also Colour Display Advertisement

LAKE DISTRICT. Lakeside Guest House, Dubwath, Bassenthwaite Lake, Bassenthwaite, Near Cockermouth CA13 9YD (017687 76358; Fax: 01768 776163). Elegant country house offering friendly and relaxing hospitality, set in peaceful surroundings near the shore of Bassenthwaite Lake. Magnificent views of the lake and surrounding mountain scenery. Keswick seven miles, western fells and Lake of Buttermere and Crummock Water, with the Solway Coast and the border city of Carlisle within easy reach. The house has a panelled hall and oak floors with eight comfortably furnished bedrooms (seven of which are en suite), offering colour TV, radio/alarm, hair drying, shoe cleaning and tea and coffee making facilities. The smaller eighth room has its own private bathroom. Delicious home cooking using local produce. Self-catering accommodation in the lodge sleeping four is also available. Residential licence. No smoking. No pets. Please telephone for brochure. **ETC ◆◆◆◆**

DERBYSHIRE

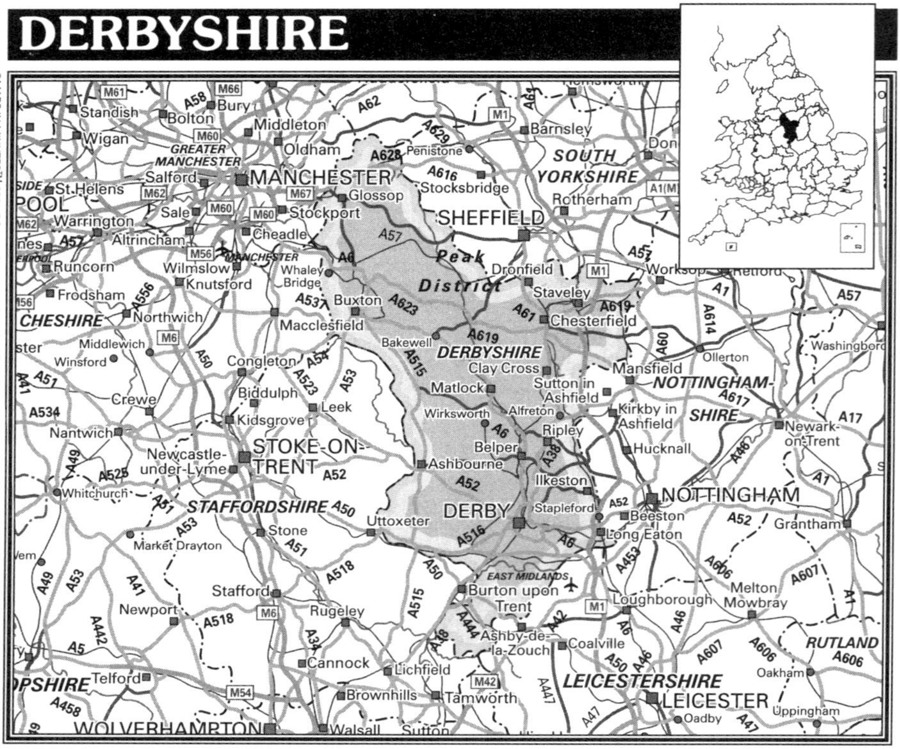

Farmhouse 1-12 &

ASHBOURNE. The Courtyard, Dairy House Farm, Alkmonton, Longford, Ashbourne DE6 3DG (Tel & Fax: 01335 330187). Grazing farm. Victorian cowshed tastefully converted and furnished to a very high standard. Tranquil location, yet within easy reach of Alton Towers, Chatsworth House, Calke Abbey and many other historic houses. The Potteries are close to hand, as is the American Adventure Theme Park. We are surrounded by beautiful countryside which includes Dovedale and the many other lovely Dales which make up the Derbyshire Dales. A newly opened 18 hole, par-three golf course is only four miles away. Good farmhouse fare served on our 18 acre farm. Stay in one of our seven rooms – five double, one twin and a family suite, all with en suite facilities. Children welcome. Regret, no pets. Bed and Breakfast from £24; family suite from £75. Winter breaks October 20–March 20: Dinner, Bed and Breakfast £34 per person per night, minimum two nights. **AA/RAC ◆◆◆◆, RAC** *SPARKLING DIAMOND AWARD, CATEGORY 1 DISABLED.*
e-mail: andy@dairyhousefarm.org.uk
website: www.dairyhousefarm.org.uk/

FREE or REDUCED RATE entry to Holiday Visits and Attractions — see our READERS' OFFER VOUCHERS on pages 35-54

BOARD

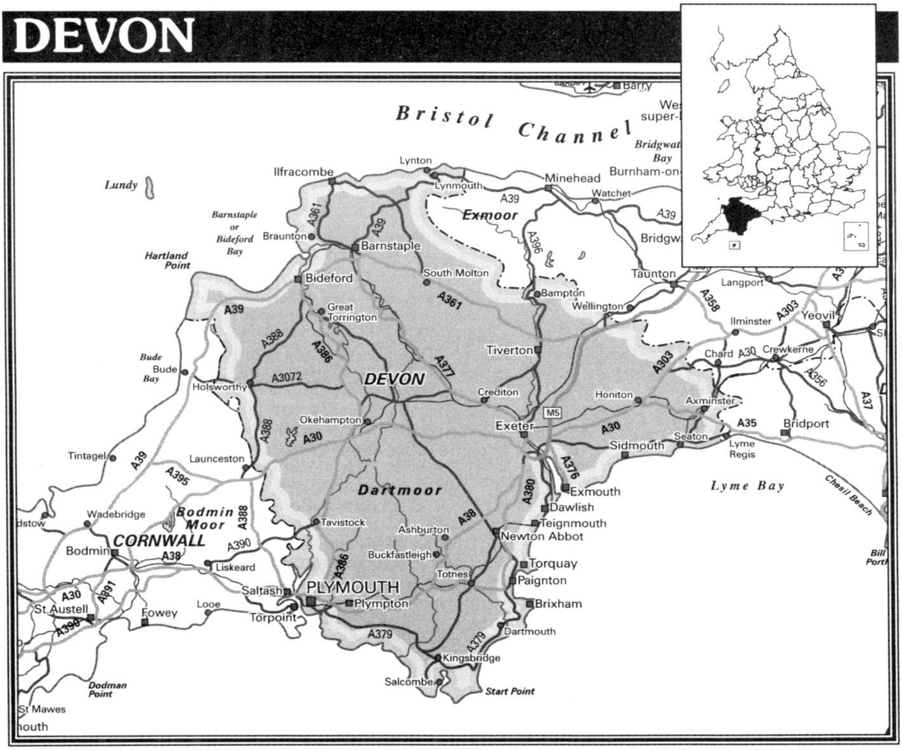

Devon 67

DEVON

SANDY COVE HOTEL ETC ★★★

See also Colour Advertisement

HOW would you like to arrive for a week's holiday at a hotel overlooking a beautiful bay, the sea and Exmoor? It has acres of gardens and woods running down to the cliff edge. The restaurant has an extensive à la cârte menu and on Saturdays you can enjoy the hot carvery and Swedish Smorgasbord, live entertainment (in the height of season) and dancing. Guests have use of the 80°F heated indoor pool and recreation centre with sauna, sunbed, gym equipment and whirlpool. Children free accommodation, under 5 years old – completely free including meals. Babysitting facilities. Pets welcome. Invalids catered for. Open all year. See also our Advertisement in the Colour Section.

Combe Martin Bay, Berrynarbor, Devon EX34 9SR Tel: 01271 882243 or 882888

Visit the  website

www.holidayguides.com

for details of the wide choice of accommodation featured in the full range of FHG titles

68 Devon **BOARD**

Hotel 1-12

See also Colour Display Advertisement — **BERRYNARBOR. Sandy Cove Hotel, Combe Martin Bay, Berrynarbor EX34 9SR (01271 882243; Fax: 01271 883830).** Sandy Cove Hotel has acres of gardens and woods running down to the cliff edge. The restaurant has an extensive à la cârte menu and on Saturdays you can enjoy the hot carvery and Swedish Smorgasbord, live entertainment (in the height of season) and dancing. Guests have use of the 80°F heated indoor pool and recreation centre with sauna, sunbed, gym equipment and whirlpool. Children free accommodation, under 5 years old – completely free including meals. Babysitting facilities. Pets welcome. Invalids catered for. Open all year. **ETC ★★★**

Guesthouse 2-11

HOLSWORTHY. Mrs Cole, Highbre Crest, Whitstone, Holsworthy EX22 6UF (01288 341002). Stunning views to coasts and moors make this very spacious house a special destination for your holiday with the added bonus of peace, tranquillity and delicious homemade country cooking. How can you resist paying us a visit? We are well situated for the coast and moors in Devon and Cornwall. Two double and one twin room - all en suite. Games room with full size snooker table, diningroom with separate tables, comfortable large conservatory with spectacular coastal views. Garden for guests' use, car parking. Non-smoking establishment. Children over 12 years welcome. Bed and Breakfast from £20, optional Evening Meal from £10. Open February to November.

Hotel

See also Colour Display Advertisement — **ILFRACOMBE. The Avoncourt Hotel, Torrs Walk Avenue, Ilfracombe (01271 862543).** Chris and Tony welcome you to their friendly family-run hotel. The hotel is situated in a quiet private road adjacent to National Trust land. It faces south with panoramic views of town and countryside. All bedrooms are on first or ground floor and the excellent food and relaxed atmosphere will make your holiday a memorable one. The heated rooms are en suite with tea/coffee making facilities and colour TV. There is also a cosy licensed bar and a TV lounge. Ample parking.

Hotel

PAIGNTON. Freda Dwane and Steve Bamford, Clifton Hotel, 9-10 Kernou Road, Paignton TQ4 6BA (Tel & Fax: 01803 556545). In the heart of the English Riviera. A friendly, licensed, no-smoking hotel in an ideal level location just off the sea front and close to shops, rail and coach stations. All rooms en suite with TV and beverages. Superb evening meals available. A perfect spot to leave the car and explore on foot or by public transport South Devon, Dartmoor etc. Welcome Host and Commitment to Quality Award Holders. Open Easter to October. Bed and Breakfast from £21 per person. Spring Breaks available.
e-mail: b&b@cliftonhotelpaignton.co.uk
website: www.cliftonhotelpaignton.co.uk

1-12 Months open	Pets welcome	Suitable for disabled
Sporting/special interests provided	Coast under two miles	Car essential
Licensed	Babysitting available	Children welcome
		Central heating

A useful Index of Towns/Villages and Counties appears on page 217 – please also refer to Contents Page 31.

Devon 69

Guesthouse 1-12

SLAPTON. Jane and Bryan Ashby, Start House, Start, Slapton, Kingsbridge TQ7 2QD (01548   580254).
Spacious and comfortable, Start House is situated in a quiet hamlet, one mile from Slapton. All the bedrooms overlook a beautiful valley running south-east to Slapton Ley and the sea. The delicious breakfasts, traditional or vegetarian, are cooked to order using local produce. Evening meals are available by arrangement. We are an ideal base for walkers and wildlife enthusiasts, and garden lovers will find much of interest in our large garden. Open all year for Bed and Breakfast from £23, we also have a self-catering flat for two people. Non-smokers only. Full details on request. **ETC ♦♦♦**

Hotel 3-11

WOOLACOMBE. Crossways Hotel, The Seafront, Woolacombe EX34 7DJ (Tel & Fax: 01271 870395).
Cosy, family-run licensed Hotel situated in one of the finest seafront positions in Woolacombe, overlooking the pretty Combesgate Beach and Lundy Island, and surrounded by National Trust land. Bathing and surfing from the hotel and ideally situated for golf, horse riding and beautiful walks. Menu choice for breakfast and evening dinner, and children's menu. Varied bar snacks available at lunchtime. All bedrooms individually refurbished to a high standard, many en suite and with fabulous sea views. Colour TV and tea/coffee making facilities in all rooms. Children half price or FREE. Pets welcome. Non-smoking establishment. Free on-site parking. RAC Dining Award. Why not find out why many of our guests return year after year? **ETC/AA/RAC ★** *SILVER AWARD*

VISITS & ATTRACTIONS

Quince Honey Farm • *South Molton, Devon* • *01769 572401*
The world's largest living honey bee exhibition, where the hives can be viewed in complete safety. Ideal for all ages, with fascinating videos and well-stocked shop.

National Marine Aquarium • *Plymouth, Devon* • *01752 220084*
website: www.national-aquarium.co.uk
Come face to face with thousands of marine creatures in settings including a wall of ocean 15 metres high and 5 metres wide, a shark theatre with over 700,000 litres of water, a living coral reef and a seawater wave-tank.

PLEASE MENTION THIS GUIDE WHEN YOU WRITE
OR PHONE TO ENQUIRE ABOUT ACCOMMODATION

IF YOU ARE WRITING, A STAMPED, ADDRESSED
ENVELOPE IS ALWAYS APPRECIATED

DORSET

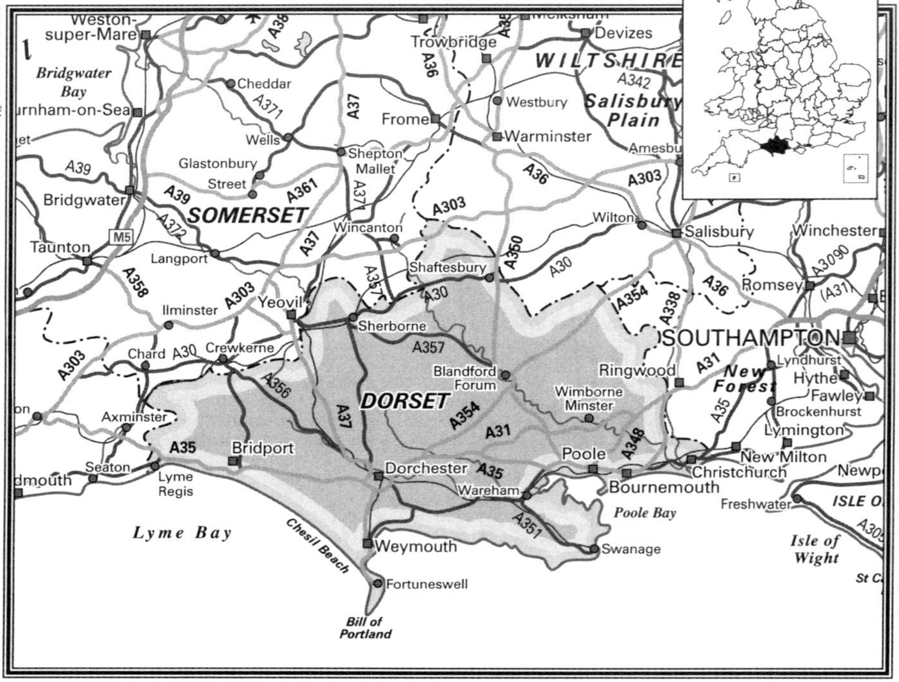

The Cobb at Lyme Regis, Dorset

Dorset

THE KNOLL HOUSE

A CIVILISED AND RELAXING HOLIDAY FOR ALL AGES.
AN INDEPENDENT COUNTRY-HOUSE HOTEL IN AN UNRIVALLED POSITION ABOVE
THREE MILES OF GOLDEN BEACH

STUDLAND BAY DORSET BH19 3AH
01929 450450 (FAX-450423)
e-mail: enquiries@knollhouse.co.uk   www.knollhouse.co.uk

Inn 1-12

See also Colour Display Advertisement

DORCHESTER. The Poachers Inn, Piddletrenthide DT2 7QX (01300 348358; Fax: 01300 348153). Country Inn set in the heart of the lovely Piddle Valley within easy reach of all Dorset's attractions. All rooms en suite and have colour TV, tea/coffee making facilities, telephone. Swimming pool, riverside garden. Restaurant. Half Board guests choose from our à la carte menu at no extra cost. Bed and Breakfast £30 per person; Dinner, Bed and Breakfast £42 per person. 10% discount for seven nights or more. Low Season Breaks - two nights Dinner, Bed and Breakfast £84 per person, third night free (October – April). Send for brochure. **ETC/AA ♦♦♦♦**.

Guesthouse 1-12

See also Colour Display Advertisement

DORCHESTER. Mrs V.A. Bradbeer, Nethercroft, Winterbourne Abbas, Dorchester DT2 9LU (01305 889337). This country house with its friendly and homely atmosphere welcomes you to the heart of Hardy's Wessex. Central for touring the many places of interest that Dorset has to offer, including Corfe Castle, Lyme Regis, Dorchester, Weymouth, Lulworth Cove, etc. Lovely country walks and many local attractions. Two double rooms, one single, washbasins or en suite. Separate bathroom, shower and toilets. TV lounge, dining room. Large garden. Open all year. Central heating. Car essential, ample parking. Bed and Breakfast from £18. Take A35 from Dorchester, we are the last house at the western edge of the village.

72 Dorset

BOARD

Hotel   4-10

STUDLAND BAY. The Knoll House Hotel, Studland Bay BH19 3AH (01929 450450; Fax: 01929 450423). A country house hotel situated within a National Trust reserve overlooking three miles of golden beaches and native heath. Six fine lounges; restaurant and separate children's restaurant. Family suites available and the many ground floor and single rooms are a popular all-age asset. Facilities include tennis courts, golf course, outdoor heated pool, Jacuzzi, sauna, Turkish room, plunge pool and gym. Children's play room and fabulous SAFE adventure playground. Full Board from £93 to £125 per day inclusive of VAT and service. Further information available. Also see Display Advertisement in this Guide.
e-mail: enquiries@knollhouse.co.uk
website: www.knollhouse.co.uk

Hotel   1-12

WAREHAM. Cromwell House Hotel, Lulworth Cove, Wareham BH20 5RJ (01929 400253/400332; Fax: 01929 400566). Catriona and Alistair Miller welcome guests to their comfortable family-run hotel, set in secluded gardens with spectacular sea views. Situated 200 yards from Lulworth Cove, with direct access to the Dorset Coastal Footpath. A heated swimming pool is available for guests' use from May to October. Accommodation is in 17 en suite bedrooms, with TV, direct-dial telephone, and tea/coffee making facilities, most have spectacular sea views. Restaurant, bar, wine list. Two nights dinner, bed and breakfast (fully en suite) from £75. Off peak mid week breaks. Open all year except Christmas. **ETC/AA/RAC ★★**.
website: www.lulworthcove.co.uk

1-12 Months open	Pets welcome	Suitable for disabled	Car essential
[S] Sporting/special interests provided		Coast under two miles	Children welcome
Licensed	Babysitting available		Central heating

VISITS & ATTRACTIONS

Sherborne Castle • Sherborne, Dorset • *01935 813182*
website: www.sherbornecastle.com
Built by Sir Walter Raleigh in 1594 and home to the Digby family since the early 17th century. Splendid collection of art, furniture and porcelain.

The Blue Pool • Furzebrook, Dorset • *01929 551408*
Sandy paths wander through 20 acres of heather, gorse and pine trees or down to the water's edge, which varies in colour from green to turquoise. Cream teas, children' s play area, gift shop, museum, plant centre.

Visit the **FHG** website
www.holidayguides.com
for details of the wide choice of accommodation featured in the full range of FHG titles

GLOUCESTERSHIRE

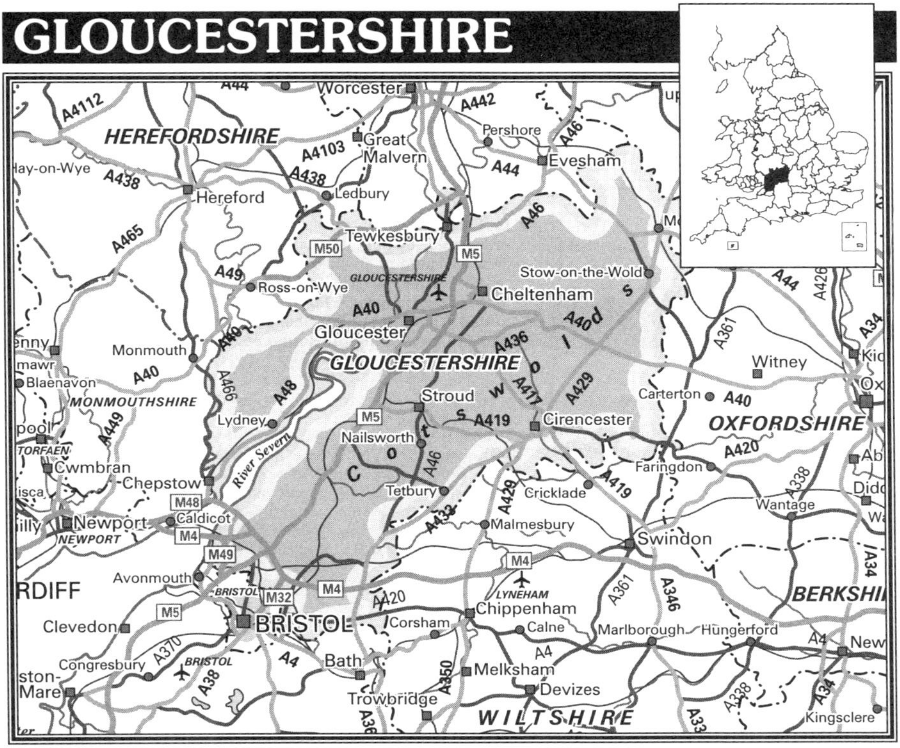

Guesthouse   1-12

GLOUCESTER near. S. J. Barnfield, Kilmorie Smallholding, Gloucester Road, Corse, Staunton, Near Gloucester GL19 3RQ (Tel & Fax: 01452 840224). QUALITY ALL GROUND FLOOR ACCOMMODATION. Kilmorie is Grade II Listed (c.1848) within conservation area in a lovely part of Gloucestershire. Deceptively spacious yet cosy, tastefully furnished: double, twin, family or single bedrooms all with tea trays, colour TVs, radios, mostly en suite. Very comfortable guests' lounge; traditional home cooking is served in the separate dining room overlooking large garden where there are seats to relax, watch our free range hens (who provide excellent eggs for breakfast!!) or the wild birds and butterflies which we encourage to visit. Perhaps walk waymarked farmland footpaths which start here. Children may "help" with our child's pony and free range hens. Rural yet ideally situated to visit Cotswolds, Royal Forest of Dean, Wye Valley and Malvern Hills. Children over five years welcome. Three-course Evening Dinner, Bed and Breakfast from £25; Bed and full English Breakfast from £17. Ample parking. **ETC** ♦♦♦
e-mail: sheila-barnfield@supanet.com

The FHG **Directory of Website Addresses** on pages 182-216 is a useful quick reference guide for holiday accommodation with e-mail and/or website details

74 Gloucestershire

BOARD

Inn   1-12

See also Colour Display Advertisement

LYDNEY. The Fountain Inn, Parkend, Royal Forest of Dean, Gloucestershire GL15 4JD (01594 562189; Fax: 01594 564438) A traditional village inn, well known locally for its excellent meals and real ales. A Forest Fayre menu offers such delicious main courses as Lamb Steak in Woodland Berry Sauce and Gloucester Sausage in Onion Gravy, together with a large selection of curries, vegetarian dishes and other daily specials. Centrally situated in one of England's foremost wooded areas, the inn makes an ideal base for sightseeing, or for exploring some of the many peaceful forest walks nearby. All bedrooms (including one especially adapted for the less able) are en suite, decorated and furnished to an excellent standard, and have television and tea/coffee making facilities. Various half-board breaks are available throughout the year. **ETC** ◆◆◆
e-mail: TheFountainInn@aol.com
website: www.SmoothHound.co.uk/hotels/fount.html

Guesthouse

STOW-ON-THE-WOLD. (Cotswolds). Graham and Helen Keyte, The Limes, Evesham Road, Stow-on-the-Wold GL54 1EN (01451 830034/831056). Large Victorian House (established over 30 years) in the centre of the Cotswolds. Large attractive garden has ornamental pond and waterfall and overlooks fields. Four minutes' walk to town centre and central for visiting such interesting places as Stratford-upon-Avon, Burford, Cheltenham, Broadway, Tewkesbury, Cirencester, Bourton-on-the-Water, Chipping Campden, etc all within a 20 mile radius. Four en suite, one four-poster, with colour TV and tea/coffee making facilities, hair dryer; TV lounge; diningroom, cot, high chair. Children and pets welcome. Car park. Bed and Breakfast from £20 to £25 per night. Full English Breakfast or vegetarians catered for. **AA** ◆◆◆.

Farmhouse   1-12

STOW-ON-THE-WOLD. Robert and Dawn Smith, Corsham Field Farmhouse, Bledington Road, Stow-on-the-Wold GL54 1JH (01451 831750). Homely farmhouse with traditional features and breathtaking views, one mile from Stow-on-the-Wold. Ideally situated for exploring all the picturesque Cotswold villages such as Broadway, Bourton-on-the-Water, Upper and Lower Slaughter, Chipping Campden, Snowshill, etc. Also central point for places of interest such as Blenheim Palace, Cotswold Wildlife Park, Stratford and many stately homes and castles in the area. Twin, double and family rooms, most with en suite facilities, others with washbasins, TV and tea/coffee making facilities. Pets and children welcome. Good pub food five minutes' walk away. Bed and full English Breakfast from £17 to £23 per person. **ETC/AA** ◆◆◆.

B&B

TEWKESBURY. Gantier, 12 Church Road, Alderton, Near Tewkesbury GL20 8NR (01242 620343; Fax:07787 504872). A warm welcome awaits you at our traditional stone house which is situated on the edge of the village with lovely views accross the meadowland to the Cotswold hills. All our bedrooms benefit from a colour television, tea and coffee making facilities, radio/alarm, hairdryer and a private bathroom. Another double room with en suite is planned for spring 2002. Breakfast time is flexible and special diets can be catered for with prior notice. Evening Meals are not provided although there is a local village pub providing excellent food within walking distance and several other highly recommended establishments close by. We are a non-smoking household (we do have a lovely garden and covered porch if you are desperate!) and we do not usually take children under four years old. Terms:double room; £45 per night, single room £25 per night (one person only in a double room £27.50 per night).

PUBLISHER'S NOTE

While every effort is made to ensure accuracy, we regret that FHG Publications cannot accept responsibility for errors, omissions or misrepresentations in our entries or any consequences thereof. Prices in particular should be checked because we go to press early. We will follow up complaints but cannot act as arbiters or agents for either party.

HAMPSHIRE

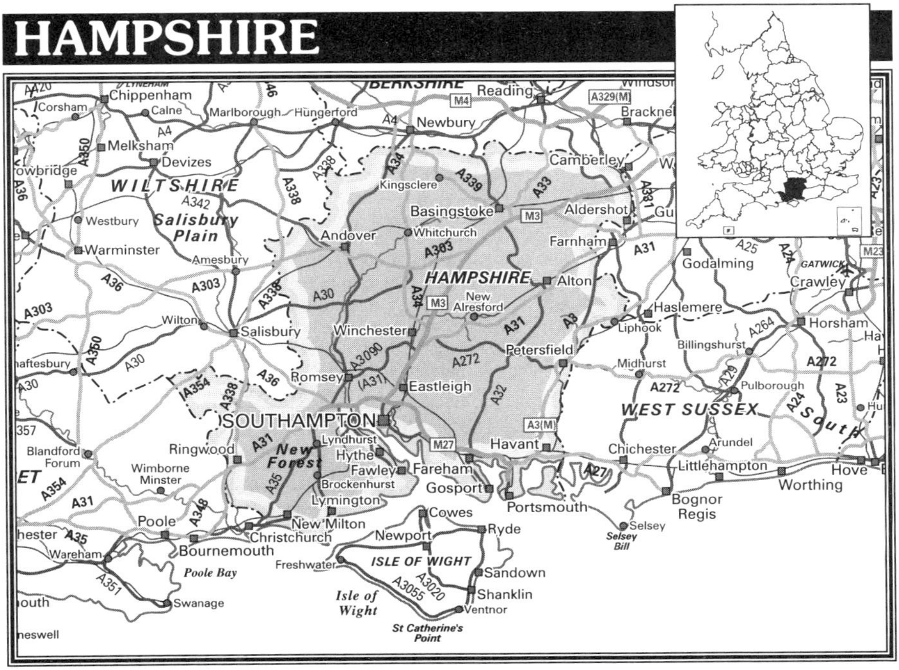

Guesthouse   1-12

LYMINGTON. (New Forest). Jane and Mike Finch, "Dolphins", 6 Emsworth Road, Lymington SO41 9BL (01590 676108 or 679545; Fax: 01590 688275).

"Dolphins" is a very comfortable and homely Victorian cottage offering warm hospitality and the highest standard of accommodation. Single, twin, double and family rooms all have colour TV and tea/coffee making facilities; kingsize and twin en suite available if required. Spacious and very comfortable sitting room with open log fire (in winter) and colour TV with satellite. Choice of breakfast; traditional home-cooked evening meals optional. Very quiet position, centrally located, just five minutes' walk from railway/bus/coach stations and ferry. Beautiful Forest walks, excellent cycle rides in and around Lymington and the New Forest (maps provided, mountain bikes with hats available). Open all year. From £18 per person per night. Children half price. Use of Leisure Club facilities, beach chalet and mountain bikes. Visa/Mastercard accepted. Please write, telephone or fax for brochure. **ETC** ♦♦♦♦
website: www.DolphinsNewForestBandB.co.uk

Guesthouse   1-12

STOCKBRIDGE. Mr and Mrs A.P. Hooper, Carbery Guest House, Stockbridge SO20 6EZ (01264 810771).

Ann and Philip Hooper welcome you to Carbery Guest House situated on A30, just outside the village of Stockbridge, overlooking the famous trout fishing River Test. This fine old Georgian house has one acre of landscaped gardens, with swimming pool. Stonehenge and numerous other places of interest nearby; sporting and recreational facilities close at hand. Accommodation includes double, twin, family and single rooms with private facilities, central heating, colour TV, tea/coffee makers, hair dryers and radio alarms. Cots, high chairs available. Car essential, parking. Open January to December for Evening Dinner, Bed and Breakfast or Bed and Breakfast only. RAC Acclaimed, AA Listed. Terms on application. **AA/RAC** ♦♦♦.

ISLE OF WIGHT

Windcliffe Manor Hotel & Restaurant
SANDROCK ROAD, NITON UNDERCLIFFE PO38 2NG Tel/Fax: 01983 730215

The hotel is situated in its own grounds at the most southerly part of the island overlooking the English Channel and offers lovely walks along the coastal paths and through unspoilt countryside. The many places of interest are all within an easy drive, and after a day out, guests can enjoy a dip in the heated outdoor pool before dinner. Windcliffe dining is of the highest standard, with à la carte and vegetarian menus and excellent breakfasts; light lunches and afternoon teas are served. Our well stocked bar and extensive wine list complements the food. All rooms are en suite with colour television, video and tea/coffee making facilities. Fishing, golf and horse riding are all available locally. Colour brochure.
website: www.windcliffe.co.uk

Hotel   1-12

NITON UNDERCLIFFE. Windcliffe Manor Hotel & Restaurant, Sandrock Road, Niton Undercliffe PO38 2NG (Tel & Fax: 01983 730215). Situated in its own grounds at the most southerly part of the island overlooking the English Channel in an area of outstanding natural beauty and bordering National Trust land. We offer lovely walks along the coastal paths and through unspoilt countryside. The many places of interest are all within an easy drive. After a day out, enjoy a dip in the heated outdoor pool before dinner. Windcliffe dining is to the highest standards with the à la carte or vegetarian menus served to all guests and a choice breakfast menu. Our well stocked bar and extensive wine list complement the food. The Hotel offers a high degree of comfort and gentility with Victorian grace and charm. All rooms en suite with TV, video and tea/coffee facilities. Light lunches and afternoon teas served. Free private car parking. Open all year. Phone for fully detailed colour brochure by return of post. **ETC ★★★**.
website: www.windcliffe.co.uk

VISITS & ATTRACTIONS

Isle of Wight Waxworks • *Brading, Isle of Wight* • *01983 487286*
See the Rectory Mansion, The Chamber of Horrors, The World of Nature, Professor Copperthwaite's Exhibition of Oddities, and demonstrations of the fascinating art of candle carving.

The FHG GOLF GUIDE
Where to Play Where to Stay
2002

Available from most bookshops, the 2002 edition of **THE GOLF GUIDE** covers details of every UK golf course – well over 2800 entries – for holiday or business golf. Hundreds of hotel entries offer convenient accommodation, accompanying details of the courses – the 'pro', par score, length etc.

In association with 'Golf Monthly' and including Holiday Golf in Ireland, France, Portugal, Spain, The USA, South Africa and Thailand.

£9.99 from bookshops or from the publishers (postage charged outside UK) • FHG Publications, Abbey Mill Business Centre, Paisley PA1 1TJ

Lancashire 77

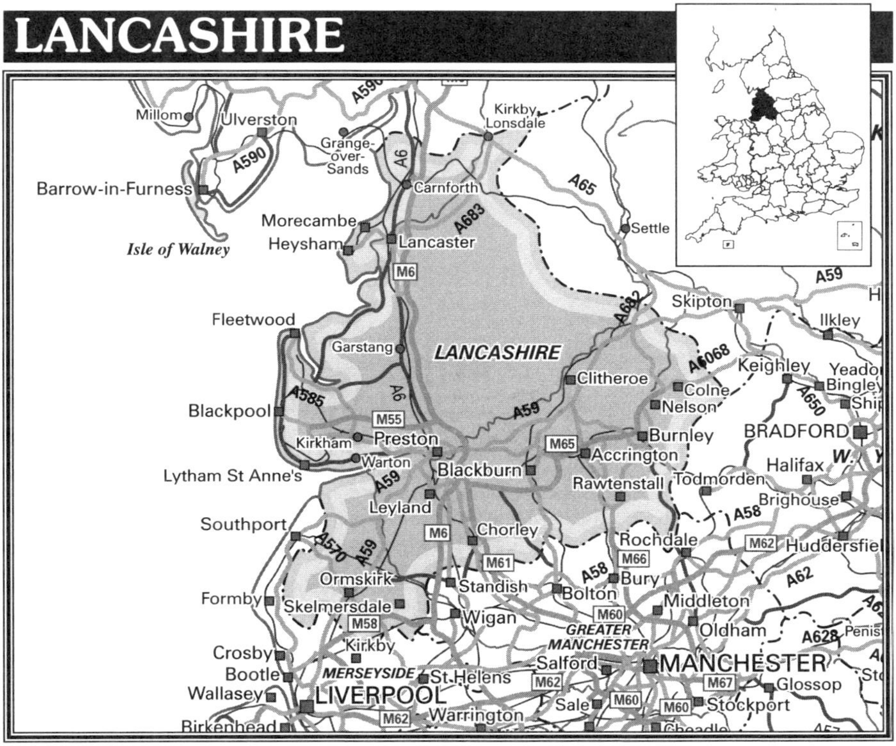

LANCASHIRE

The Golf Links Hotel
85, The Promenade, Southport PR9 0JN
Tel: 01704 530405

Privately owned and personally managed. An elegant Victorian house standing in its own grounds, ideally situated on the promenade overlooking the golf course and beach. Easy walking distance to town, theatre, marine lake, park and beach. The hotel has a comfortable public bar which offers excellent bar meals, a sun patio overlooking 18 hole golf course. Open all year. Families welcome. Pets welcome. Excellent value for money and a friendly service.
Terms from £19.50 to £23.50.

See also Colour Advertisement

NOTE

All the information in this book is given in good faith in the belief that it is correct. However, the publishers cannot guarantee the facts given in these pages, neither are they responsible for changes in policy, ownership or terms that may take place after the date of going to press. Readers should always satisfy themselves that the facilities they require are available and that the terms, if quoted, still apply.

Lancashire		BOARD

Hotel 1-12

See also Colour Display Advertisement

SOUTHPORT. **The Golf Links Hotel, 85 The Promenade, Southport PR9 0JN (01704 530405).** An elegant Victorian house standing in its own grounds, ideally situated on the promenade overlooking the golf course and beach, within easy walking distance of the town theatre, marine lake, park and beach. The hotel is privately owned, has a comfortable public bar which offers excellent bar meals and a sun patio overlooking an 18-hole golf course. Open all year. Families welcome. Excellent value for money and very friendly service. Terms: £25 en suite, £19.50 standard.

The FHG Diploma

HELP IMPROVE BRITISH TOURIST STANDARDS

You are choosing holiday accommodation from our very popular FHG Publications. Whether it be a hotel, guest house, farmhouse or self-catering accommodation, we think you will find it hospitable, comfortable and clean, and your host and hostess friendly and helpful.

Why not write and tell us about it?

As a recognition of the generally well-run and excellent holiday accommodation reviewed in our publications, we at FHG Publications Ltd. present a diploma to proprietors who receive the highest recommendation from their guests who are also readers of our Guides. If you care to write to us praising the holiday you have booked through FHG Publications Ltd. – whether this be board, self-catering accommodation, a sporting or a caravan holiday, what you say will be evaluated and the proprietors who reach our final list will be contacted.

The winning proprietor will receive an attractive framed diploma to display on his premises as recognition of a high standard of comfort, amenity and hospitality. FHG Publications Ltd. offer this diploma as a contribution towards the improvement of standards in tourist accommodation in Britain. Help your excellent host or hostess to win it!

We nominate ....

....

Because

Your Name ....

Address ....

....

Telephone No..

NORFOLK

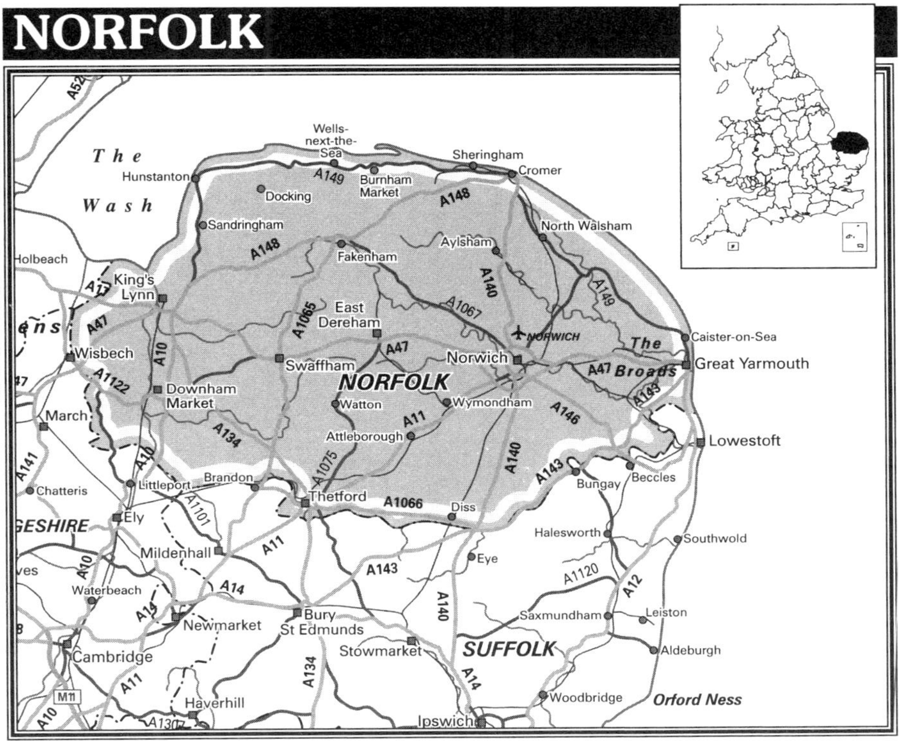

Norfolk

Hotel

See also Colour Display Advertisement

HORNING. Petersfield House Hotel, Horning NR12 8PF (01692 630741). The Petersfield House Hotel is a family owned Country House Hotel situated in a peaceful location in the heart of the Norfolk Broads and within easy reach of the North Norfolk coast. Our landscaped gardens and moorings are an ideal setting to relax and enjoy the beautiful Broadland surroundings. Our restaurant offers light lunches, table d'hôte and an extensive à la carte menu. Saturday night dinner dances and themed evenings are held regularly. Bargain breaks are available from £55 per person. For further information and a brochure please call us on the above number or visit our website.
website: www.petersfieldhotel.co.uk

VISITS & ATTRACTIONS

Norfolk Lavender • *Caley Mill, Heacham, Norfolk* • *01485 570384*
website: www.norfolk-lavender.co.uk
Learn about the ancient process of lavender distillation – a gift shop stocks a wide range of products. The Herb Shop has a selection of lavender and herb plants, plus unusual gifts.

Pensthorpe Waterfowl Trust • *Fakenham, Norfolk* • *01328 851465*
Over 120 species of waterfowl from all over the world make this Europe's finest collection of endangered and exotic waterbirds, with over 200 acres of lakes, woodland and meadows.

NORTHUMBERLAND

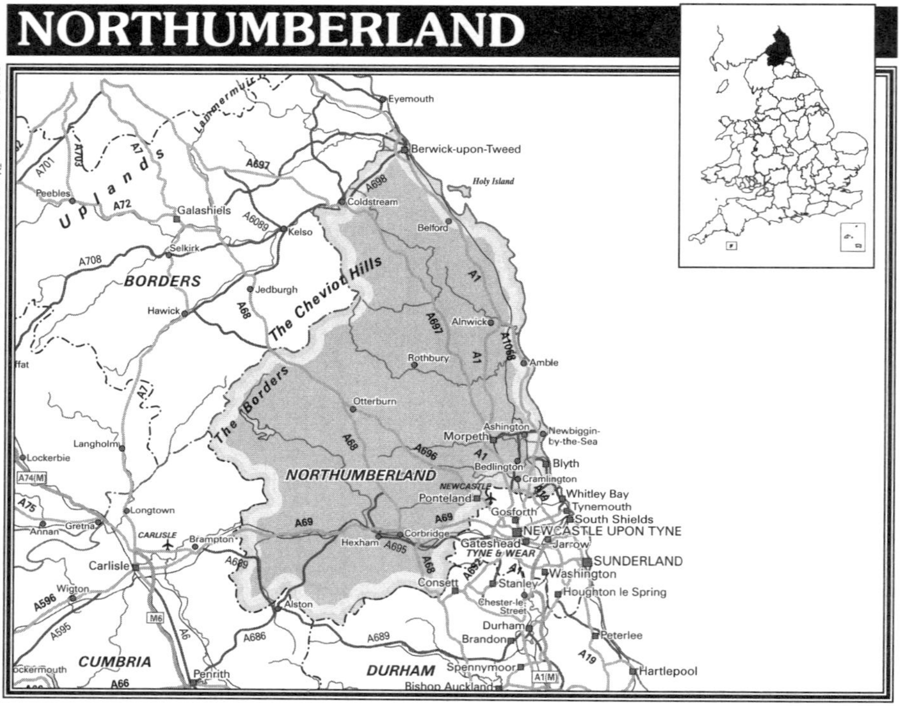

B&B

ALNWICK. Mrs J.W. Bowden, "Anvil-Kirk", 8 South Charlton Village, Alnwick NE66 2NA (01665 579324). A very characterful cottage offering a friendly, homely atmosphere and a welcome to match. Former Smithy built in 1771, completely modernised in 1974, affording very comfortable accommodation comprising a double bedroom and one twin bedded room with washbasin, shower and shaver points. Open wood-burning fire in communal lounge. Full English Breakfast. Good value meals at local pubs. A peaceful village surrounded by farmland plus moorland walks with views of the Cheviot Hills, Bamburgh and Dunstanburgh Castles and, of course, our lovely clean beaches. Three-quarters of a mile from the A1 and very easy to locate. Pets welcome. Ample parking. Bed and Breakfast terms from £18 to £20. Also available, a 39 ft. Residential Caravan for hire weekly from £165 to £195. Please phone for details.

VISITS & ATTRACTIONS

Grace Darling Museum • *Bamburgh, Northumberland* • *01668 214465*
Commemorates the rescue by Grace and her father of the nine survivors of the wreck of the *Forfarshire*. Many original relics, including the cable used in the rescue, plus books, paintings etc.

- 1-12 Months open
- Pets welcome
- Suitable for disabled
- Car essential
- Sporting/special interests provided
- Coast under two miles
- Children welcome
- Licensed
- Babysitting available
- Central heating

OXFORDSHIRE

Hotel

FARINGDON. Faringdon Hotel, 1 Market Place, Faringdon SN7 7HL (01367 240536; Fax: 01367 243250) The Faringdon Hotel is a delightful 17th century coaching inn and authentic Thai restaurant situated in the historic town of Faringdon. We are located just south of the famous city of Oxford and close to the Cotswolds. For that quiet country break we provide traditional hospitality that allows you to relax in the beauty of the English countryside. **ETCAA/RAC ★★**, *LES ROUTIERS*.

FHG PUBLICATIONS

publish a large range of well-known accommodation guides. We will be happy to send you details or you can use the order form at the back of this book.

The Water Terrace, Blenheim Palace, Woodstock, Oxfordshire

SOMERSET

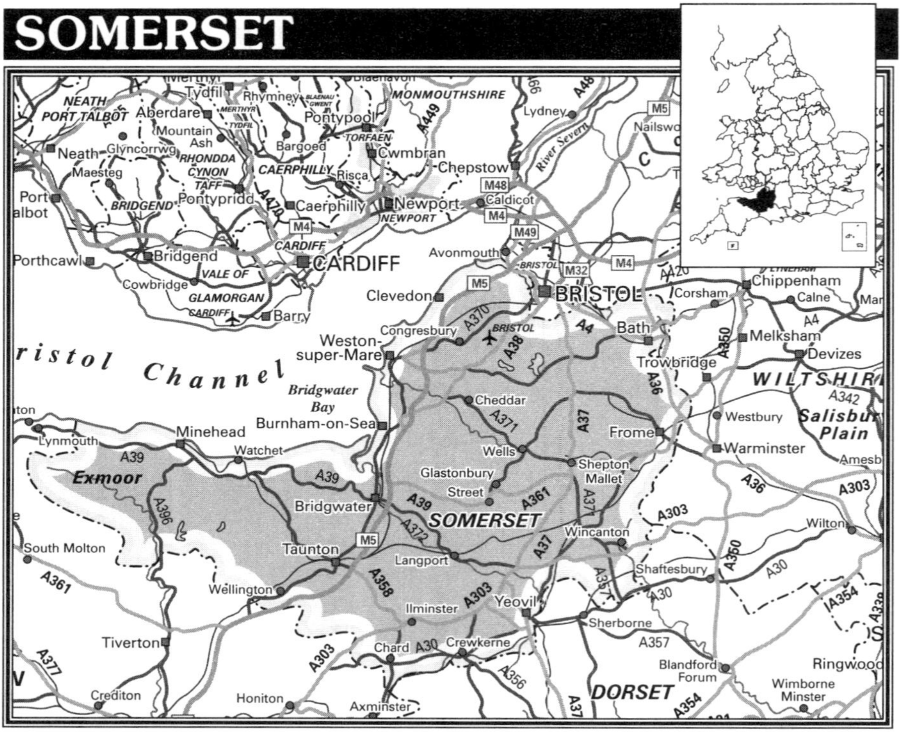

Guesthouse

BATH. Mrs D. Strong, Wellsway Guest House, 51 Wellsway, Bath BA2 4RS (01225 423434). A comfortable Edwardian house with all bedrooms centrally heated; washbasins and colour televisions in the rooms. On bus route with buses to and from the city centre every few minutes or an eight minute walk down the hill. Alexandra Park, with magnificent views of the city, is five minutes' walk. Bath is ideal for a short or long holiday with many attractions in and around the city; Longleat, Wells and Bristol are all nearby. Parking available. Bed and Breakfast from £18–£20 per night, with a pot of tea to welcome you on arrival. ETC ♦♦.

See also Colour Display Advertisement

EXMOOR. Court Farm, Exford, Exmoor TA24 7LY (01643 831207). For Bed and Breakfast, our cosy farmhouse can be reached down a quiet lane and has much character, with inglenook fireplaces and exposed beams. Our two bedroomed cottages each take five people. They have large kitchen/diner, sittingroom, two bedrooms (double with Gothic four-poster and twin with bunk-beds). Snowdrop Cottage sleeps two people. There is sitting/diningroom and well-equipped kitchen. The double bedroom has en suite bathroom and the garden has rustic furniture. We provide all electricity, full oil central heating and all bed linen in the price. Cottages are open 52 weeks and we have ample parking. Stabling and grazing available for horses. Well behaved pets are welcome in cottages. For more details visit our website. **ETC ★★★**
e-mail: beth@courtfarm.co.uk
website: www.courtfarm.co.uk

1-12 Months open	Pets welcome	Suitable for disabled	Car essential
[S] Sporting/special interests provided		Coast under two miles	Children welcome
Licensed	Babysitting available		Central heating

Ralegh's Cross Inn
Brendon Hill, Exmoor, Somerset TA23 0LN

**Tel: 01984 640343
Fax: 01643 851227**

Perched high in the beautiful Brendon Hills, Exmoor National Park, Ralegh's Cross Inn offers comfortable and tastefully refurbished en suite rooms, some with four-poster beds, all non-smoking with colour TVs and hospitality trays.

A full and à la carte menu with freshly prepared starters, home-cooked main courses and home-made desserts is available daily. We're also famous locally for our tasty Farmer's Carvery.

A walker's, rider's and fisherman's paradise with many nearby places of interest for the tourist too.

Open all year, terms from £20 per night. Colour brochure available.

See also Colour Advertisement

Guesthouse

ILMINSTER. Mrs G Phillips, "Hermitage", 29 Station Road, Ilminster TA19 9BE (01460 53028).
Enjoy the friendly atmosphere of a lovely Listed 17th century house with beams and inglenook. Four-poster beds. Two acres of delightful gardens, with wood and hills beyond. Twin or double rooms with washbasins, en suite available. Lounge with log fire and colour TV. Tea or coffee with homemade biscuits on arrival. Full English breakfast. Traditional inns nearby for evening meals. Ideal touring centre for Quantock Hills, Wells, Glastonbury, Lyme Regis and many picturesque villages. Several National Trust properties, gardens and historic houses within a few miles; 10 miles from M5, half-a-mile from A303. Bed and Breakfast from £38 for two double, £43 double en suite. **ETC ♦♦♦**.
website: www.home.freeuk.net/hermitage

Country House

PORLOCK. Margery and Henry Dyer, West Porlock House, West Porlock, Near Minehead TA24 8NX (01643 862880). Imposing country house in Exmoor National Park on the wooded slopes of West Porlock commanding exceptional sea views of Porlock Bay and countryside. Set in five acres of beautiful woodland gardens unique for its variety and size of unusual trees and shrubs and offering a haven of rural tranquillity. The house has large spacious rooms with fine and beautiful furnishings throughout. Two double, two twin and one family bedrooms, all with en suite or private bathrooms, TV, radio/alarm, tea/coffee making facilities and shaver points. Licensed. Non-smoking. Private car park. Bed and Breakfast from £26 to £28 per person. Credit cards accepted. Sorry, no pets.
ETC ♦♦♦♦

VISITS & ATTRACTIONS

Wookey Hole Caves • *Wells, Somerset* • *01749 672243* • *website: www.wookey.co.uk*
Spectacular showcaves with ancient history and legends. Victorian papermill with traditional papermaking, magical mirror maze, old penny arcade, caves museum

West Somerset Railway • *Bishops Lydeard (near Taunton) to Minehead* • *01643 704996*
Enjoy 20 miles of glorious Somerset countryside as the steam train gently rolls back the years.
Break your journey at any one of ten restored stations along the route.
For 24hr talking timetable call 01643 707650.

Dunster Water Mill • *Dunster, Somerset* • *01643 821759*
The West Country's finest working water mill, set alongside the River Avill. See how flour is produced, then visit the Mill Shop where stoneground flour, home-made muesli and other products are available.

'LANA'

Hollow Farm, Westbury-sub-Mendip, Near Wells, Somerset BA5 1HH
Tel: 01749 870635
Mrs Sheila Stott

Modern farmhouse accommodation on working farm. Gently elevated site offering beautiful views over the moors and Somerset Levels, Glastonbury Tor in the distance and the Mendip Hills. En suite rooms including fridge, hair dryer, tea/coffee making facilities, shaver point, colour TV and central heating. Non-smoking. Terms from £21 pppn (reduced rates 3 nights or more), children under 12 years old £15.

See also Colour Advertisement

Inn 1-12 ♀

See also Colour Display Advertisement

WATCHET. Ralegh's Cross Inn, Brendon Hill, Exmoor TA23 0LN (01984 640343; Fax: 01643 851227) Perched high in the beautiful Brendon Hills, Exmoor National Park, Ralegh's Cross Inn offers comfortable and tastefully refurbished en suite rooms (some with four-poster beds), all non-smoking with colour TV and hospitality tray. A full à la carte menu with freshly prepared starters, home-cooked main courses and home-made desserts is available daily. We are also famous locally for our tasty Farmer's Carvery. A walker's, rider's and fisherman's paradise with many nearby places of interest for the tourist too. Open all year. Colour brochure available. Terms from £20 per night.

B&B

See also Colour Display Advertisement

WELLS. Mrs Sheila Stott, "Lana", Hollow Farm, The Hollow, Westbury-sub-Mendip, Near Wells BA5 1HH (01749 870635). Modern farmhouse accommodation on working farm. Gently elevated site offering beautiful views over the moors and Somerset Levels, Glastonbury Tor in the distance and the Mendip Hills. En suite rooms including fridge, hairdryer. tea/coffee facilities, shaver point, colour TV and central heating. Attractively furnished and comfortable. Breakfast room - sole use of guests, breakfasts served at separate tables in the farmhouse style room. Full English breakfast and a varied menu. Browse through the tourist information and relax in comfort. Non-smoking. Two double rooms, one twin room, all en suite with shower facilities. Prices from £21 per person per night, £15 children under 12 years old. Reduced rates for three nights or more.

FREE or REDUCED RATE entry to Holiday Visits and Attractions — see our READERS' OFFER VOUCHERS on pages 35-54

A useful Index of Towns/Villages and Counties appears on page 217 – please also refer to Contents Page 31

SUFFOLK

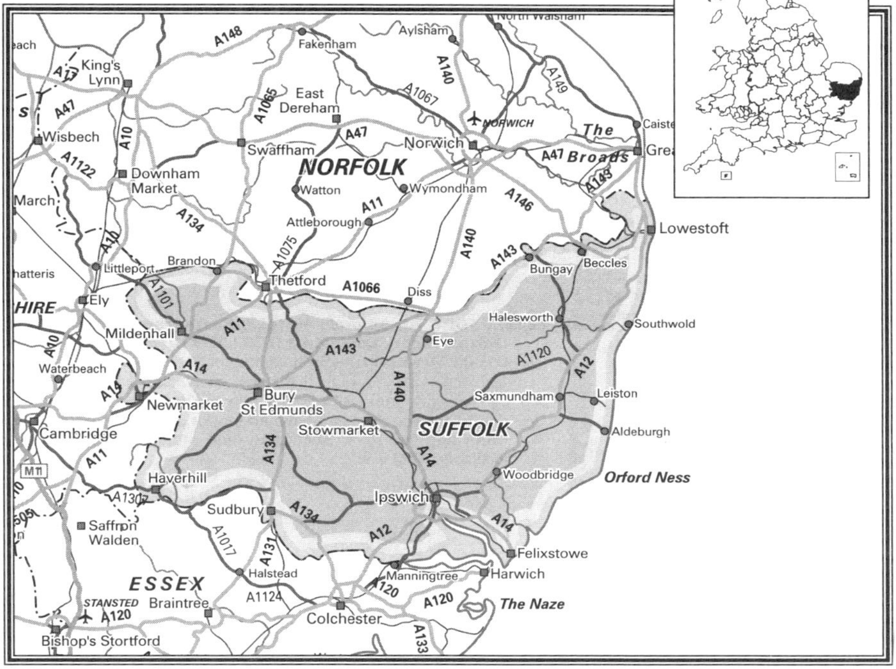

Suffolk 85

BROADLANDS HOTEL & LEISURE

**BRIDGE ROAD,
OULTON BROAD
LOWESTOFT
SUFFOLK
NR32 3LN**

The Broadlands Hotel is located within walking distance of Lake Lothing in the area known as the Norfolk Broads. We have 50 rooms, all en suite, with hospitality tray, hairdryer, TV and telephone. We also have an indoor swimming pool, steam room and spa bath, restaurant and residents' bar. Car park available.

Tel: 01502 516031 • Fax: 01502 501454

See also Colour Advertisement

VISITS & ATTRACTIONS

National Horse Racing Museum • *Newmarket, Suffolk* • *01638 667333*
website: www.nhrm.co.uk
Five permanent galleries tell the story of the development of the "sport of kings" over 400 years. Guided tours by arrangement to the studs, racing yards and training facilities.

East Anglia Transport Museum • *Lowestoft, Suffolk* • *01502 5184599*
The working museum where the past comes to life. Travel as often as you like on the preserved historic vehicles through the museum street scene or take a trip on the narrow gauge railway (all rides included in entry price).

Hotel

COLCHESTER. The Stoke by Nayland Club Ltd, Keepers Lane, Leavenheath, Colchester CO6 4PZ (01206 262836; Fax: 01206 263356). Set in the heart of Dedham Vale, an area captured in the paintings of Gainsborough and Constable, Stoke by Nayland offers some of the finest golfing and leisure facilities in East Anglia. Accommodation is now also available with the opening in 2000 of a 30 bedroomed hotel with fabulous views of the surrounding courses and lakes. Other than the two golf courses, which provide an outstanding and enjoyable experience for all standards of golfers, facilities include a leisure complex with gym, indoor pool, sauna and spa, and health/beauty treatments. Also available is a 20 bay covered driving range and 300 seater banqueting facility.
e-mail: info@golfclub.co.uk
website: www.stokebynaylandclub.co.uk

Hotel

LOWESTOFT. Broadlands Hotel & Restaurant, Bridge Road, Oulton Broad, Lowestoft NR32 3LN (01502 516031; Fax: 01502 501454). The Broadlands Hotel is located within walking distance of Lake Lothing, in the area known as the Norfolk Broads. We have 50 rooms, all with en suite including hospitality tray, TV and telephone. We also have an indoor swimming pool, steam room and spa bath. Restaurant and residents' bar. Car park available. **ETC ★★**

•• *Some Useful Guidance for Guests and Hosts* ••

Every year literally thousands of holidays, short breaks and overnight stops are arranged through our guides, the vast majority without any problems at all. In a handful of cases, however, difficulties do arise about bookings, which often could have been prevented from the outset.

It is important to remember that when accommodation has been booked, both parties – guests and hosts – have entered into a form of contract. We hope that the following points will provide helpful guidance.

GUESTS:
- When enquiring about accommodation, be as precise as possible. Give exact dates, numbers in your party and the ages of any children.
- State the number and type of rooms wanted and also what catering you require – bed and breakfast, full board etc. Make sure that the position about evening meals is clear – and about pets, reductions for children or any other special points.
- Read our reviews carefully to ensure that the proprietors you are going to contact can supply what you want. Ask for a letter confirming all arrangements, if possible.
- If you have to cancel, do so as soon as possible. Proprietors do have the right to retain deposits and under certain circumstances to charge for cancelled holidays if adequate notice is not given and they cannot re-let the accommodation.

HOSTS:
- Give details about your facilities and about any special conditions. Explain your deposit system clearly and arrangements for cancellations, charges etc. and whether or not your terms include VAT.
- If for any reason you are unable to fulfil an agreed booking without adequate notice, you may be under an obligation to arrange suitable alternative accommodation or to make some form of compensation.

While every effort is made to ensure accuracy, we regret that FHG Publications cannot accept responsibility for errors, omissions or misrepresentations in our entries or any consequences thereof. Prices in particular should be checked because we go to press early. We will follow up complaints but cannot act as arbiters or agents for either party.

East Sussex

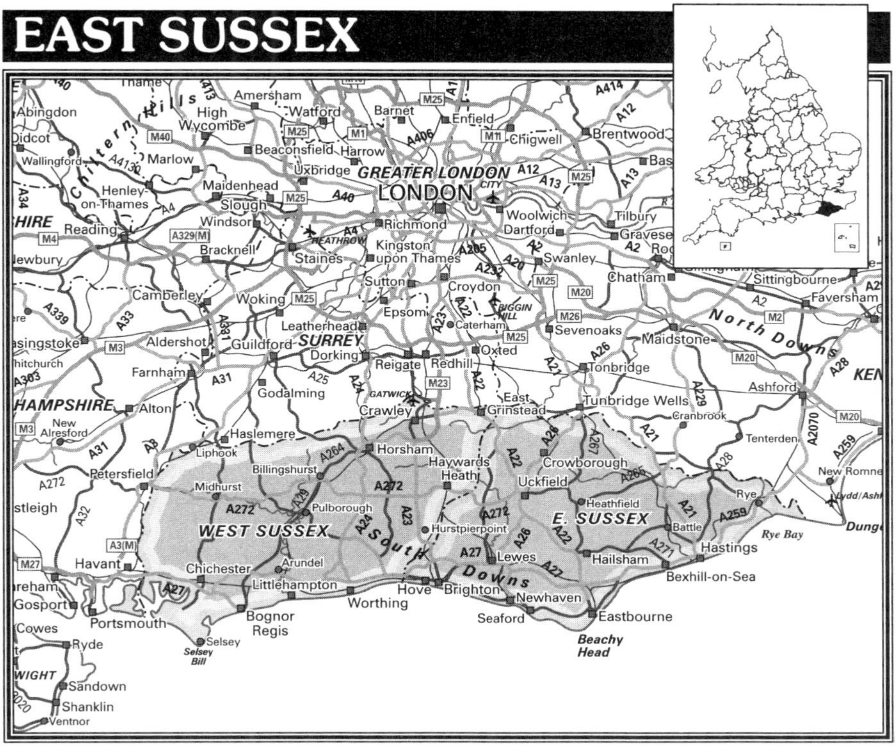

FAIRLIGHT COTTAGE

Warren Road (via Coastguard Lane), Fairlight, East Sussex TN35 4AG

Peace, tranquillity and a warm welcome await you at our comfortable country house, adjoining 650 acres of country park in an area of outstanding natural beauty, close to the ancient towns of Rye, Battle, Winchelsea and Hastings.. Panoramic sea views from large balcony. Centrally heated en suite bedrooms with beverage trays and colour TV. Comfortable guest lounge. Delicious breakfasts; dinner by arrangement – bring your own drinks. No smoking. Ample parking. Pets welcome.

B&B from £25 pppn. • Single supplement • Dinner £15.00
Janet & Ray Adams • 01424 812545 • e-mail: *fairlightcottage@supanet.com*

See also Colour Advertisement

The FHG **Directory of Website Addresses**
on pages 182-216 is a useful quick reference guide for
holiday accommodation with e-mail and/or website details

East Sussex

Hotel 3-12

BRIGHTON. Mrs M.A. Daughtery, Ma'on Hotel, 26 Upper Rock Gardens, Brighton BN2 1QE (01273

694400). This is a completely non-smoking Grade II Listed building run by proprietors who are waiting with a warm and friendly welcome. No children. Established over 20 years. Our standard of food has been highly recommended by many guests who return year after year. Two minutes from the sea and within easy reach of conference and main town centres. All nine bedrooms are furnished to a high standard and have colour TV, radio alarm clock, hospitality tray and hairdryer and most are en suite. A lounge with colour TV is available for guests' convenience. Diningroom. Full central heating. Access to rooms at all times. Terms from £30. Brochure on request with SAE.

B&B 1-12

BRIGHTON. Brighton Marina House Hotel, 8 Charlotte Street, Brighton BN2 1AG (01273

605349; Fax: 01273 679484). As a premier Bed & Breakfast we offer our guests a unique and innovative experience during their stay with us. Pivotally located just off the sea front and walking distance from the major attractions such as the Royal Pavilion, Lanes, Sea Life Centre, Brighton Pier, restaurants, shopping, Conference Centres, cinema and theatre. Luxuriously appointed rooms, unrivalled in their look and decor, are fully equipped for business and leisure with en suite facilities. Our French, Swedish and Tudor style rooms offer a fresh look in today's bed and breakfast for couples. We cater for families and are happy to provide cots and high chairs. In the Breakfast Room, we are committed to creating the ultimate breakfast experience. Catering for vegans, vegetarians, Continental and English cooked breakfast. Bed and Breakfast from £25 to £49 per person per night. For more information please contact us or take a look at our website. **ETC/AA/RAC ◆◆◆**.
e-mail: rooms@jungs.co.uk
website: www.brighton-mh-hotel.co.uk

Hotel

EASTBOURNE. Tony and Trish Callaghan, Far End Private Hotel, 139 Royal Parade, Eastbourne BN22

7LH (01323 725666). From the moment you arrive you are assured of a warm welcome and 'home from home' atmosphere. Our centrally heated bedrooms with colour TV and tea/coffee making facilities are tastefully decorated; most have en suite facilities and sea views. Residents have their own lounge and private car park. Enjoy freshly prepared traditional home cooking. Special diets can be catered for. We are adjacent to the popular Princes Park with boating lake, lawns, bowlings greens and pitch'n'putt; close by you can enjoy sailing, fishing, bowling, tennis and swimming. We are within easy reach of Beachy Head, the South Downs and Newhaven. We will be delighted to provide information on the many local attractions and services and shall do our best to make your stay as memorable and pleasant as possible. Bed and Breakfast from £19; Evening Meals available. Low season short breaks. Please call or write for colour brochure.

1-12 Months open	🐕 Pets welcome	♿ Suitable for disabled	🚗 Car essential
S Sporting/special interests provided		≋ Coast under two miles	🐎 Children welcome
♀ Licensed	🍼 Babysitting available		🎋 Central heating

Readers are requested to mention this guidebook
when seeking accommodation (and please enclose
a stamped addressed envelope).

| BOARD | East Sussex 89 |

Country House 1-12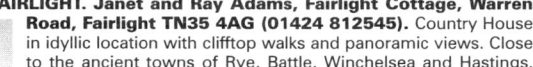

See also Colour Display Advertisement

FAIRLIGHT. Janet and Ray Adams, Fairlight Cottage, Warren Road, Fairlight TN35 4AG (01424 812545). Country House in idyllic location with clifftop walks and panoramic views. Close to the ancient towns of Rye, Battle, Winchelsea and Hastings. Centrally heated en suite rooms with beverage trays and colour TV; comfortable guest lounge. Large balcony. Delicious home cooking, generous breakfasts. Dinner by arrangement, bring your own drinks. No smoking. Ample parking. Pets welcome. ETC ♦♦♦♦

VISITS & ATTRACTIONS

Royal Pavilion • *Brighton, East Sussex* • *01273 290900*
website: www.royalpavilion.brighton.co.uk
Decorated in Chinese taste with an Indian exterior, this Regency Palace was built for George IV and features superb craftsmanship and extravagant decoration. Guided tours, tearooms and shop.

Fishbourne Roman Palace • *Near Chichester, West Sussex* • *01243 785859*
website: www.sussexpast.co.uk
Largest Roman residence excavated in Britain, with re-created garden, museum, and audio-visual programme.

Weald & Downland Open Air Musem *Chichester, West Sussex* • *01243 811348*
Over 40 historic buildings carefully re-constructed, including medieval farmstead, working flour mill, Victorian rural school, and 16th century market place. Visitors can see working horses and demonstrations of building crafts and countryside skills.

FHG

Other specialised

FHG PUBLICATIONS

Published annually: available in all good bookshops or direct from the publisher.

- Recommended COUNTRY HOTELS OF BRITAIN   £5.25
- Recommended WAYSIDE & COUNTRY INNS OF BRITAIN   £5.25
- Recommended SHORT BREAK HOLIDAYS IN BRITAIN   £5.25
- PETS WELCOME!   £6.75 • B&B IN BRITAIN   £4.25
- THE GOLF GUIDE Where to Play / Where to Stay   £9.99

FHG PUBLICATIONS LTD, Abbey Mill Business Centre, Seedhill, Paisley, Renfrewshire PA1 lTJ
Tel: 0141-887 0428 • Fax: 0141-889 7204
e-mail: fhg@ipcmedia.com • website: www.holidayguides.com

YORKSHIRE

BOARD

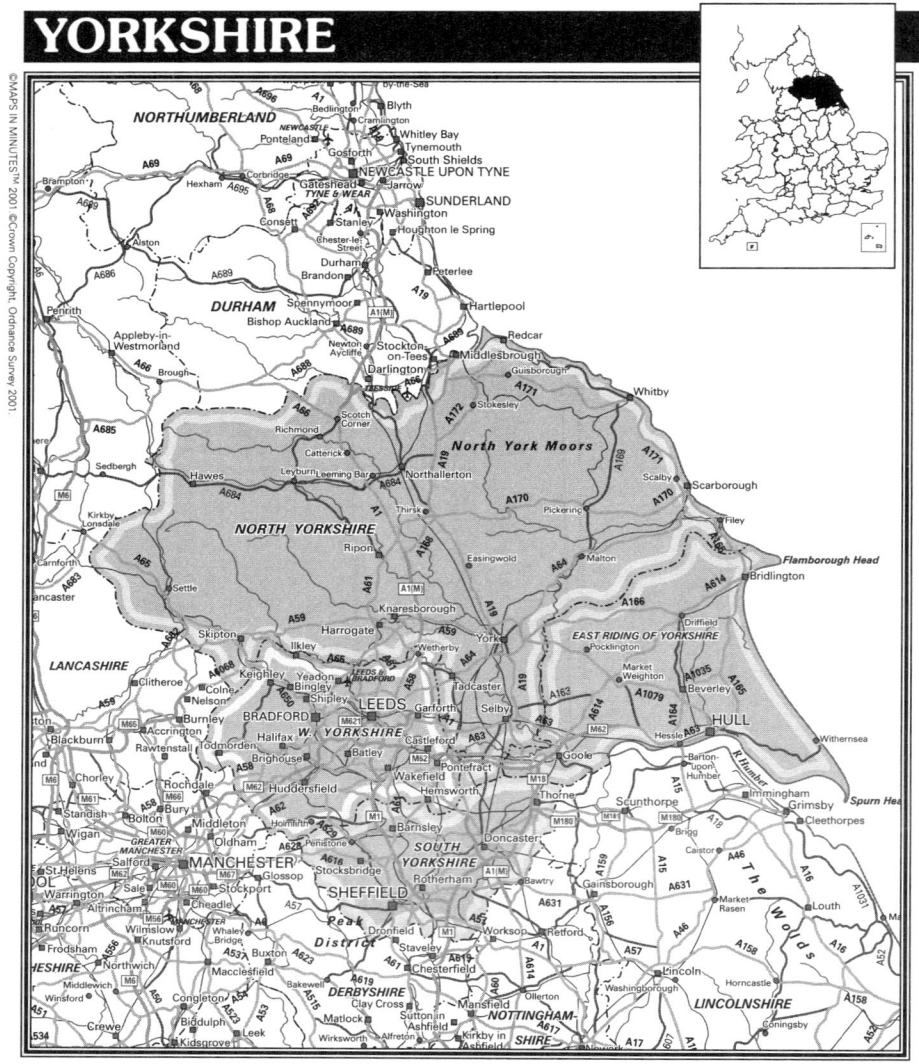

FREE or REDUCED RATE entry to Holiday Visits and Attractions — see our READERS' OFFER VOUCHERS on pages 35-54

EAST YORKSHIRE

White Lodge Guest House

9 Neptune St, Bridlington, Yorkshire YO15 3DE Tel & Fax: 01262 670903

White Lodge is a friendly, relaxing guest house, personally run by owners Caitlyn and Toni Greene. Situated near the superb South Beach and Conference Centre, we have an excellent reputation for food, hospitality and variety of service. 7 bedrooms, 5 en suite, with sky TV and tea/coffee facilities. Extra facilities for elderly or disabled patrons, and special reductions for children and senior citizens.

E-mail: Caitlyn@whitelodgeguesthouse.fsnet.co.uk
Website: www.whitelodgeguesthouse.co.uk   **Open All Year**

Guesthouse   1-12

BRIDLINGTON. Caitlyn and Toni Greene, White Lodge Guest House, 9 Neptune Street, Bridlington YO15 3DE (01262 670903). Very relaxing guest house, personally run by Caitlyn and Toni Greene. We have an excellent reputation for food and can cater for all diets, with adequate notice. Situated opposite South Beach and Conference Centre, with the harbour and town only a short walk away. The ground floor room has its own patio area, garden furniture and purpose built store for motorised wheelchair. All seven bedrooms are centrally heated and have colour TV with satellite, tea/coffee facilities and five rooms en suite. Guests' lounge; diningroom and toilet on ground floor. Own keys. Special reductions for children and Senior Citizens. Special offers on Christmas breaks. Ideal base for conference delegates, golfers, fishing trips, bird watchers, walkers and in fact everyone! Open all year.

e-mail: Caitlyn@whitelodgeguesthouse.fsnet.co.uk
website: www.whitelodgeguesthouse.co.uk

FHG

PLEASE MENTION THIS GUIDE WHEN YOU WRITE OR PHONE TO ENQUIRE ABOUT ACCOMMODATION

IF YOU ARE WRITING, A STAMPED, ADDRESSED ENVELOPE IS ALWAYS APPRECIATED

1-12 Months open	🐕 Pets welcome	♿ Suitable for disabled	🚗 Car essential
[S] Sporting/special interests provided		〰 Coast under two miles	🧸 Children welcome
♀ Licensed	➡ Babysitting available		ⅢⅢ Central heating

NORTH YORKSHIRE

Inn   1-12   ♀

See also Colour Display Advertisement   **DANBY. The Fox and Hounds Inn, Ainthorpe, Danby YO21 2LD (01287 660218; Fax: 01287 660030).** Residential 16th century Coaching Inn. Freshly prepared dishes served every lunchtime and evening. Superb en suite bedrooms with glorious views. Open all year. An ideal base for exploring moors and coast. **ETC** ♦♦♦♦.
website: www.foxandhounds-ainthorpe.com

Guesthouse   1-12

YORK. Mont-Clare Guest House, 32 Claremont Terrace, Gillygate, York YO31 7EJ (01904 627054; Fax: 01904 651011). Take advantage and enjoy the convenience of City Centre accommodation in a quiet location close to the magnificent York Minster. A warm and friendly welcome awaits you at the Mont-Clare. All rooms are en suite, tastefully decorated, with colour TV (Satellite), radio alarm, direct-dial telephone, hairdryer, tea/coffee tray, shoe cleaning, etc. Some are four-poster. All of York's attractions are within walking distance and we are ideally situated for the Yorkshire Dales, Moors and numerous stately homes. Fire and Hygiene Certificates. Cleanliness, good food, pleasant surroundings and friendliness are our priorities. Private car park with CCTV. Open all year. Bed and Breakfast from £25 per person per night. Reduced rates for weekly stays.
e-mail: MontclareY@aol.com
website: www.mont-clare.co.uk

Guesthouse   1-12   ♿

YORK. Mr & Mrs G. Hudson, Orillia House, 89 The Village, Stockton on Forest, York YO3 9UP (01904 400600). A warm welcome awaits you at Orillia House, conveniently situated in the centre of the village, three miles north east of York, one mile from A64. The house dates back to the 17th century and has been restored to offer a high standard of comfort with modern facilities yet retaining its original charm and character. All rooms have private facilities, colour TV and tea/coffee making facilities. Our local pub provides excellent evening meals. We also have our own private car park. Bed and Breakfast from £19. Telephone for our brochure. **ETC** ♦♦♦.

VISITS & ATTRACTIONS

Mount Grace Priory • *Northallerton, North Yorkshire* • *01609 883494*
The best preserved Carthusian monastery in the country, set in beautiful woodlands.
Restored monk's cell and herb garden.

Visit the **FHG** website
www.holidayguides.com
for details of the wide choice of accommodation featured in the full range of FHG titles

SCOTLAND BOARD

Dunvegan Castle on the Isle of Skye

BOARD

THE FHG DIPLOMA

HELP IMPROVE BRITISH TOURIST STANDARDS

You are choosing holiday accommodation from our very popular FHG Publications. Whether it be a hotel, guest house, farmhouse or self-catering accommodation, we think you will find it hospitable, comfortable and clean, and your host and hostess friendly and helpful.

Why not write and tell us about it?

As a recognition of the generally well-run and excellent holiday accommodation reviewed in our publications, we at FHG Publications Ltd. present a diploma to proprietors who receive the highest recommendation from their guests who are also readers of our Guides. If you care to write to us praising the holiday you have booked through FHG Publications Ltd. – whether this be board, self-catering accommodation, a sporting or a caravan holiday, what you say will be evaluated and the proprietors who reach our final list will be contacted.

The winning proprietor will receive an attractive framed diploma to display on his premises as recognition of a high standard of comfort, amenity and hospitality. FHG Publications Ltd. offer this diploma as a contribution towards the improvement of standards in tourist accommodation in Britain. Help your excellent host or hostess to win it!

FHG DIPLOMA

We nominate ....

....

Because

Name ....

Address..

....

Telephone No..

Argyll & Bute

ARGYLL & BUTE

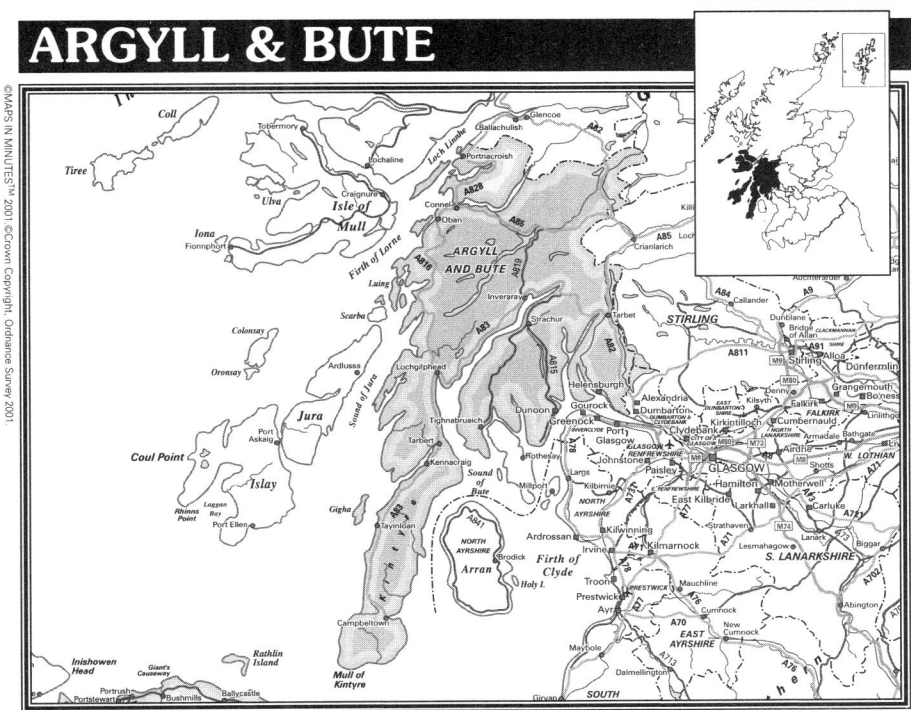

Hotel

See also Colour Display Advertisement ISLE OF GIGHA. **Gigha Hotel, Isle of Gigha PA41 7AA (01583 505254; Fax: 01583 505244).** Spend a relaxing holiday on the Isle of Gigha (pronounced Gee-a). Meaning God's Isle, it is surely a little piece of heaven. Explore the sandy bays, lochs, easy walks, cycling, golf, birds and wildlife, but for the jewel in the crown, visit Achamore Gardens with rhododendrons, azaleas and semi-exotic plants. Grass airstrip, 9-hole golf course and a regular ferry service. Holiday cottages also available. Details on request. STB ★★★ *HOTEL.*
website: www.isle-of-gigha.co.uk

- 1-12 Months open
- Pets welcome
- Suitable for disabled
- Car essential
- [S] Sporting/special interests provided
- Coast under two miles
- Children welcome
- Licensed
- Babysitting available
- Central heating

Visit the **FHG** website
www.holidayguides.com
for details of the wide choice of accommodation
featured in the full range of FHG titles

AYRSHIRE & ARRAN

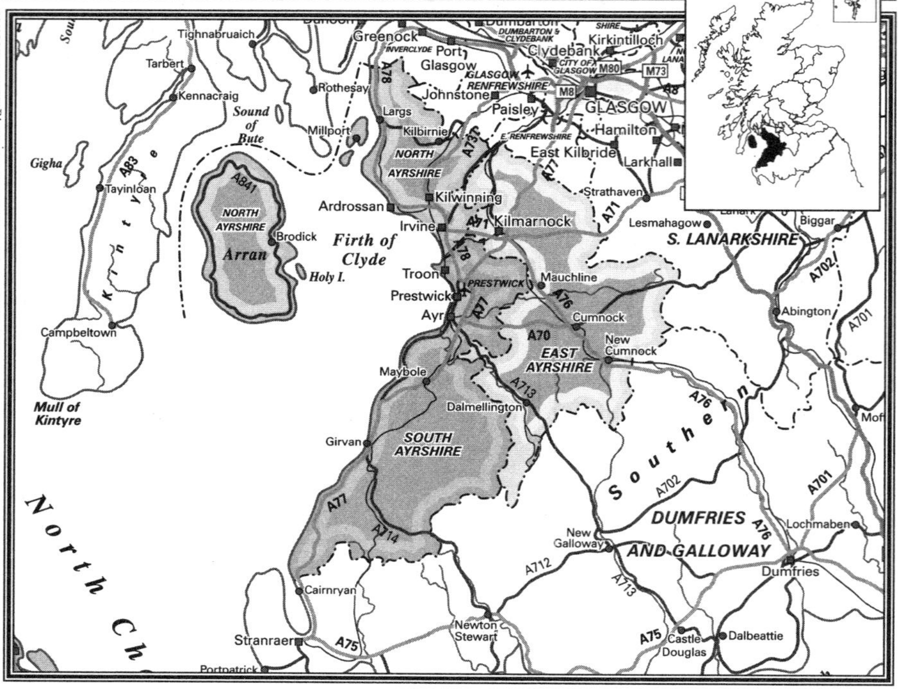

B&B

AYR near. Mrs Agnes Gemmell, Dunduff Farm, Dunure, Ayr KA7 4LH (01292 500225). Welcome to Dunduff Farm where a warm friendly atmosphere awaits you. Situated just south of Ayr at the coastal village of Dunure, this family-run beef and sheep unit of 600 acres is only 15 minutes from the shore providing good walks and sea fishing and enjoying close proximity to Dunure Castle and Park. Accommodation is of a very high standard yet homely and comfortable. Bedrooms have washbasins, radio alarm, tea/coffee making facilities, central heating, TV, hair dryer and en suite facilities (the twin room has private bathroom). There is also a small farm cottage available sleeping two/four people. Bed and Breakfast from £23 per person, weekly rate £130. Cottage £250 per week. Colour brochure available. **STB** ★★★★ *B&B*, **AA/RAC** ◆◆◆◆

VISITS & ATTRACTIONS

Culzean Castle and Country Park • *Maybole, Ayrshire* • *01655 884400*
website: www.nts.org.uk/culzean.html
Robert Adam's masterpiece set in beautifully landscaped gardens. Investigate the Eisenhower connection and visit the Interpretation Centre, swan pond and aviary. Restaurant and tea rooms, picnic areas.

BORDERS

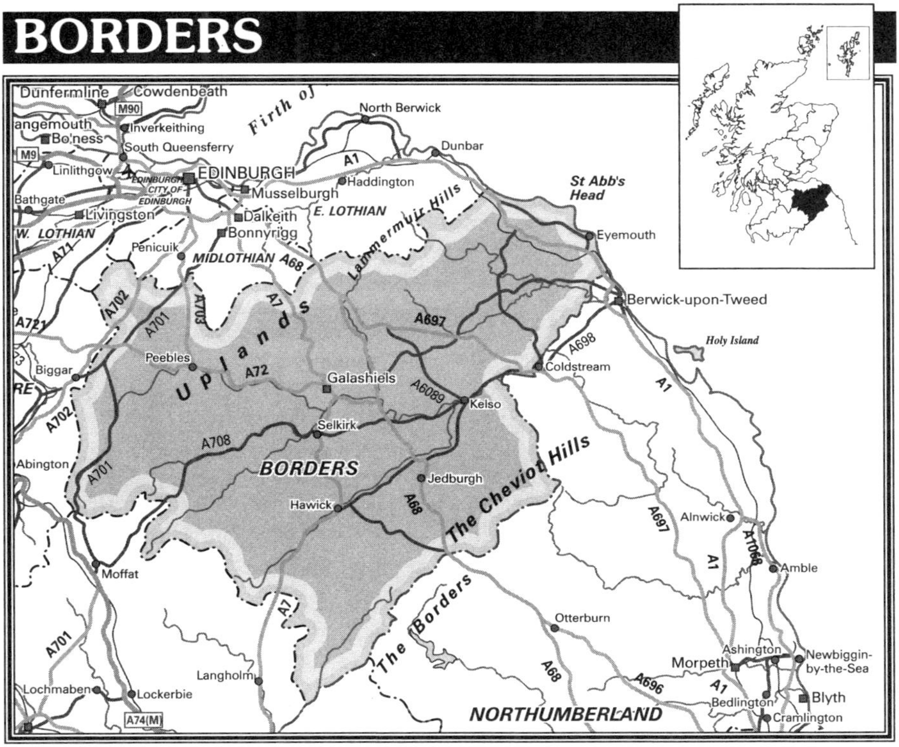

Ashkirktown Farm, Ashkirk, Selkirk TD7 4PB

Situated off the A7 midway between Hawick and Selkirk. Ashkirktown Farm offers a warm welcome in a peaceful and tranquil setting. Whether en route to Edinburgh or exploring the beautiful Borders area of Scotland, a comfortable stay is assured. The old farmhouse has been tastefully furnished. Large private lounge with colour TV, tea/coffee making facilities. Non-smoking accommodation available. **Open all year**. Bed and Breakfast from £20. Reduced rates for children.

Tel & Fax : 01750 32315

Farm 1-12

ASHKIRK. Ashkirkton Farm Ashkirk, Selkirk TD7 4PB (Tel & Fax 01750 32315). Situated off the A7 midway between Hawick and Selkirk, Ashkirktown Farm offers a warm welcome in a peaceful and tranquil setting. Whether en route to Edinburgh or exploring the beautiful Borders area of Scotland, a comfortable stay is assured. The old farmhouse has been tastefully furnished. Large private lounge with colour TV, tea/coffee making facilities. Non-smoking accommodation available. Bed and Breakfast from £20. Reduced rates for children. Open all year.

98   Dumfries & Galloway   **BOARD**

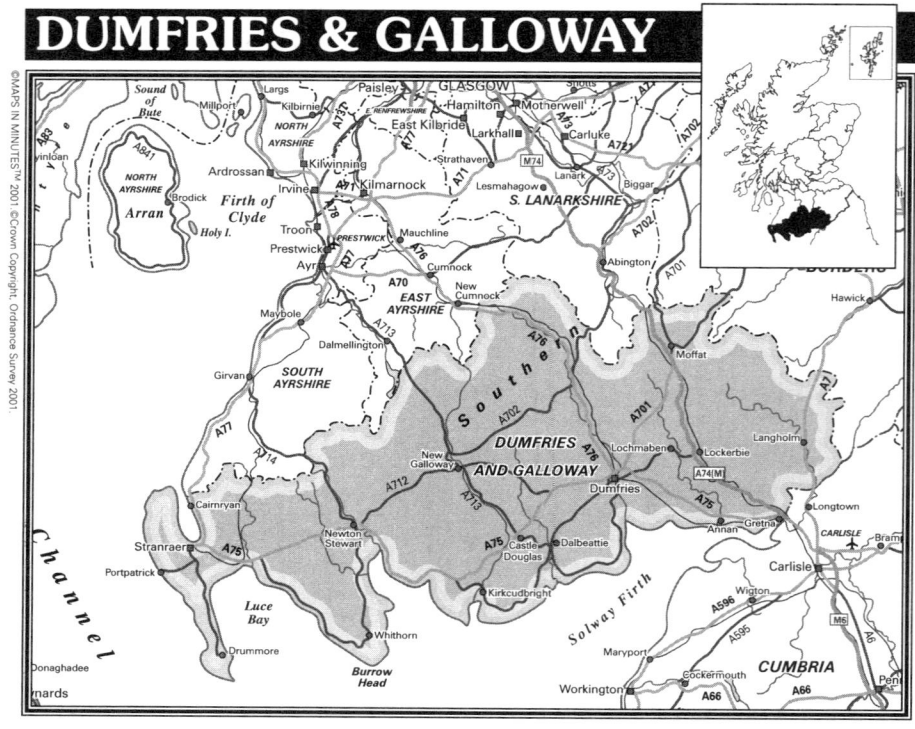

Hotel   ♀
See also Colour Display Advertisement   **CASTLE DOUGLAS. The Urr Valley Hotel, Ernespie Road, Castle Douglas DG7 3JG (01556 502188; Fax: 01556 504055).** Privately owned, and set in 14 acres of mature woodland and gardens within walking distance of Castle Douglas, its situation makes the Urr Valley Hotel extremely popular with visitors wishing to explore and enjoy the beauty and tranquillity of the countryside without being too remote. 17 en suite rooms, all with colour TV, tea/coffee facilities, hairdryer, trouser press and direct dial telephone. Enjoy some of the region's finest produce in our restaurant including seafood, venison, pheasant and haggis complemented by our extensive selection of wines. Bar meals also available in the lounge. **AA ★★.**
e-mail: info@urrvalleyhotel.co.uk
website: www.urrvalleyhotel.co.uk

VISITS & ATTRACTIONS

Shambellie Museum of Costume • *Dumfries, Dumfriesshire* • *01387 850375*
Step back in time and experience Victorian and Edwardian grace and refinement.
Set in attractive wooded grounds, it offers visitors the chance to see period clothes
in appropriate settings.

The **FHG** **Directory of Website Addresses**
on pages 182-216 is a useful quick reference guide for
holiday accommodation with e-mail and/or website details

DUNDEE & ANGUS

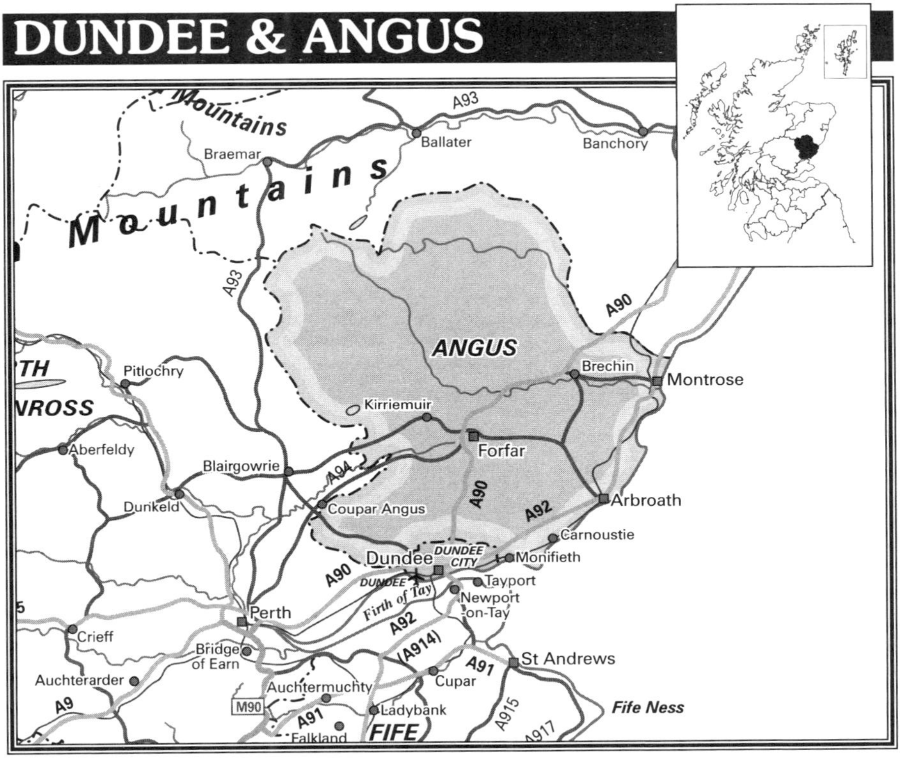

The Glenesk Hotel Edzell, Angus

AA ★★★   RAC ★★★

This splendid family-run hotel is situated in its own grounds ADJOINING THE 18 HOLE GOLF COURSE. 25 comfortable bedrooms all with modern facilities. Recommended by both golf parties and families who enjoy the friendly atmosphere and Scottish hospitality given by resident directors.

ENJOY OUR LEISURE COMPLEX
Indoor Pool, Sauna, Spa Bath, Solarium and Games Room. Special Breaks always available.

Telephone: (01356) 648319   Fax: (01356) 647333

STB ★★★ Hotel

See also Colour Advertisement

Hotel

See also Colour Display Advertisement EDZELL. **The Glenesk Hotel, High Street, Edzell DD9 7TF (01356 648319; Fax: 01356 647333).** Set in some of Scotland's loveliest countryside and offering traditional three star luxury. Situated only a short wedge away from a championship golf course, and within a short drive from Carnoustie and St Andrews. Luxurious country club with beautiful indoor pool and leisure facilities to relax in, not to mention the wide variety of outdoor pursuits available making the Glenesk Hotel the perfect place to get away from it all. Whether you come for an overnight stay, a long weekend or a two week break you will see why guests who visit the Glenesk come back again. **STB ★★★** *HOTEL*, **AA/RAC ★★★.**

Terms quoted in this publication may be subject to increase if rises in costs necessitate

EDINBURGH & LOTHIANS

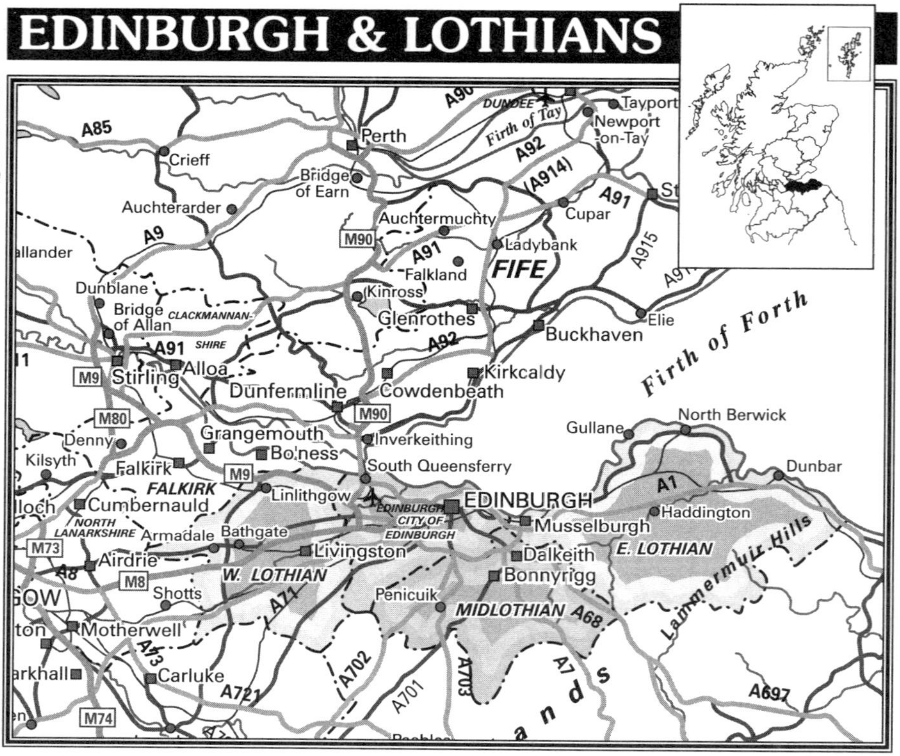

Guesthouse

EDINBURGH. Kenvie Guest House, 16 Kilmaurs Road, Edinburgh EH16 5DA (0131-668 1964; Fax: 0131-668 1926). A charming and comfortable Victorian town house situated in a quiet and pleasant residential part of the city, approximately one mile south of the centre and one small block from Main Road (A7) leading to the City and Bypass to all routes. Excellent bus service. We offer for your comfort, complimentary tea/coffee, central heating, colour TV and No Smoking rooms. En suite rooms available. Lovely breakfasts and lots of additional caring touches. A warm and friendly welcome is guaranteed from Richard and Dorothy.
e-mail: dorothy@kenvie.co.uk

VISITS & ATTRACTIONS

Royal Yacht Britannia • *Leith, Edinburgh* • 0131- 555 5566
website: www.royalyachtbritannia.co.uk
One of the most famous ships in the world, serving the Royal Family for over 40 years and one million miles. A purpose-built visitor centre at Ocean Terminal tells its history.

Scottish Mining Museum • *Newtongrange, Midlothian* • 0131- 663 7519
Ex-miners take you on a tour of Scotland's most famous colliery, award winning talking tableaux, audio-visual presentation and new life-size reconstruction of coal-face. Tearoom.

FIFE

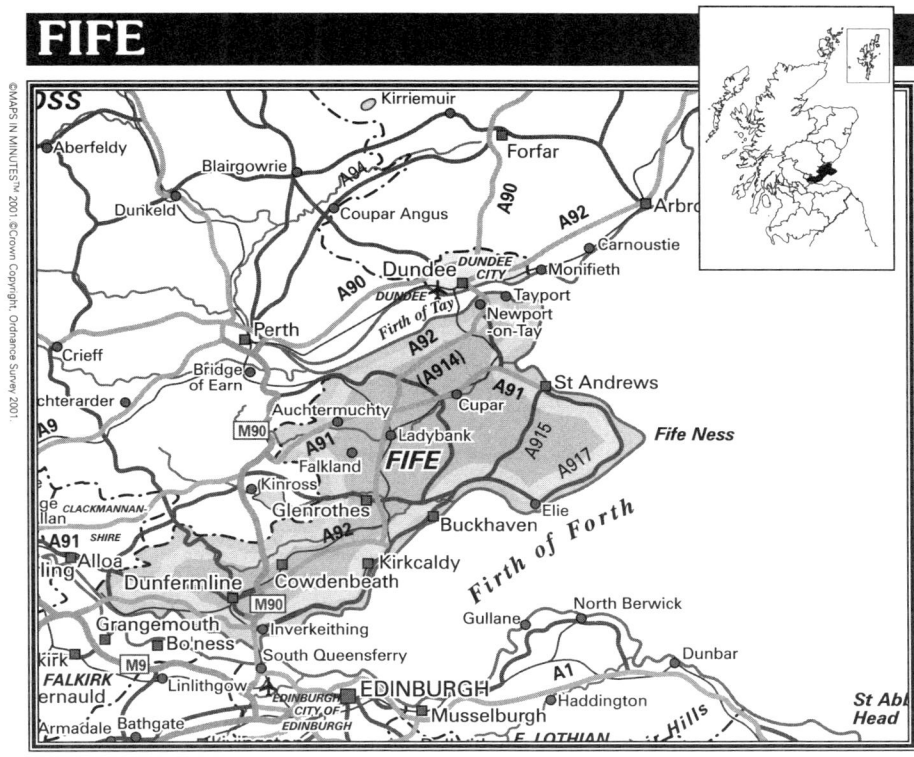

Hotel

See also Colour Display Advertisement **DUNFERMLINE. The Pitfirrane Arms Hotel, Crossford, Dunfermline KY12 8NJ (01383 736132; Fax: 01383 621760).** The hotel is conveniently situated for touring, within easy access of Edinburgh, Glasgow and the M90 motorway. We have 38 comfortable bedrooms - 16 twin, 12 double and 10 single-bedded rooms. All rooms have private en suite facilities, colour television, tea/coffee maker, telephone and radio. We have 10 golf courses within 10 miles. **STB ★★★** *HOTEL,* **AA/RAC ★★★**
e-mail: info@scothotels.com
website: www.scothotels.com

VISITS & ATTRACTIONS

Scotland's Secret Bunker • *Near St Andrews, Fife* • *01333 310301*
website: www.secretbunker.co.uk
An amazing labyrinth built 100ft below ground, from where the country would have been run in the event of nuclear war. The command centre with its original equipment can be seen, and there is an AV theatre and two cinemas.

1-12 Months open	⚐ Suitable for disabled	🚗 Car essential
ⓢ Sporting/special interests provided	〰 Coast under two miles	⛄ Children welcome
♀ Licensed	🍼 Babysitting available	ⅢⅢ Central heating
🐾 Pets welcome		

4-10

CUPAR (Near St. Andrews). Mrs M. Chrisp, Scotstarvit Farm, By Cupar KY15 5PA (Tel & Fax: 01334 653591). Just off the A916, nestled by the 16th century ancient monument of Scotstarvit Tower and National Trust places of interest, our traditional stockrearing farm is five minutes from the market town of Cupar and the historic village of Ceres, with St Andrews only ten minutes' drive away. Explore the quaint, bustling fishing villages of the East Neuk of Fife after a fifteen minute drive. The cities of Edinburgh, Glasgow, Perth, Dundee and Aberdeen are all within easy reach for a day trip. Scotstarvit is a peaceful, unspoilt scenic spot giving you the best of both worlds by being in an enviable central location for all leisure activities and entertainment including the numerous golf courses on our doorstep, or you may enjoy the relaxing, peaceful atmosphere and wonderful panoramic scenery in our comfortable characteristic farmhouse, where you will enjoy a hearty breakfast. Open April to October. From £16 per night. Delightful self-catering cottage also available - prices from £140 to £395 per week. (**STB** ★★★ *SELF-CATERING*)
e-mail: chrisp.scotstarvit@uk.gateway.net   website: www.scotstarvitfarm.co.uk

Hotel   ♀

FALKLAND. The Covenanter Hotel, Falkland KY15 7BU (01337 857224; Fax: 01337 857163). George and Margaret Menzies have run this Hotel for the past 20 years and have upgraded the restaurant and bistro as well as the comfortable en suite rooms. The location of the hotel in the historic village makes it the ideal base from which to discover Fife. Bed and Breakfast Double £26 per person. Bed and Breakfast Single £39. In addition to the hotel, self-catering cottages are available.
website: www.covenanterhotel.com

The **FHG**
GOLF
GUIDE
Where to Play
Where to Stay
2002

Available from most bookshops, the 2002 edition of
THE GOLF GUIDE covers details of every UK golf course – well over 2800 entries – for holiday or business golf. Hundreds of hotel entries offer convenient accommodation, accompanying details of the courses – the 'pro', par score, length etc.

In association with 'Golf Monthly' and including Holiday Golf in Ireland, France, Portugal, Spain, The USA, South Africa and Thailand .

£9.99 from bookshops or from the publishers (postage charged outside UK) • FHG Publications, Abbey Mill Business Centre, Paisley PA1 1TJ

NOTE

All the information in this book is given in good faith in the belief that it is correct. However, the publishers cannot guarantee the facts given in these pages, neither are they responsible for changes in policy, ownership or terms that may take place after the date of going to press. Readers should always satisfy themselves that the facilities they require are available and that the terms, if quoted, still apply.

HIGHLANDS

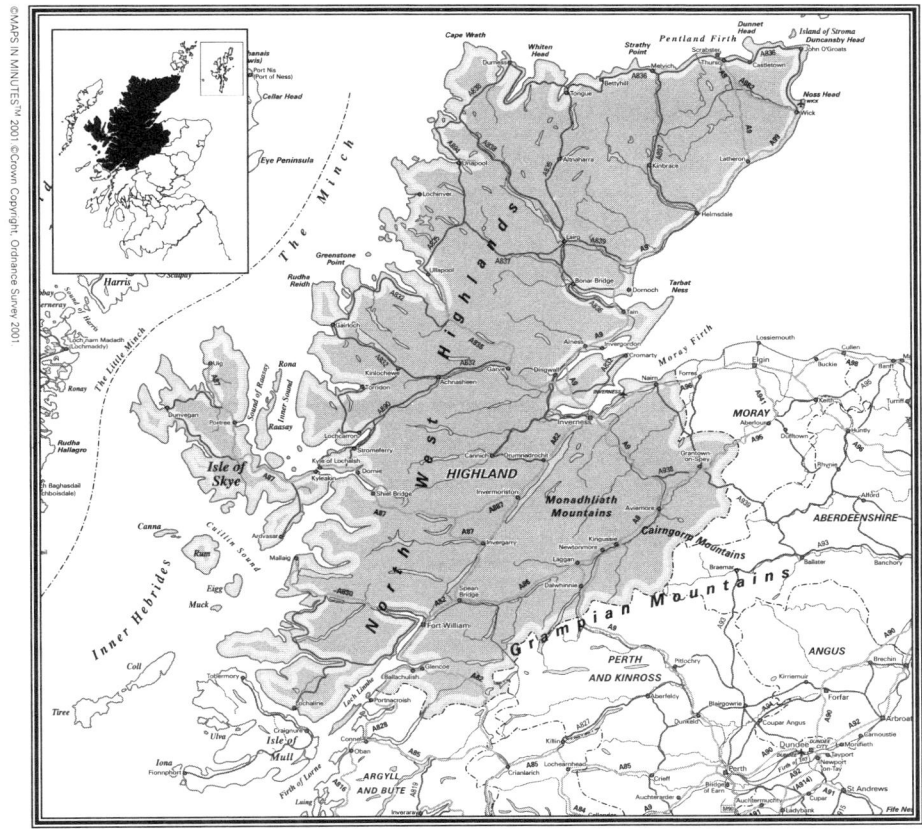

FREE or REDUCED RATE entry to Holiday Visits and Attractions — see our READERS' OFFER VOUCHERS on pages 35-54

Visit the **FHG** website
www.holidayguides.com
for details of the wide choice of accommodation
featured in the full range of FHG titles

HIGHLANDS (SOUTH)

Guesthouse   4-10

FORT WILLIAM. Mrs A. Grant, Glen Shiel House, Achintore Road, Fort William PH33 6RW (01397 702271). Modern purpose-built guest house situated near the shore of Loch Linnhe with panoramic views of the surrounding mountains. Accommodation comprises two double bedrooms and one twin-bedded room, all en suite, with colour TV and tea making facilities. Non-smoking. Large car park. Garden. Bed and Breakfast from £17 to £21. Directions: on the A82 one-and-a-half-miles south of Fort William. **STB** ★★ *GUEST HOUSE.*

Guesthouse

KINGUSSIE. Arden House, Newtonmore Road, Kingussie PH21 1HE (Tel & Fax: 01540 661369). Arden House combines two holiday essentials - central location with comfortable accommodation. Ideal base for touring, friendly and relaxed atmosphere and easy walking distance to centre of town. Choose from a full Scottish breakfast or serve yourself Continental buffet. Just step back in time and enjoy the unrushed atmosphere and friendly Highland welcome. **STB** ★★★ *GUEST HOUSE.*
e-mail: ardenhouse@compuserve.com
website: www.ardenhouse.org

FHG

Other specialised

FHG PUBLICATIONS

Published annually: available in all good bookshops or direct from the publisher.

- Recommended COUNTRY HOTELS OF BRITAIN   £5.25
- Recommended WAYSIDE & COUNTRY INNS OF BRITAIN   £5.25
- Recommended SHORT BREAK HOLIDAYS IN BRITAIN   £5.25
- PETS WELCOME!   £6.75 • B&B IN BRITAIN   £4.25
- THE GOLF GUIDE Where to Play / Where to Stay   £9.99

FHG PUBLICATIONS LTD, Abbey Mill Business Centre, Seedhill, Paisley, Renfrewshire PA1 ITJ
Tel: 0141-887 0428 • Fax: 0141-889 7204
e-mail: fhg@ipcmedia.com • website: www.holidayguides.com

PERTH & KINROSS

Perth & Kinross 105

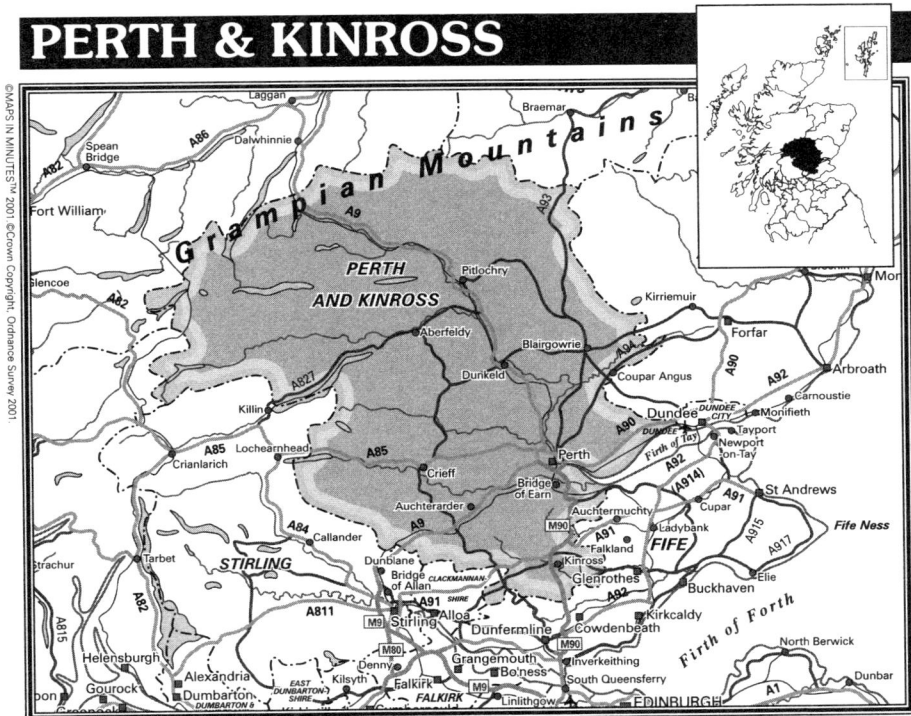

•• *Some Useful Guidance for Guests and Hosts* ••

Every year literally thousands of holidays, short breaks and overnight stops are arranged through our guides, the vast majority without any problems at all. In a handful of cases, however, difficulties do arise about bookings, which often could have been prevented from the outset.

It is important to remember that when accommodation has been booked, both parties – guests and hosts – have entered into a form of contract. We hope that the following points will provide helpful guidance.

GUESTS:
- When enquiring about accommodation, be as precise as possible. Give exact dates, numbers in your party and the ages of any children.
- State the number and type of rooms wanted and also what catering you require – bed and breakfast, full board etc. Make sure that the position about evening meals is clear – and about pets, reductions for children or any other special points.
- Read our reviews carefully to ensure that the proprietors you are going to contact can supply what you want. Ask for a letter confirming all arrangements, if possible.
- If you have to cancel, do so as soon as possible. Proprietors do have the right to retain deposits and under certain circumstances to charge for cancelled holidays if adequate notice is not given and they cannot re-let the accommodation.

HOSTS:
- Give details about your facilities and about any special conditions. Explain your deposit system clearly and arrangements for cancellations, charges etc. and whether or not your terms include VAT.
- If for any reason you are unable to fulfil an agreed booking without adequate notice, you may be under an obligation to arrange suitable alternative accommodation or to make some form of compensation.

While every effort is made to ensure accuracy, we regret that FHG Publications cannot accept responsibility for errors, omissions or misrepresentations in our entries or any consequences thereof. Prices in particular should be checked because we go to press early. We will follow up complaints but cannot act as arbiters or agents for either party.

Perth & Kinross

Farmhouse 1-12

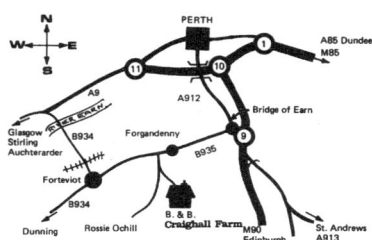

PERTH. Mrs Mary Fotheringham, Craighall Farmhouse, Forgandenny, Near Bridge of Earn, Perth PH2 9DF (01738 812415). Working farm. Come and stay in a modern and warm farmhouse with a cheerful, friendly atmosphere situated in lovely Earn Valley, half-a-mile west of village of Forgandenny on B935 and only six miles south of Perth. True Highland hospitality and large choice of breakfast served in dinningroom overlooking fields where a variety of cattle, sheep and lambs graze. Farm produce used. Open all year, the 1000 acre arable and stock farm is within easy reach of Stirling, Edinburgh, St. Andrews, Glasgow and Pitlochry. Fishing, golf, tennis, swimming locally. Hill walking and lovely scenery. All rooms en suite. Tea making facilities. Sitting room. Cot, and reduced rates for children. Sorry, no pets. Central heating. Car not essential; parking. Bed and Breakfast from £19.50. Midweek bookings taken.
STB ★★★ *FARMHOUSE*.

Farm

See also Colour Display Advertisement

STANLEY. Mrs Ann Guthrie, Newmill Farm, Stanley PH1 4QD (01738 828281). This 330 acre farm is situated on the A9, six miles north of Perth. Accommodation comprises twin and double en suite rooms and a family room with private bathroom; lounge, sittingroom, diningroom; bathroom, shower room and toilet. Bed and Breakfast from £18; Evening Meal on request. The warm welcome and supper of excellent home baking is inclusive. Reductions and facilities for children. Pets accepted. The numerous castles and historic ruins around Perth are testimony to Scotland's turbulent past. Situated in the area known as "The Gateway to the Highlands", the farm is ideally placed for those seeking some of the best unspoilt scenery in Western Europe. Many famous golf courses and trout rivers in the Perth area.
STB ★★★ *B&B*.
e-mail: guthrienewmill@sol.co.uk
website: www.newmillfarm.co.uk

1-12 Months open	Pets welcome	Suitable for disabled	Car essential
S Sporting/special interests provided	Coast under two miles		Children welcome
Licensed	Babysitting available		Central heating

PLEASE NOTE

All the information in this book is given in good faith in the belief that it is correct. However, the publishers cannot guarantee the facts given in these pages, neither are they responsible for changes in policy, ownership or terms that may take place after the date of going to press. Readers should always satisfy themselves that the facilities they require are available and that the terms, if quoted, still apply.

Stirling & The Trossachs 107

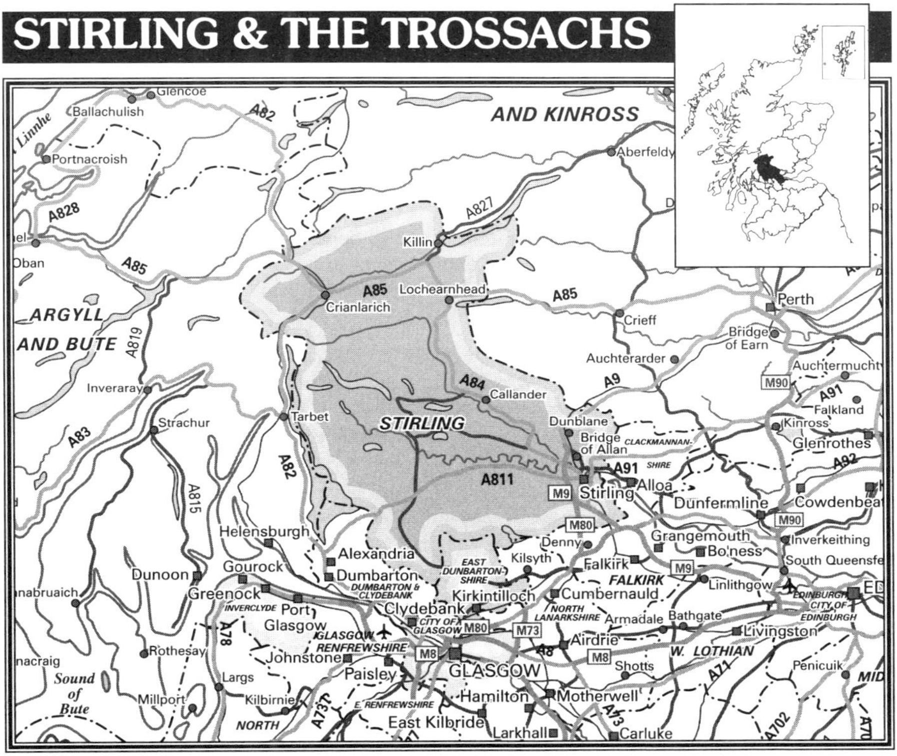

STIRLING & THE TROSSACHS

INVERTROSSACHS COUNTRY HOUSE Invertrossachs Road, Near Callander, Perthshire FK17 8HG
Tel: 01877 331126; Fax: 01877 331229

Relax in our lovely loch-side family home and grounds within the beautiful Invertrossachs Estate in stunning Perthshire. Family pets are most welcome and will enjoy the varied walks in our woodland, lochside and hill trails. Your pets will be welcomed by ours and there is always room for a few more at the log fire, after a great day out.

Website:www.invertrossachs.co.uk

CALLANDER. Invertrossachs Country House, Invertrossachs Road, Callander FK17 8HG (01877 331126; Fax: 01877 331229) Relax in our lovely loch-side family home and grounds within the beautiful Invertrossachs Estate in stunning Perthshire. Family pets are most welcome and will enjoy the varied walks in our woodland, lochside and hill trails. Your pets will be welcomed by ours and there is always room for a few more at the log fire, after a great day out. Short break details on request. **STB ★★★★**
website: www.invertrossachs.co.uk

THE FHG DIPLOMA

HELP IMPROVE BRITISH TOURIST STANDARDS

You are choosing holiday accommodation from our very popular FHG Publications. Whether it be a hotel, guest house, farmhouse or self-catering accommodation, we think you will find it hospitable, comfortable and clean, and your host and hostess friendly and helpful.

Why not write and tell us about it?

As a recognition of the generally well-run and excellent holiday accommodation reviewed in our publications, we at FHG Publications Ltd. present a diploma to proprietors who receive the highest recommendation from their guests who are also readers of our Guides. If you care to write to us praising the holiday you have booked through FHG Publications Ltd. – whether this be board, self-catering accommodation, a sporting or a caravan holiday, what you say will be evaluated and the proprietors who reach our final list will be contacted.

The winning proprietor will receive an attractive framed diploma to display on his premises as recognition of a high standard of comfort, amenity and hospitality. FHG Publications Ltd. offer this diploma as a contribution towards the improvement of standards in tourist accommodation in Britain. Help your excellent host or hostess to win it!

FHG DIPLOMA

We nominate ....

....

Because

Name ....

Address...

....

Telephone No..

WALES BOARD

Powis Castle, near Welshpool, Powys

ANGLESEY & GWYNEDD

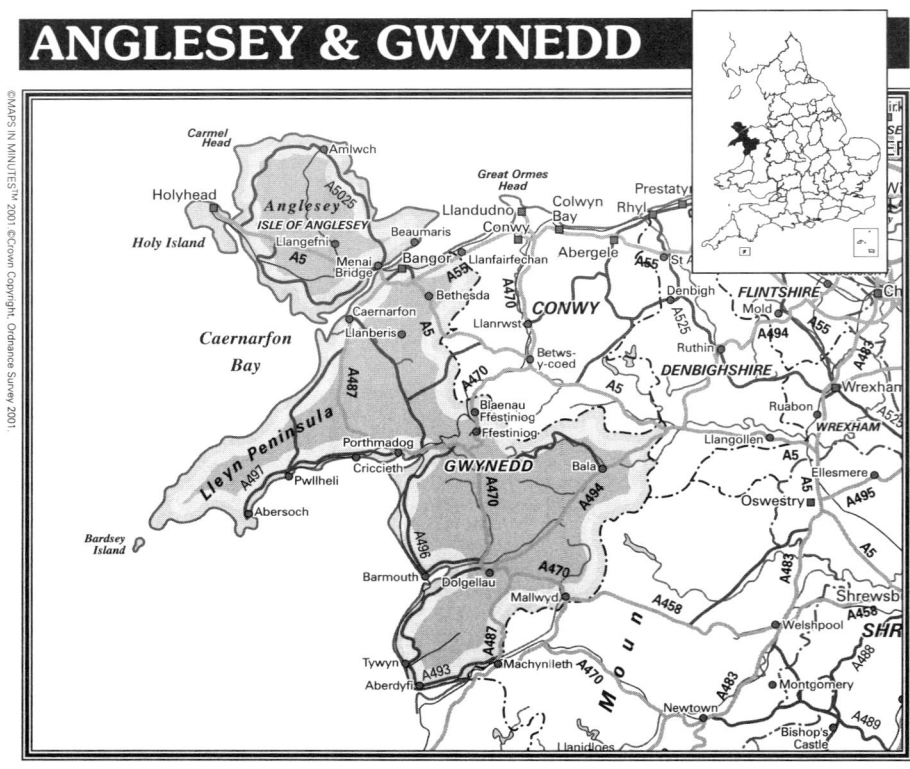

Hotel 1-12

CRICCIETH. Mrs Reynolds, Glyn-y-Coed Hotel, Porthmadoc Road, Criccieth LL52 0HL (01766 522870; Fax: 01766 523341). Lovely Victorian family-run hotel overlooking sea, mountains, Criccieth and Harlech castles. Fully centrally heated, cosy bar. Parking in our grounds. Special diets catered for; highly recommended home cooking. Separate tables in our pretty pink restaurant. All bedrooms en suite with colour TV and tea-making facilities. Fire Certificate. Moderate rates from £20 for Bed and Breakfast. Good reductions for children. Brochure sent with pleasure on receipt of SAE. Parties and groups catered for. Most credit cards accepted. Les Routiers, Good Food Guide, AA/RAC. **WTB ★★★** *HOTEL.*

VISITS & ATTRACTIONS

Gwynfynydd Gold Mine • *Dolgellau, Gwynedd* • *01341 423332*
Explore the underground workings of the only operational gold mine in Wales open to the public. Compare today's mining with past methods and see how gold ore is smelted. Pan for gold – any you find is yours to keep!

The FHG Directory of Website Addresses

on pages 182-216 is a useful quick reference guide for holiday accommodation with e-mail and/or website details

POWYS

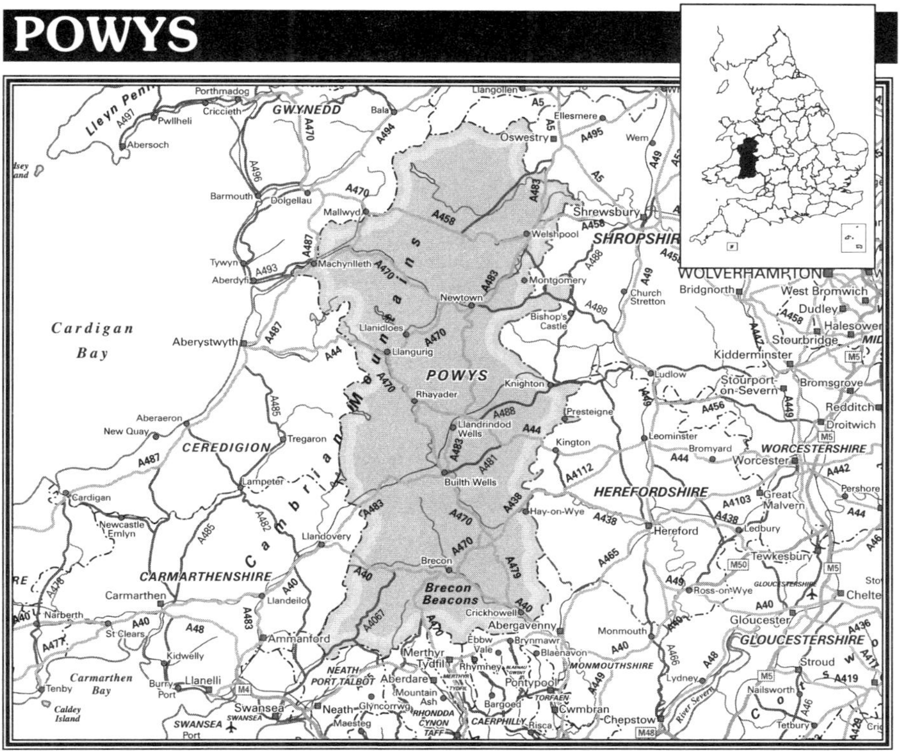

THE BEACONS

WTB ★★★ Guest House
AA ♦♦♦ RAC ♦♦♦

Recently restored, listed Georgian house, offering beautifully appointed standard, en suite, and luxury period rooms. The candlelit restaurant offers fine food and wines (five nights). Cosy cellar bar, elegant lounge, private parking, bike lock-up. Excellently situated for Brecon's historic centre and National Park exploration. A lovely house with a welcoming atmosphere.

Ring Stephen or Melanie for more information.

**16 Bridge Street, Brecon, Powys LD3 8AH
Telephone & Fax: 01874 623339
E-mail: beacons@brecon.co.uk
Website: www.beacons.brecon.co.uk**

Guesthouse

See also Colour Display Advertisement **BRECON. The Beacons Accommodation and Restaurant, 16 Bridge Street, Brecon LD3 8AH (Tel & Fax: 01874 623339).** Recently restored 17th/18th century house offering a variety of beautifully appointed standard, en suite and luxury period rooms. The candlelit restaurant offers fine food and wines (five nights). Relax in the elegant lounge or cosy Cellar Bar. Situated just two minutes' walk from Brecon's historic centre in the heart of the magnificent Brecon Beacons National Park. Two night break: Dinner, Bed and Breakfast from £65.90 to £88.90 per person. Please phone for further information. **WTB ★★★ *GUESTHOUSE*, AA/RAC ♦♦♦**.
e-mail: beacons@brecon.co.uk
website: www.beacons.brecon.co.uk

SOUTH WALES

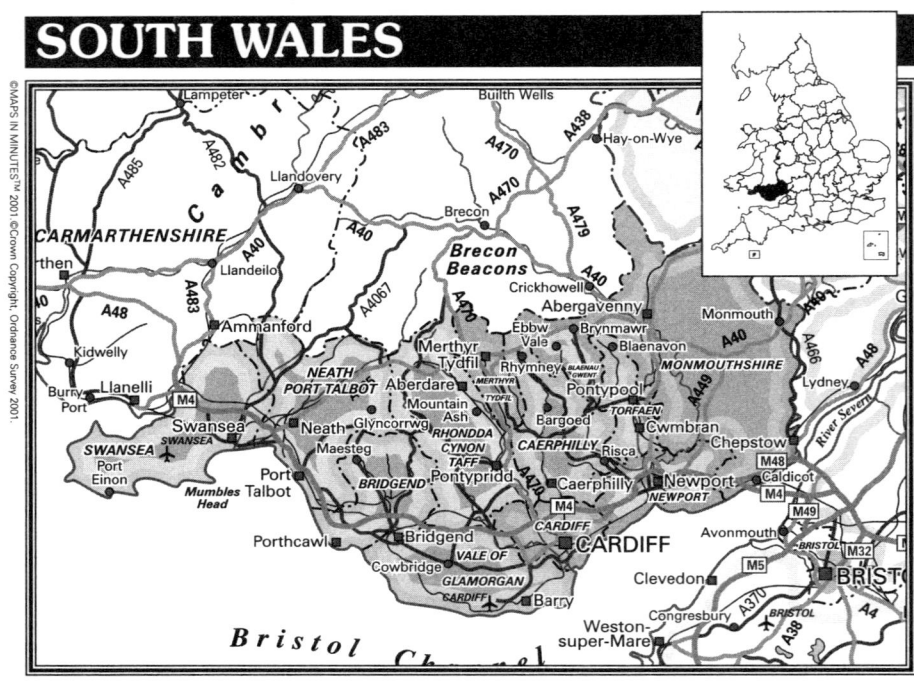

Guesthouse

ST. BRIDES WENTLOOG (Near Newport). Mr David W. Bushell, Chapel Guest House, Church Road, St. Brides Wentloog, Near Newport NP10 8SN (01633 681018; Fax: 01633 681431) Comfortable accommodation in a converted chapel situated in a village between Newport/Cardiff, near Tredegar House. Restaurant and inn adjacent, car park available. Guest lounge with TV. Single, double and twin rooms en suite or private bathroom. Beverage trays, TV, shaver points in all rooms. From £20. Children under three years FREE, three to 12 year olds half price sharing parents' room. Pets by arrangement. Leave M4 at Junction 28, take A48 towards Newport, at roundabout take third exit signposted St. Brides, B4239. Drive to centre of village, turn right into Church Road and left into Church House Inn car park; the guest house is on the left and a warm welcome awaits.
WTB ★★★ *GUEST HOUSE.*
e-mail: chapelguesthouse@hotmail.com
website: www.SmoothHound.co.uk

VISITS & ATTRACTIONS

Rhondda Heritage Park • *Trehafod, South Wales* • *01443 682036*
website: www.netwales.co.uk/rhondda-heritage
A living testament to the coal mining valleys of the Rhondda, and to the spirit of the people who dug for "Black Gold". Special effects and life-like models bring to life this unique story.

Carreg Cennen Castle • *Near Landeilo, South Wales* • *01558 822291*
website: www.cadw.wales.gov.uk
In the Brecon Beacons National Park, this 'eagle's nest' of a castle is an adventure below and above ground, with passageways cut into the cliff face leading to natural caves.

Centre for Visual Arts • *Cardiff, South Wales* • *029 20394040*
Wales' largest gallery with regularly changing exhibitions and 'Fantasmic', an interactive gallery with over 100 hands-on exhibits to push, pull, touch and see.

SELF CATERING

ENGLAND
SELF-CATERING

The old Packhorse Bridge, Bakewell, Derbyshire

Ratings You Can Trust

ENGLAND

The *English Tourism Council* (formerly the English Tourist Board) has joined with the *AA* and *RAC* to create a new, easily understood quality rating for serviced accommodation, giving a clear guide of what to expect.

HOTELS are given a rating from One to Five *Stars* – the more Stars, the higher the quality and the greater the range of facilities and level of services provided.

GUEST ACCOMMODATION, which includes guest houses, bed and breakfasts, inns and farmhouses, is rated from One to Five *Diamonds*. Progressively higher levels of quality and customer care must be provided for each one of the One to Five Diamond ratings.

HOLIDAY PARKS, TOURING PARKS and CAMPING PARKS are now also assessed using *Stars*. Standards of quality range from a One Star (acceptable) to a Five Star (exceptional) park.

Look out also for the new *SELF-CATERING* Star ratings. The more *Stars* (from One to Five) awarded to an establishment, the higher the levels of quality you can expect. Establishments at higher rating levels also have to meet some additional requirements for facilities.

*NB Some self-catering properties had not been assessed at the time of going to press and in these cases the old-style **KEY** symbols will still be shown.*

SCOTLAND

Star Quality Grades will reflect the most important aspects of a visit, such as the warmth of welcome, efficiency and friendliness of service, the quality of the food and the cleanliness and condition of the furnishings, fittings and decor.

THE MORE STARS, THE HIGHER THE STANDARDS.

The description, such as Hotel, Guest House, Bed and Breakfast, Lodge, Holiday Park, Self-catering etc tells you the type of property and style of operation.

WALES

Places which score highly will have an especially welcoming atmosphere and pleasing ambience, high levels of comfort and guest care, and attractive surroundings enhanced by thoughtful design and attention to detail

STAR QUALITY GUIDE FOR

HOTELS, GUEST HOUSES AND FARMHOUSES
SELF-CATERING ACCOMMODATION
(Cottages, Apartments, Houses)
CARAVAN HOLIDAY HOME PARKS
(Holiday Parks, Touring Parks, Camping Parks)

★★★★★ Exceptional quality
★★★★ Excellent quality
★★★ Very good quality
★★ Good quality
★ Fair to good quality

In England, Scotland and Wales, all graded properties are inspected annually by Tourist Authority trained Assessors.

SELF CATERING — Greater London 115

GREATER LONDON

Citadines Apart'hotel

Experience the freedom of an Apart'hotel in the heart of London!

- A fully equipped apartment with a choice of "à la carte" services and a personalised welcome
- Adaptability to meet your business or leisure stay needs, alone or with your family or friends
- The ideal locations in the heart of London – Trafalgar Square, Barbican, Kensington, Covent Garden
- Reception, parking, cleaning, breakfast
- Kitchen, TV, telephone, hi-fi, house linen, even a dishwasher – nothing is missing

Information / Central Reservation London
Tel: 0800 376 3898 - Fax: 020 7766 3866
Internet: www.citadines.com • e-mail: reslondon@citadines.com
49 Apart'hotels Citadines in Europe: Paris (17), London (4), Brussels (2), Barcelona and Berlin...

See also Outside Back Cover

VISITS & ATTRACTIONS

London Aquarium • *South Bank, London SE1* • *020 7967 8000*
Experience the array of tropical sharks, sting rays, deadly stonefish and piranhas. Don't miss the new 2m Zebra Shark.

Bramah Museum of Tea & Coffee • *Butler's Wharf, London SE1* • *020 7378 0222*
Set amongst atmospheric warehouses, telling the story of 400 years of social and commercial history in ceramics, metal and graphic arts.

National Portrait Gallery • *St Martin's Place, London WC2* • *0870 0660597*
The largest collection of portraiture in the world, with over 10, 000 images of men and women who have shaped the history and culture of the nation. Varied programme of special exhibitions.

FHG PUBLICATIONS

publish a large range of well-known accommodation guides. We will be happy to send you details or you can use the order form at the back of this book.

Greater London

SELF CATERING

See also Outside Back Cover

LONDON. Citadines Trafalgar Square, 18-21 Northumberland Avenue, London WC2N 5BJ (020-7766 3700; Fax: 020-7766 3766). This new Apartment Hotel offers 130 comfortable studios, which can sleep up to two people, 46 one-bedroom apartments sleeping up to 4 and 13 two-bedroom apartments sleeping up to 6. Each apartment has bathroom and fully equipped kitchen. Well-equipped, including air conditioning, direct-dial telephone and TV with satellite channels. A baby cot is available on request. In the heart of the Ministries' district, near the Thames, St. James' Park and Trafalgar Square, it is ideally situated in the city centre for business and tourist visits. Terms on request.

1-12 Months open	Pets welcome	Suitable for disabled	Car essential
[S] Sporting/special interests provided		Coast under two miles	Children welcome
1-6 Number accommodated		Shops nearby	Linen supplied (may be charge)

• • *Some Useful Guidance for Guests and Hosts* • •

Every year literally thousands of holidays, short breaks and overnight stops are arranged through our guides, the vast majority without any problems at all. In a handful of cases, however, difficulties do arise about bookings, which often could have been prevented from the outset.

It is important to remember that when accommodation has been booked, both parties – guests and hosts – have entered into a form of contract. We hope that the following points will provide helpful guidance.

GUESTS:

- When enquiring about accommodation, be as precise as possible. Give exact dates, numbers in your party and the ages of any children.
- State the number and type of rooms wanted and also what catering you require – bed and breakfast, full board etc. Make sure that the position about evening meals is clear – and about pets, reductions for children or any other special points.
- Read our reviews carefully to ensure that the proprietors you are going to contact can supply what you want. Ask for a letter confirming all arrangements, if possible.
- If you have to cancel, do so as soon as possible. Proprietors do have the right to retain deposits and under certain circumstances to charge for cancelled holidays if adequate notice is not given and they cannot re-let the accommodation.

HOSTS:

- Give details about your facilities and about any special conditions. Explain your deposit system clearly and arrangements for cancellations, charges etc. and whether or not your terms include VAT.
- If for any reason you are unable to fulfil an agreed booking without adequate notice, you may be under an obligation to arrange suitable alternative accommodation or to make some form of compensation.

While every effort is made to ensure accuracy, we regret that FHG Publications cannot accept responsibility for errors, omissions or misrepresentations in our entries or any consequences thereof. Prices in particular should be checked because we go to press early. We will follow up complaints but cannot act as arbiters or agents for either party.

CORNWALL

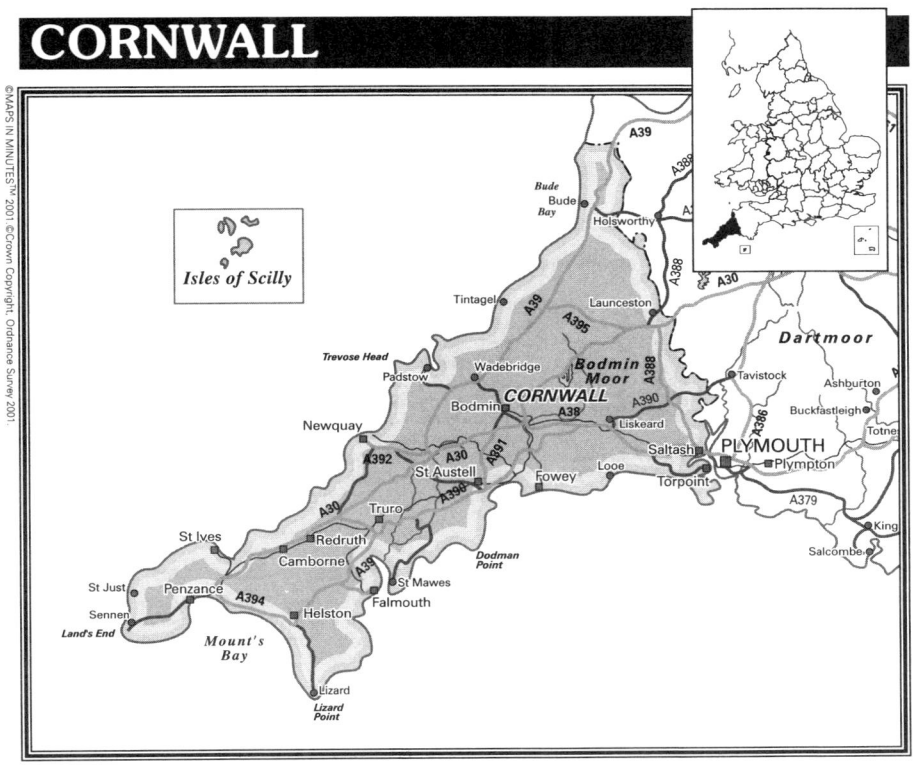

POLPERRO
CORNWALL

Spectacularly situated holiday cottages in picturesque Cornish fishing village.

Sleeping from 2 to 8 persons - £100 to £395 per cottage per week.

With terraced gardens and fabulous outlook over harbour, encompassing 15 mile sea views. Private parking, two minutes shops, beach, quay and National Trust cliff walks. Open all year. Children and pets most welcome. All cottages are fully furnished and equipped to include a colour television, microwave, electric oven, refrigerator, duvets and pillows.

Graham Wright, Guardian House,
Barras Street, Liskeard, Cornwall PL14 6AD

01579 344080

VISITS & ATTRACTIONS

The Eden Project • *Near St Austell, Cornwall* • *01726 811911*
website: www.edenproject.com

A gateway into the fascinating interaction of plants and people. Two gigantic geodesic conservatories - the Humid Tropics Biome and the Warm Temperate Biome - set amidst landscaped outdoor terraces.

118 Cornwall — SELF CATERING

1-12   2/6

See also Colour Display Advertisement **BUDE. Mr K.H. Freestone, Langfield Manor, Broadclose, Bude EX23 8DP (01288 352415; Fax: 01288 353416).** Treat yourself to a special holiday amidst the magnificent splendours of the North Cornwall coastline. Seven quality apartments in this fine Edwardian house with its lovely games room situated in one-and-a-half acres of delightful, sheltered, south-facing gardens. Come and enjoy the conservatory and the sun terrace set around the 36 ft swimming pool. A superb centre for any holiday, out in the country yet only three minutes' walk to the shops and ten minutes' walk to Bude's sandy beaches. Here we are just across the lane from the Bude and North Cornwall Golf Club. Children welcome. Sorry, no pets.
e-mail: info@langfieldmanor.co.uk
website: www.langfieldmanor.co.uk

LOOE near. The Cottages at Trefanny Hill, Near Looe. COTTAGES FOR ROMANTICS. Old world charm, log fires, antiques – beautifully furnished with the comforts of home, private gardens, spectacular views, peace – for families, friends and couples to enjoy. Nestling on a south-facing hillside, near coast. Heated pool, tennis, badminton, lake, Shire horses etc. Enchanting 70 acre estate with bluebell wood, walking, fishing and wildlife. Delicious fare also available by candlelight 'at home' or in our tiny inn. A country lover's paradise, with an abundance of country walks from your garden gate and coastal walks only four miles away. Discover the magic of Trefanny Hill. **B. Slaughter, Trefanny Hill, Duloe, Liskeard PL14 4QF (01503 220622).**
e-mail: enq@trefanny.co.uk
website: www.trefanny.co.uk

1-12   2-8

POLPERRO, CORNWALL (01579 344080). Spectacularly situated holiday cottages in picturesque Cornish fishing village with terraced gardens and fabulous outlook over harbour encompassing 15 mile sea views. Private parking, two minutes shops, beach, quay and National Trust cliff walks. Open all year, children and pets most welcome. All cottages are fully furnished and equipped, to include a colour television, microwave, refrigerator, duvets and pillows. Terms from £100 to £395 per cottage per week.

ST. KEVERNE. Treyloyan Cottage. Sleeps 7. A superb, old character cottage. Spacious with a cosy atmosphere, inglenooks, open beams and thick walls. Peace and quiet. The cottage is situated in its own three-quarter acre grounds with relaxing lawns and natural gardens, sun chairs and picnic table. Three-quarters of a mile from St Keverne village where you will find shops, pubs, bar snacks, etc. - music and laughter. Coastal walks, good fishing and a variety of good beaches. There are four bedrooms, sleeping seven people, bathroom, toilet, washbasin and shower unit. Cot, highchair, telephone, colour TV and bed linen supplied. Night storage heating and log fires, all electric modern kitchen with microwave oven, four ring cooker, automatic washing machine, spin dryer, refrigerator and large toaster. Fitted carpets everywhere. Smoke alarms. Electricity by slot meter. Car essential - ample parking. Contact: **Mrs G.J. Roskilly, Penmarth Farm, Coverack, Helston TR12 6SB (01326 280389).**

See also Colour Display Advertisement **WADEBRIDGE. Pinewood Flats, Polzeath, Wadebridge PL27 6TO (01208 862269).** Many guests, their children and pets return regularly to relax in two-and-a-half acres of Pinewood grounds. The 12 self-contained units all have colour television. Table tennis, a launderette and baby-sitting are available (cots and highchairs too). Own path to beach (surfing and rock pools), shops, tennis, crazy golf and children's playground (four-five minutes' walk). Sea-fishing trips, golf, riding, sailing and wind-surfing are within three to four miles. Superb coastal walks start right at the door so a car is not essential. Spring and Autumn are kindest for your pets. Please phone or write for colour brochure.

SELF CATERING Cumbria **119**

CUMBRIA

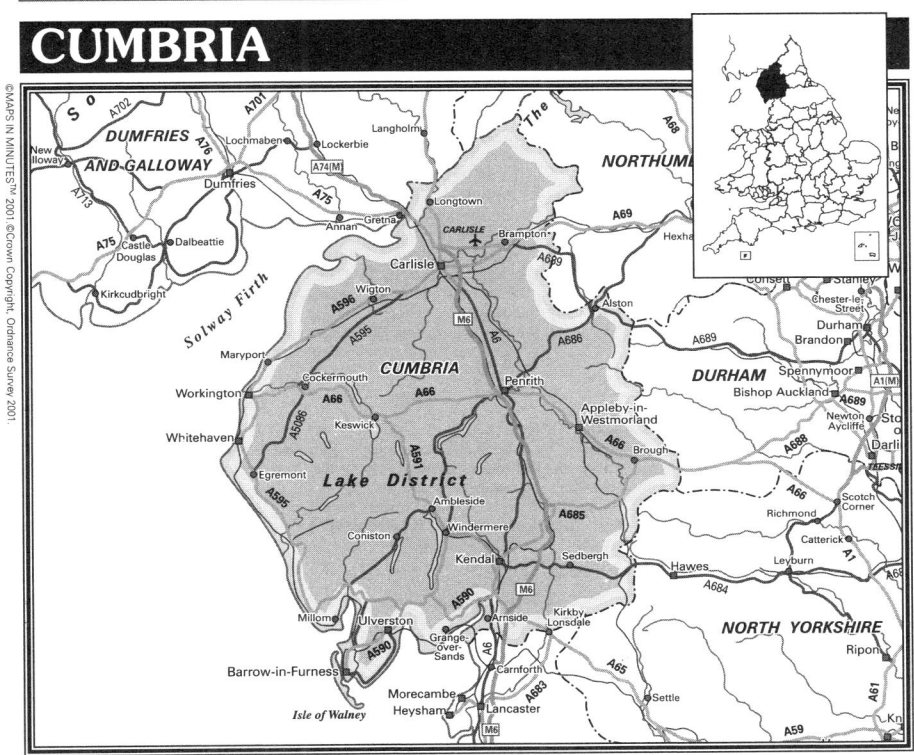

The LAKES and FELLS of CUMBRIA

Dales Holiday Cottages

Superb, personally inspected, self catering holiday properties in beautiful rural and coastal locations. Cosy cottages to country houses, many welcome pets and most are open all year.

01756 799821 & 790919

www.dalesholcot.com *on-line booking, with secure server.*

VISITS & ATTRACTIONS

Rheged Discovery Centre • *Off M6 Junction 40, A66* • *01768 868000* • *website: www.rheged.com*
The Lake District's most spectacular attraction. Six-storey high giant cinema screen takes you on a journey through 2000 years of Cumbria's history, myths and legends.
Set in Britain's largest grass-covered building.

The Dock Museum • *Barrow-in-Furness, Cumbria* • *01229 870871*
A fascinating modern museum telling how this tiny hamlet became the biggest iron and steel centre in the world, and then a major British ship-building force. Film show, galleries, shop, cafe.

Cumbria

SELF CATERING

1-12 🚗 🐎 2-4

AMBLESIDE. Bracken Fell Cottage, Outgate, Ambleside. Bracken Fell Cottage is situated in beautiful countryside between Ambleside and Hawkshead in the picturesque hamlet of Outgate. The two-bedroomed accommodation has central heating and is immaculately furnished. Fully equipped kitchen. Linen and electricity included in the price. Patio area and two acres of gardens. Ample parking. Sorry, no pets. Children over eight years are welcome. The Cottage is ideally positioned for exploring the Lake District with all major outdoor activities catered for in the immediate locality. Open all year from £160 per week. Non-smoking. Bed and Breakfast accommodation also available. Write or phone for brochure and tariff. **ETC ◆◆◆. Peter and Anne Hart, Bracken Fell, Outgate, Ambleside LA22 0NH (015394 36289).**
e-mail: hart.brackenfell@virgin.net
website: www.brackenfell.com

🐕 $ 🐎 2-6

See also Colour Display Advertisement **KIRKOSWALD. Crossfield Cottages & Leisure Fishing.** Accessible, tranquil, secluded quality cottages overlooking fishing lakes amidst Lakeland's Eden Valley countryside. Only 30 minutes' drive from Ullswater, North Pennines, Hadrian's Wall and Scotland's Borderlands. Guaranteed clean. Well-equipped and maintained. Centrally located. Good fishing - coarse and fly - for residents, and walking. Laundry area. Pets VERY welcome - no restrictions. Relax and escape to your home in the country. 24 hour brochure line. Bookings and enquiries 6pm to 10pm. **ETC ★★★. Telephone or Fax: 01768 898711 or SAE to Crossfield Cottages, Kirkoswald, Cumbria CA10 1EU.**

1-12 🚗

See also Colour Display Advertisement **NORTH CUMBRIA. Sleeps 5.** A cosy recently refurbished three-bedroomed cottage, adjoining the owner's home on a small-holding in a rural area of North Cumbria, close to the Scottish border. Surrounded by Kershope Forest, with its winding streams and endless miles of forest walks and waymarked cycle routes. Abundant with wildlife. A good central base for touring Scotland, Hadrian's Wall, Northumberland, The Eden Valley and the Lake District. Bed linen, towels, electricity, central heating and a welcome food pack are all included in the price. Car essential. Ample parking by the door. Lockable shed for cycles. Non-smoking. Children over 7 welcome. Sorry no pets. From £180 to £300 per week. Open all year. Short breaks also available. Colour brochure available from: **Mrs J. Furness, 2 Cuddy's Hall, Bailey, Newcastleton, Roxburghshire TD9 0TP (016977 48160).**

ULLSWATER. Tirril Farm Cottages. Opened in 2001, these tasteful barn conversions are set around a quiet courtyard, some with outstanding views of the fells. Situated two miles from Ullswater in the village of Tirril, and three miles from the M6 (Junction 40), this is an ideal base for visiting the Lakes and Eden Valley. Village facilities include a pub/restaurant and regular bus service. ETC ★★★★. For brochure/bookings **Tel or Fax: 01768 864767 or contact David Owens or Trish Little, Tirril View, Tirril, Penrith CA10 2JE** .
e-mail: tirril.farmcottages@btopenworld.com
website: www.tirrilfarmcottages.fsnet.co.uk

FREE or REDUCED RATE entry to Holiday Visits and Attractions — see our READERS' OFFER VOUCHERS on pages 35-54

DEVON

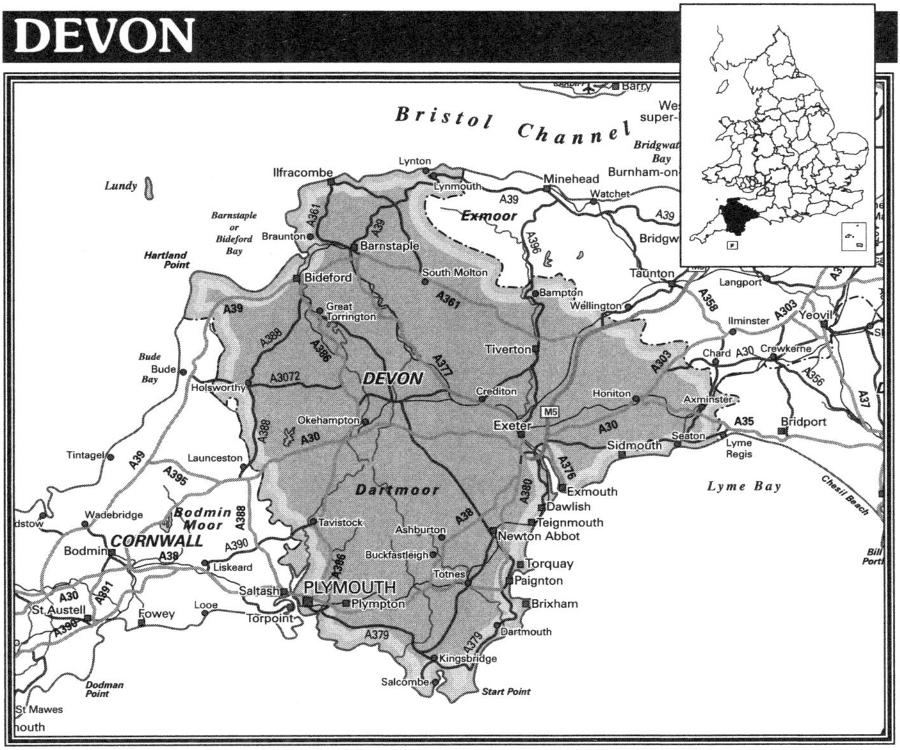

DEVON. Marsdens Cottage Holidays, 2 The Square, Braunton EX33 2JB (01271 813777). There's no better way to experience the charms of North Devon than from the comfort and luxury of a Marsdens holiday cottage. Romantic whitewashed cottages nestling in the heart of North Devon's idyllic countryside and Exmoor or secluded beach houses, just a stone's throw away from some of Britain's most spectacular and unspoilt coastlines...whatever your idea of a perfect holiday, we can help make it a reality. Little wonder then that so many of our customers come back for more. For more details call today for your free colour brochure, or see our cottages on our website (24 hour online booking available). Cottages are inspected and graded by the English Tourism Council, and most are commended for quality.
e-mail: holidays@marsdens.co.uk
website: www.marsdens.co.uk

DEVON/CORNWALL. Holiday Homes and Cottages S.W. (01803 663650: Fax: 01803 664037). Large selection of cottages in Devon and Cornwall. Choose from over 80 properties, ALL ETC inspected and graded. Many are pet-friendly and they are located both in the countryside and near to the sea. For more details visit our website.
website: www.swcottages.co.uk

SELF CATERING

Self-catering you can trust

There's no better way to experience the charms of North Devon than from the comfort and luxury of a Marsdens holiday cottage.

Our full colour brochure includes properties each inspected by our staff, as well as graded by the English Tourism Council, and most are commended for quality.

Romantic whitewashed cottages nestling in the heart of North Devon's idyllic countryside and Exmoor... secluded beach houses just a stone's throw away from some of Britain's most spectacular and unspoilt coastlines...whatever your idea of a perfect holiday, we can help make it a reality. Little wonder, then, that so many of our customers come back for more.

01271 813777 for free colour brochure
www.marsdens.co.uk
email: holidays@marsdens.co.uk

24 HOUR ON LINE BOOKING AVAILABLE

MARSDENS
COTTAGE HOLIDAYS
2 The Square, Braunton,
North Devon EX33 2JB

See also Colour Advertisement on page 00

See also Colour Display Advertisement

BARNSTAPLE. North Devon Holiday Homes, 19 Cross Street, Barnstaple EX31 1BD (01271 376322; Fax: 01271 346544). Easily the best choice of cottages in Devon and comfortably the best value. Contact us now for a free colour guide and unbiased recommendation service to the 400 best value cottages around Devon's unspoilt National Trust Coast.
e-mail: info@northdevonholidays.co.uk
website: www.northdevonholidays.co.uk

See also Colour Display Advertisement

BIDEFORD. Mrs C. A. Thompson, Rosewood, Knotty Corner, Bideford EX39 5BT (01237 451514). Rosewood is a delightful opportunity to enjoy one of the prettiest areas in Devon. Relax on the "suntrap" patio amidst a garden full of colour! Clovelly, Rosemoor Gardens, Milky Way, Tarka Trail, coastal walks, swimming, golf, surfing, canoeing and fishing nearby. Shops and pubs one-and-a-half miles. Beaches within three miles. On the perimeter of a 45 acre stock farm Rosewood offers – attractive entrance hall leading to a large, well equipped kitchen/diningroom with electric cooker and microwave. Tastefully furnished sittingroom, TV, stereo, woodburner. Downstairs bathroom. Three bedrooms, one double, one double and single, one single. Private parking. Children welcome. Sorry, no pets. Terms from £250.
e-mail: christhompson81@hotmail.com

SELF CATERING   Devon   **123**

Devoncourt is a development of 24 self-contained flats, occupying one of the finest positions in Torbay, with unsurpassed views. At night the lights of Torbay are like a fairyland to be enjoyed from your very own balcony.

EACH FLAT HAS:

Marina views	Heating	Sea Views over Torbay
Private balcony	Own front door	Separate bathroom and toilet
Separate bedroom	Bed-settee in lounge	Lounge sea views over Marina
Kitchenette - all electric	Private car park	Opposite beach
Colour television	Overlooks lifeboat	Short walk to town centre
Double glazing	Open all year	Mini Breaks October to April

**DEVONCOURT HOLIDAY FLATS, BERRYHEAD ROAD,
BRIXHAM, TQ5 9AB. Tel: 01803 853748 (24 HRS)**
After hours telephone: 07050 338889
Fax: 01803 855775   e-mail: devoncourt@devoncoast.com

PLEASE SEE OUR MAIN ADVERT IN THE COLOUR SECTION!

Welcome Family Holiday Park

······ DAWLISH WARREN SOUTH DEVON ······

FIRST rate facilities and friendly personal service provide the perfect family holiday!

 Stylish Kaleidoscope, Entertainment Centre

 Superb Indoor Heated Tropicana Water Leisure Complex

 - four feature packed Pools, and Spectator Viewing area

 Cruisers Adult Cocktail Bar with Big Screen TV

 Childrens' Jolly Roger Club with Disco and large Games Arcade

 Short, level walk to safe sandy beach

 Great value-for-money prices

 Free electricity, linen, Colour TV

 Welcome Movie Channel - great films for all the family

 3 Shops • Cafe • 2 Takeaways • Crazy Golf

 Adventure Playground

 Launderette

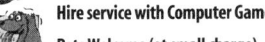 Hire service with Computer Games

 Pets Welcome (at small charge)

 Caravans, Villas, Apartments and Bungalows - Accommodation to suit all taste and pockets

 Sports Ground

Please call for your FREE colour brochure!
Enquiries / Reservations 01626 862070
www.welcomefamily.co.uk

124 Devon — SELF CATERING

1-12 [S] ≋ 🐴 1-4 🧺 🗝

BRIXHAM. Devoncourt Holiday Flats, Berry Head Road, Brixham TQ5 9AB (01803 853748 24 hours; Fax: 01803 855775; after hours tel: 07050 338889). Devoncourt is a development of 24 self-contained flats occupying one of the finest positions in Torbay, with unsurpassed sea views over the Marina. At night the lights of Torbay are like a fairyland to be enjoyed from your own balcony. Each flat has separate bedroom, bed-settee in lounge, separate bathroom and toilet. All electric kitchenette. Colour TV, heating. Private car park. Own front door. Opposite beach and only a short walk to town centre. Open all year. Mini Breaks available October to April.

1-12   ≋   2-12

HOLSWORTHY. Glebe House Cottages. Bridgerule, Holsworthy EX22 7EW (01288 381272). Grade II listed Georgian Estate with original Coach House, Stables and Barns beautifully converted into seven spacious, warm and comfortable cottages sleeping from two to twelve. Exposed beams, some four-poster beds, double sized spa baths and en suite facilities. Set in five acres of beautiful, tranquil countryside, but only 10 minutes' drive from sandy beaches. Games room, children's play area, cellar bar and à la carte restaurant with log fire. Superb home-cooked food. **ETC ★★★★**
e-mail: fhg@glebehousecottages.co.uk
website: www.glebehousecottages.co.uk

1-12 🐕   ≋ 🐴 2-10
See also Colour Display Advertisement

HOPE COVE. Mike and Judy Tromans, Hope Barton Barns, Hope Cove, Near Salcombe TQ7 3HT (01548 561393). Nestling in its own valley, close to the sandy cove, Hope Barton Barns is an exclusive group of 17 stone barns in two courtyards and three luxury apartments in the converted farmhouse. Superbly furnished and fully equipped accommodation ranges from a studio to four bedrooms. Heated indoor pool, sauna, gym, lounge bar, tennis court, trout lake and a children's play barn. We have 35 acres of pastures and streams. Farmhouse meals from our menu. Ample parking. Golf, sailing and coastal walks nearby. Open all year. A perfect setting for family Summer holidays, a week's walking in Spring/Autumn or just a get away from it all break. Free range children and well behaved dogs welcome. Open all year. For a colour brochure please contact **Mike or Judy. ★★★★**.

🐕   4-5

NEWTON ABBOT. John and Helen Griffiths, Lookweep Farm, Liverton, Newton Abbot TQ12 6HT (01626 833277; Fax: 01626 834412). Sleep 4/5. Two attractive well-equipped stone cottages. Clean, characterful and comfortable accommodation. Tranquil setting surrounded by open farmland and woods. Perfectly placed to explore Dartmoor National Park and the charming villages and coastline of South Devon. Golf, riding, fishing and outstanding walking all nearby. Heated pool. Short breaks available. Pets welcome. Mastercard and Visa accepted. **ETC ★★★**.
e-mail: holidays@lookweep.co.uk
website: www.lookweep.co.uk

1-12   🐴
See also Colour Display Advertisement

TORQUAY. Parkfield Luxury Holiday Apartments have 1, 2 or 3 bedrooms, each fully equipped with TV, video and own patio, and most have panoramic views over the Devonshire countryside. Parkfield's landscaped grounds accommodate a children's play area, ample parking and kennels for dogs, which are welcome. The tranquil setting is a short drive to beaches, coastal walks, traditional pubs, steam railways and other family attractions. Short Breaks available by arrangement. **ETC ★★★**. For more information please phone/fax or write to **Roy and June, Parkfield Luxury Holiday Apartments, Claddon Lane, Maidencombe, Torquay TQ1 4TB (Tel & Fax: 01803 328952).**
e-mail: enquiries@parkfieldapartments.co.uk
website: www.parkfieldapartments.co.uk

SELF CATERING   Devon   125

Parkfield Luxury Holiday Apartments have 1, 2 or 3 bedrooms, each fully equipped with TV, video and own patio, and most have panoramic views over the Devonshire countryside. Parkfield's landscaped grounds accommodate a children's play area, ample parking and kennels for dogs, which are welcome. The tranquil setting is a short drive to beaches, coastal walks, traditional pubs, steam railways and other family attractions.
Short Breaks available by arrangement.
For more information, please phone, fax or write to June or Roy at:

**Parkfield Luxury Apartments, Claddon Lane,
Maidencombe, Torquay TQ1 4TB   Tel: 01803 328952**

Parkfield Luxury Holiday Apartments
website: www.parkfieldapartments.co.uk

See also Colour Advertisement

The lovely village of Broadhembury, Devon

DORSET

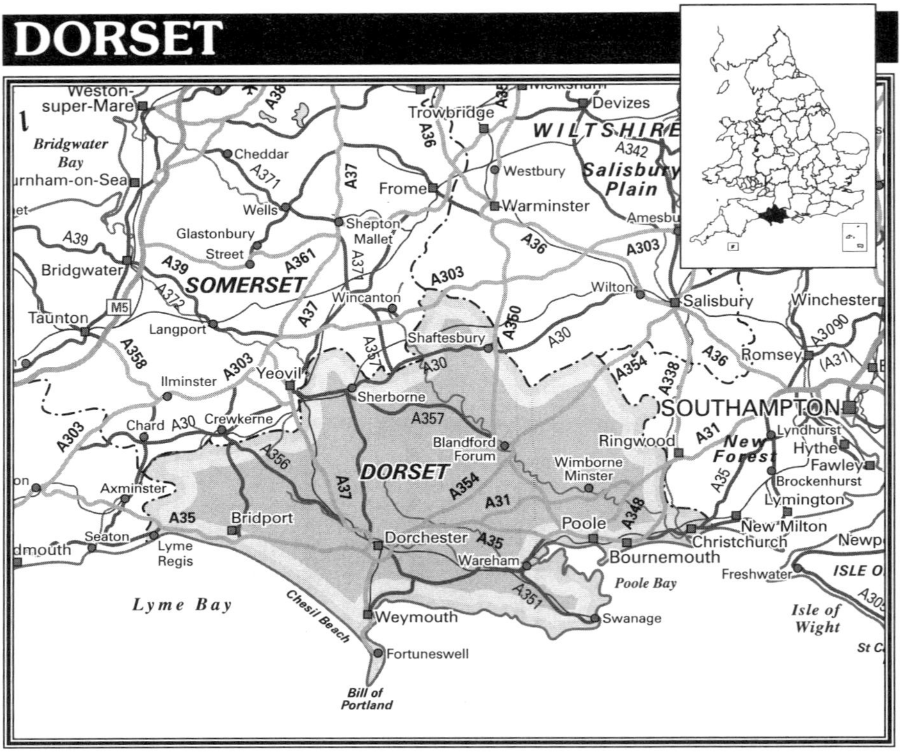

[Map of Dorset and surrounding counties]

BEAMINSTER. 33A St. Mary Well Street. Sleeps 7. Delightful two bedroomed bungalow, peacefully located in a small town, nestling in the rolling hills of West Dorset. Each bedroom has a washbasin, one has a double bed and the second has two single divans. Z-bed and cot available, also settee converts into double bed in lounge. Bathroom and toilet are separate. Well equipped kitchen/dining room. Spacious lounge overlooking patio and garden. Separate utility room. Car parking on private drive. Ideal for walking, fishing and fossil hunting, with the stunning Dorset coastline only seven miles away with picturesque harbours, beaches and coastal path. West Bay, Lyme Regis, Hardy's Cottage, Cricket St. Thomas, Forde Abbey all nearby. No pets. Terms from £140 to £330. For brochure SAE to: **Mrs L. Watts, 53 Hogshill Street, Beaminster, Dorset DT8 3AG (01308 863088).**

VISITS & ATTRACTIONS

Sherborne Castle • *Sherborne, Dorset* • *01935 813182*
website: www.sherbornecastle.com
Built by Sir Walter Raleigh in 1594 and home to the Digby family since the early 17th century. Splendid collection of art, furniture and porcelain.

The Blue Pool • *Furzebrook, Dorset* • *01929 551408*
Sandy paths wander through 20 acres of heather, gorse and pine trees or down to the water's edge, which varies in colour from green to turquoise. Cream teas, children's play area, gift shop, museum, plant centre.

SELF CATERING
Hampshire 127

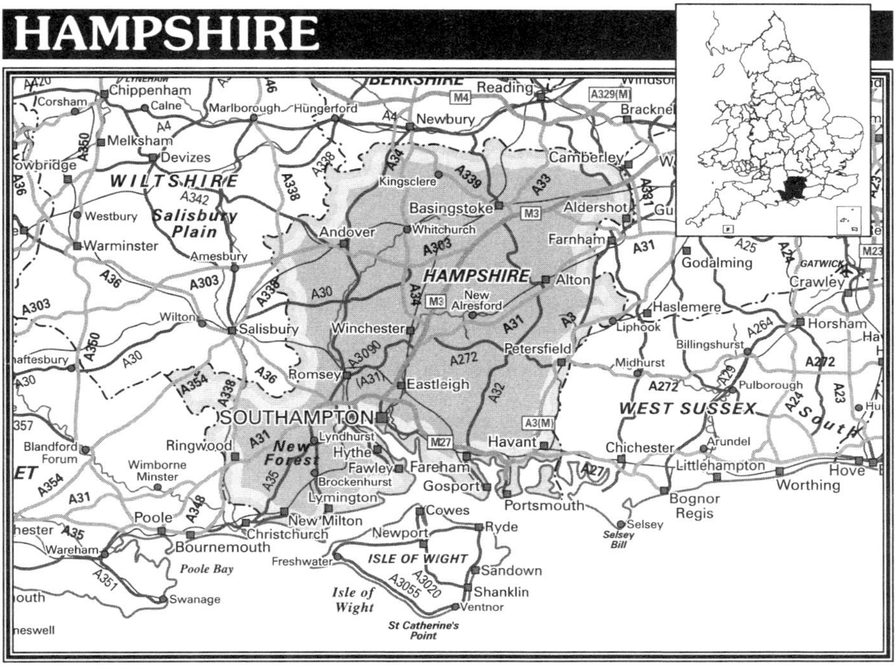

HAMPSHIRE

BENCH COTTAGE & LITTLE BENCH Self-Catering Cottages
Lodge Road, Lymington SO41 8HH • Tel: 01590 673141

Little Bench and Bench Cottage are two brand new self-catering cottages situated in the grounds of Our Bench Guest House, between the New Forest and the yachting town of Lymington. Little Bench has one bedroom sleeping two; Bench Cottage has two bedrooms sleeping up to four people. Both cottages have off-street parking and level access, making them fully accessible and wheelchair friendly. An open plan lounge/dining area and a beautiful modern fully fitted kitchen with every appliance you need. Each cottage also has a large bathroom with shower and safety grab rails fitted if required. The cottages and grounds are for non-smokers only and we are unable to take pets (working dogs for the disabled are accepted subject to conditions).   e-mail: cottages@ourbench.co.uk   website: www.ourbench.co.uk

VISITS & ATTRACTIONS

Royal Navy Submarine Museum • *Gosport, Hampshire* • 023 9252 9217
Step on board the UK's only walk-on submarine HMS *Alliance*. Discover stories of courage and sacrifice, see the heroic story of the submarine service brought to life.

128 Hampshire — SELF CATERING

&

LYMINGTON. Little Bench and Bench Cottage. Both are brand new self-catering cottages situated in the grounds of Our Bench Guest House, between the New Forest and the yachting town of Lymington. Little Bench has one bedroom sleeping two; Bench Cottage has two bedrooms sleeping up to four people. Both cottages have level access, making them fully accessible and wheelchair friendly, and off street parking. An open plan lounge/dining area and a beautiful modern fully fitted kitchen with every appliance you need. Each cottage also has a large bathroom with shower and safety grab rails fitted if required. The cottages and grounds are for non-smokers only and we are unable to take pets, but working dogs for the disabled are accepted subject to conditions. For more information or brochure telephone (01590 673141). Or vist our website.
e-mail: cottages@ourbench.co.uk
website: www.ourbench.co.uk

The FHG Diploma

HELP IMPROVE BRITISH TOURIST STANDARDS

You are choosing holiday accommodation from our very popular FHG Publications.
Whether it be a hotel, guest house, farmhouse or self-catering accommodation, we think you will find it hospitable, comfortable and clean, and your host and hostess friendly and helpful.

Why not write and tell us about it?

As a recognition of the generally well-run and excellent holiday accommodation reviewed in our publications, we at FHG Publications Ltd. present a diploma to proprietors who receive the highest recommendation from their guests who are also readers of our Guides. If you care to write to us praising the holiday you have booked through FHG Publications Ltd. – whether this be board, self-catering accommodation, a sporting or a caravan holiday, what you say will be evaluated and the proprietors who reach our final list will be contacted.

The winning proprietor will receive an attractive framed diploma to display on his premises as recognition of a high standard of comfort, amenity and hospitality. FHG Publications Ltd. offer this diploma as a contribution towards the improvement of standards in tourist accommodation in Britain. Help your excellent host or hostess to win it!

We nominate ....

....

Because

Your Name ....

Address ....

....

Telephone No..

SELF CATERING

Somerset 129

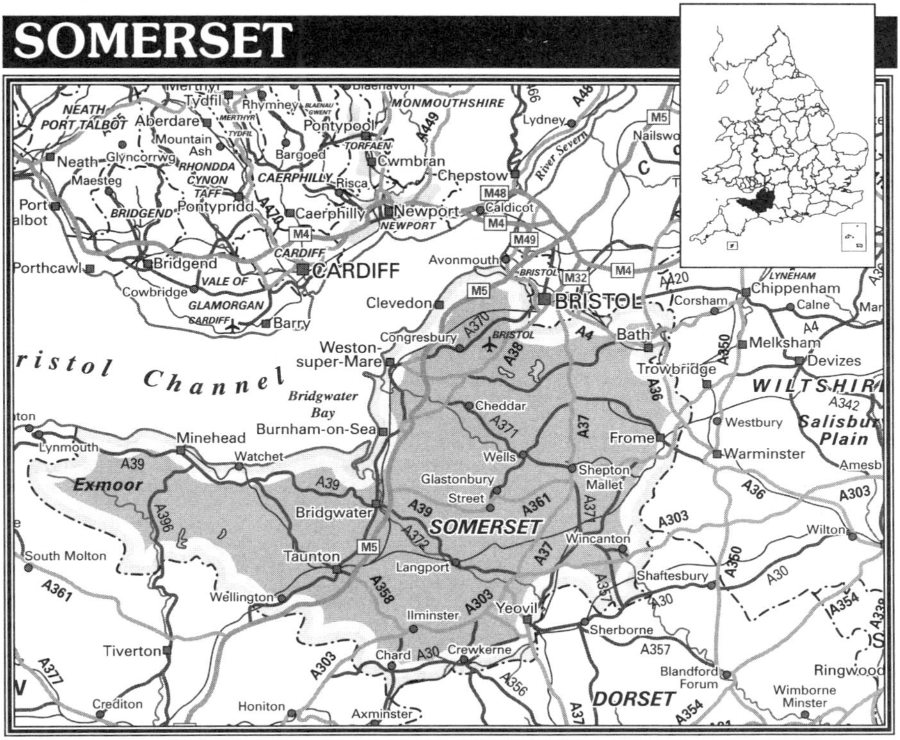

SOMERSET

BATH. Mr D.J. Beckett, Cedar Lodge, 13 Lambridge, London Road, Bath BA1 6BJ (01225 423468).

THE COACH HOUSE - a recent sympathetic luxury conversion, offers: two double and one twin bedrooms; all en suite/private bathrooms; lounge; kitchen; laundry room; full central heating; patio. Sleeps three to six. Weekly terms from £350. WEST WING CEDAR LODGE - complete wing of historic Georgian house, offers: one double and two single bedrooms; luxury bathroom; lounge; kitchen; laundry room; full central heating; lovely gardens and patio. Sleeps two to four. Weekly terms from £300. Both properties are no smoking/pets; secure parking on premises; near friendly local shops, canal walks and city centre. Ideal touring base for Bath, Avebury and Stonehenge, Salisbury, Wells and Wales, Longleat, Cotswolds, The Severn Estuary and many other places of interest. Short breaks can be arranged.

A useful Index of Towns/Villages and Counties appears on page 217 – please also refer to Contents Page 31.

FREE or REDUCED RATE entry to Holiday Visits and Attractions — see our READERS' OFFER VOUCHERS on pages 35-54

130 Somerset — SELF CATERING

Court Farm

Exford, Exmoor, Somerset TA24 7LY
Tel/Fax: 01643 831207 E-mail: beth@courtfarm.co.uk
ETC ★★★

See also Colour Advertisement

For B&B our cosy farmhouse reached down a quiet lane has much character with inglenook fireplaces and exposed beams. Our two bedroom cottages each take five people. They have large kitchen/diners, sitting room, two bedrooms (double with gothic four-poster and twin with bunk-beds). Snowdrop Cottage sleeps two people. There is a sitting/dining room and well-equipped kitchen. The double bedroom has en suite bathroom and the garden has rustic furniture.

We provide all electricity, full oil central heating and all bed-linen in the price. Cottages are open 52 weeks and we have ample parking. Horses, pets: we have stabling and grazing available. Well behaved pets are welcome in cottages.

For more details visit our website: www.courtfarm.co.uk

See also Colour Display Advertisement

MINEHEAD near. St Audries Bay Holiday Club, Dept FHG, West Quantoxhead, Near Minehead TA4 4DY (01984 632515; Fax: 01984 632785). The family holiday centre on the Somerset coast. Facilities include indoor heated pool, family entertainment programme, wide range of sports and leisure facilities, licensed bar and restaurant and all day snack bar. Situated only 15 miles from the M5, near Exmoor at the foot of the Quantock Hills. Well maintained level site with sea views. On site shop. Family owned and managed. Half board holidays available in comfortable chalets, self-catering in luxury caravans. Touring caravans and tents welcome. Luxury holiday homes for sale. No hidden extras, children FREE most weeks.
website: www.staudriesbay.co.uk

VISITS & ATTRACTIONS

Wookey Hole Caves • *Wells, Somerset* • *01749 672243* • *website: www.wookey.co.uk*
Spectacular showcaves with ancient history and legends. Victorian papermill with traditional papermaking, magical mirror maze, old penny arcade, caves museum

West Somerset Railway • *Bishops Lydeard (near Taunton) to Minehead* • *01643 704996*
Enjoy 20 miles of glorious Somerset countryside as the steam train gently rolls back the years. Break your journey at any one of ten restored stations along the route.
For 24hr talking timetable call 01643 707650.

Dunster Water Mill • *Dunster, Somerset* • *01643 821759*
The West Country's finest working water mill, set alongside the River Avill. See how flour is produced, then visit the Mill Shop where stoneground floor, home-made muesli and other products are available.

The FHG Directory of Website Addresses
on pages 182-216 is a useful quick reference guide for holiday accommodation with e-mail and/or website details

SUFFOLK

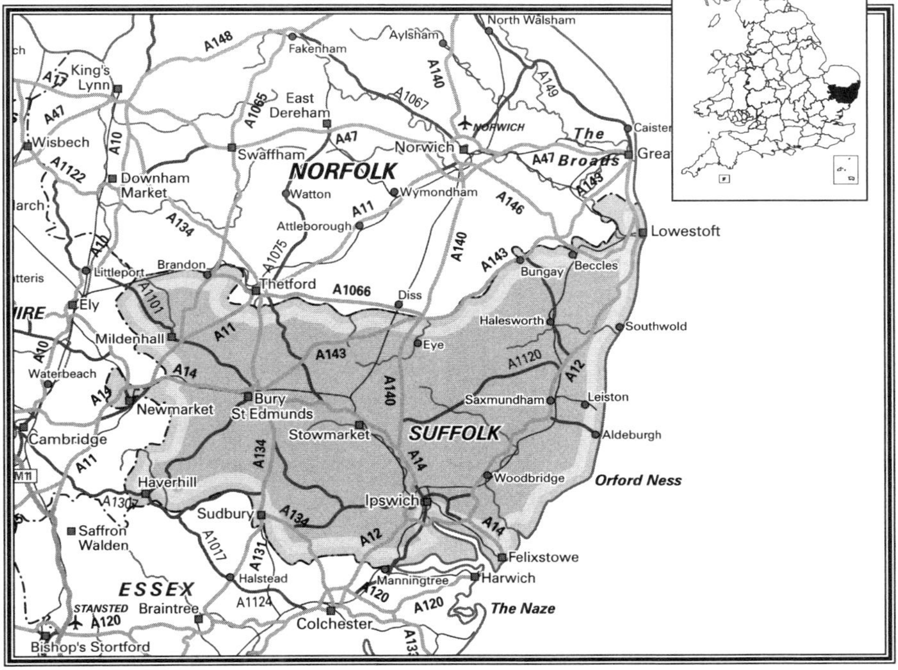

3-12 🐕 ♿ 🚗 ≋ 🐎 1-6

KESSINGLAND. Kessingland Cottages, Rider Haggard Lane, Kessingland, Near Lowestoft. An exciting three-bedroom recently built semi-detached cottage situated on the beach, three miles south of sandy beach of Lowestoft. Fully and attractively furnished with colour TV and delightful sea and lawn views from floor to ceiling windows of lounge. Accommodation for up to six people. Well equipped kitchen with electric cooker, fridge, hot and cold water; electric heater. Electricity by £1 coin meter. Luxurious bathroom with coloured suite. No linen or towels provided. Only a few yards to beach and sea fishing. One mile to wildlife country park with mini-train. Buses quarter-of-a-mile and shopping centre half-a-mile. Parking, but car is not essential. Children and disabled persons welcome. Available 1st March to 7th January. Weekly terms from £50 in early March and late December to £225 in peak season. SAE to **Mr S. Mahmood, 156 Bromley Road, Beckenham, Kent BR3 6PG (Tel & Fax: 020-8650 0539).**
e-mail: jeeptrek@kjti.freeserve.co.uk

VISITS & ATTRACTIONS

National Horse Racing Museum • *Newmarket, Suffolk* • *01638 667333*
website: www.nhrm.co.uk
Five permanent galleries tell the story of the development of the "sport of kings" over 400 years.
Guided tours by arrangement to the studs, racing yards and training facilities.

YORKSHIRE

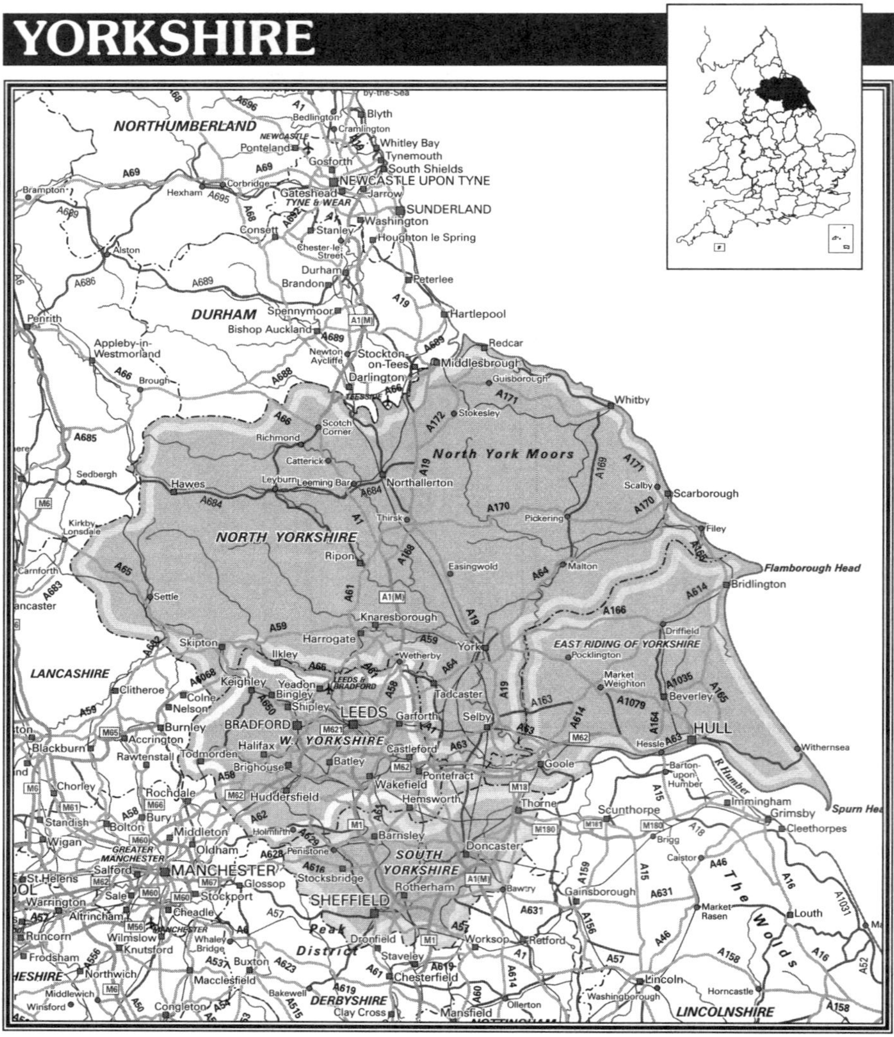

SELF CATERING

YORKSHIRE'S DALES, MOORS & COAST

Superb, personally inspected, self catering holiday properties in beautiful rural and coastal locations. Cosy cottages to country houses, many welcome pets and most are open all year.

01756 799821 & 790919

www.dalesholcot.com *on-line booking, with secure server*

North Yorkshire

1-12

HARROGATE. Mrs Alison Hartwell, Harrogate Holiday Cottages, Crimple Head, Beckwithshaw, Harrogate HG3 1QU (01432 523333; Fax: 01432 526683). Harrogate Holiday Cottages offer accommodation in and around Harrogate, the Dales of Nidderdale, Wensleydale and Herriot Country - all are excellent touring bases for the Moors, Dales, York, Knaresborough, the coast and many lovely places. A friendly, efficient company, with good local knowledge. We book all year round and have apartments, chalets, houses, caravans and courtyard cottages with a swimming pool, all personally inspected by the owner of the company (many by the Tourist Board). Good quality, excellent value, peaceful locations in which to relax and enjoy a superb holiday. Send for free colour brochure. ETC ★★ - ★★★★
e-mail: bookings@harrogateholidays.co.uk
website: www.harrogateholidays.co.uk

4-12   2-8

YORK. Orillia Cottages, Stockton-on-Forest, York. Four converted farm workers' cottages in a courtyard setting at the rear of the 300-year-old farmhouse in Stockton-on-Forest three miles from York. Golf course nearby, pub 200 yards away serving good food; post office, newsagents and general stores within easy reach. Convenient half-hourly bus service to York and the coast. Fully furnished and equipped for two to eight, the cottages comprise lounge with colour TV, etc; kitchen area with microwave, oven, grill and hob; bedrooms have double or twin beds Gas central heating. Non-smokers preferred. Children and pets welcome. Available Easter to October; short breaks may be available. Terms from £150 to £360 weekly includes heating, linen, etc. Please contact: **Mr & Mrs G. Hudson, Orillia House, 89 The Village, Stockton-on-Forest, York YO3 9UP (01904 400600).**

Other specialised

FHG PUBLICATIONS

Published annually: available in all good bookshops or direct from the publisher.

- Recommended COUNTRY HOTELS OF BRITAIN   £5.25
- Recommended WAYSIDE & COUNTRY INNS OF BRITAIN   £5.25
- Recommended SHORT BREAK HOLIDAYS IN BRITAIN   £5.25
- PETS WELCOME!   £6.75
- B&B IN BRITAIN   £4.25
- THE GOLF GUIDE Where to Play / Where to Stay   £9.99

FHG PUBLICATIONS LTD
Abbey Mill Business Centre, Seedhill, Paisley, Renfrewshire PA1 1TJ

Tel: 0141-887 0428 • Fax: 0141-889 7204
e-mail: fhg@ipcmedia.com • website: www.holidayguides.com

FHG Diploma Winners 2001

Each year we award a small number of diplomas to holiday proprietors whose services have been specially commended by our readers. The following were our FHG Diploma Winners for 2001.

England

CUMBRIA

- Mr & Mrs Haskell, Borwick Lodge, Outgate, Hawkshead, Cumbria LA22 0PU (015394 36332).

- Mrs Sue Coleman, Rockside Guest House, Ambleside Road, Windermere, Cumbria LA23 1AQ (015394 45343).

DEVON

- Mr & Mrs Menzies, Beachdown Chalet, Challaborough Bay, Kingsbridge, Devon TQ7 4JB (01548 810089).

KENT

- Mrs Pateman, Pine Lodge Touring Park, Near Bearsted, Maidstone, Kent ME17 1XH (016227 30018).

NORTHUMBERLAND

- Mr & Mrs Fearns, Bounder House, Belsay, Newcastle-upon-Tyne, Northumberland NE20 0JR (01661 881267).

SOMERSET

- Pat & Sue Weir, Slipper Cottage, 41 Bishopston, Montacute, Somerset TA15 6UX (01935 823073)

Scotland

DUMFRIES & GALLOWAY

- Mr Tweedie, Annandale Arms, High Street, Moffat, Dumfriesshire DG10 9HF (01683 220013)

HIGHLANDS

- Mrs Morrison, Nether Lochaber Hotel, Onich, Near Fort William, Inverness-shire PH33 6SE (01855 821235)

PERTH & KINROSS

- Mrs J. MacLaren, Blackcraig Castle, Bridge of Cally, Perthshire PH10 7PX (01250 886251)

HELP IMPROVE BRITISH TOURISM STANDARDS

Why not write and tell us about the holiday accommodation you have chosen from one of our popular publications? Complete a nomination form giving details of why you think YOUR host or hostess should win one of our attractive framed diplomas and send it to:

FHG Publications, Abbey Mill Business Centre, Seedhill, Paisley PA1 1TJ

Visit the FHG website
www.holidayguides.com
for details of the wide choice of accommodation featured in the full range of FHG titles

SCOTLAND
SELF-CATERING

On the shores of Loch Lomond, Scotland's largest loch

SCOTLAND from Borders to Highlands and Islands

Superb, personally inspected, self catering holiday properties in beautiful rural and coastal locations. Cosy cottages to country houses, many welcome pets and most are open all year.

01756 799821 & 790919

www.dalesholcot.com *on-line booking, with secure server.*

ABERDEEN, BANFF & MORAY

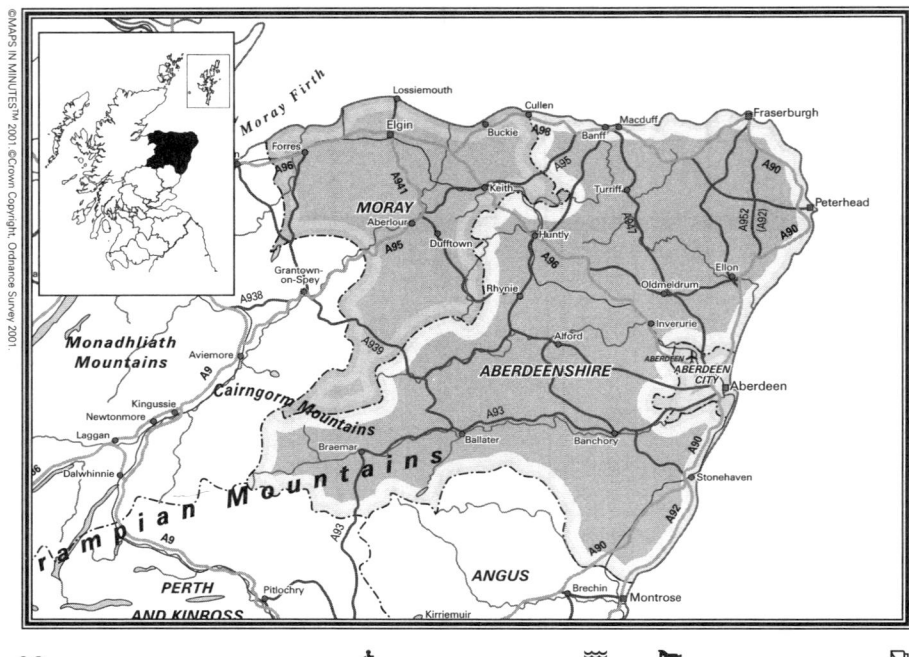

6-8

See also Colour Display Advertisement **ABERDEEN. The Robert Gordon University, Business and Vacation Accommodation, Customer Services Dept, Schoolhill, Aberdeen AB10 1FR (01224 262134; Fax: 01224 262144).** Situated in the heart of Aberdeen and offering a wide variety of accommodation to visitors from June through to August. Aberdeen is ideal for visiting Royal Deeside, castles and historic buildings, playing golf or visiting the Malt Whisky Trail. The city itself is a place to discover and Aberdonians are a friendly and welcoming people. Self-catering accommodation available for individuals or groups of people at superb rates. Each flat is self-contained, centrally heated, fully furnished and suitable for children or disabled guests. All have colour TV and some have microwave facilities. Bed linen and cooking utensils are provided, as is a 'welcome pack' of basic groceries. Each residence has laundry facilities and a telephone as well as car parking. **STB ★ & ★★** *SELF-CATERING.* ASSC MEMBER.
e-mail: accommodation@rgu.ac.uk
website: www.scotland2000.com/rgu

2-6

See also Colour Display Advertisement **ELGIN. Mrs J.M. Shaw, North East Farm Chalet, Sheriffston, Elgin IV30 8LA (01343 842695).** An "A" frame chalet near Elgin situated on a working farm. "Habitat" furnished, fully equipped for two to six people, colour TV, bed linen, duvets. Beautiful rural location in Moray - famous for flowers - district of lowlands, highlands, rivers, forests, lovely beaches, historic towns, welcoming people. Excellent local facilities. Moray golf tickets available. From £180 to £300. January to December. **STB ★★** *SELF-CATERING.* ASSC MEMBER.
e-mail: jennifer.shaw@moray.gov.uk

3-11   1-4

See also Colour Display Advertisement **INVERURIE. Mr and Mrs P. A. Lumsden, Kingsfield House, Kingsfield Road, Kintore, Inverurie AB51 0UD (01467 632366; Fax: 01467 632399).** 'The Greenknowe' is a comfortable detached and renovated cottage in a quiet location at the southern edge of the village of Kintore. It is in an ideal situation for touring castles, historic sites and distilleries, or for walking, fishing and even golf. The cottage is all on one level with a large south-facing sittingroom overlooking the garden. It sleeps four people in one double and one twin room. A cot is available. Parking adjacent. Open from March to November. Prices from £225 to £350 per week, inclusive of electricity (the cottage is all-electric) and linen. Walkers Welcome Scheme. **STB ★★★** *SELF-CATERING.* ASSC MEMBER.
e-mail: kfield@clara.net

ARGYLL & BUTE

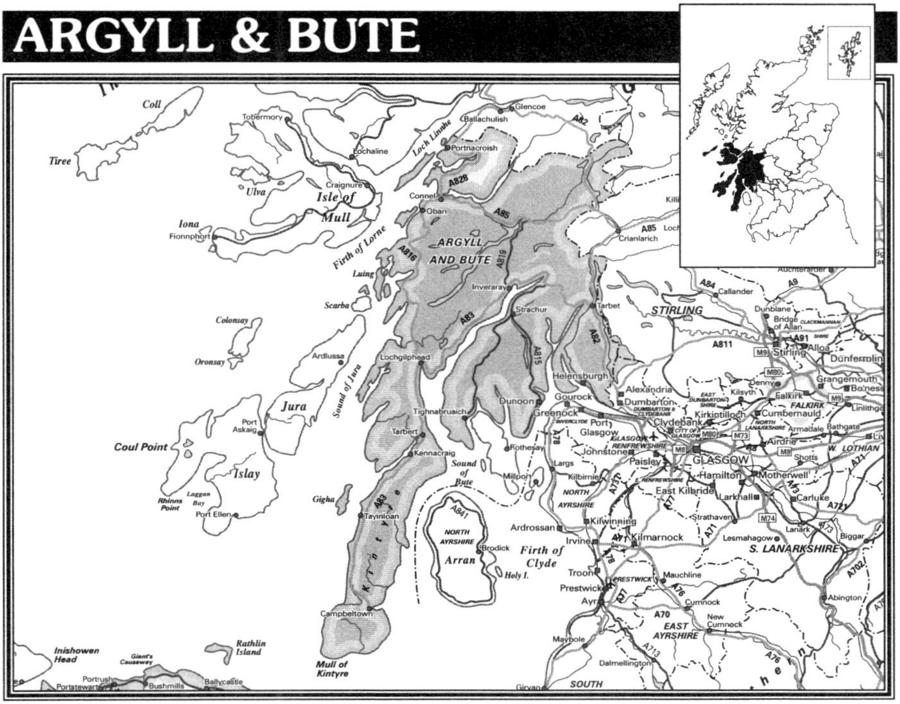

APPIN HOLIDAY HOMES
Midway between Oban and Fort William ... in the Scottish Highlands

Fine hill and shoreline walks amid natural beauty. Warm welcoming lodges and lochside caravan, set apart within landscaped park. Fishing (FREE), boating, cycling, pony trekking, Sealife Centre, Castle Stalker, licensed inn, all nearby. Lots to do and see. Price guide £165 to £395 per unit weekly. Sleeps two to five. Free colour brochure.

MR & MRS I. F. WEIR, APPIN HOLIDAY HOMES, APPIN, ARGYLL PA38 4BQ
TEL: 01631 730287 – WEB: www.appinholidayhomes.co.uk • E-MAIL: info@appinholidayhomes.co.uk

See also Colour Advertisement

FHG PUBLICATIONS

publish a large range of well-known accommodation guides. We will be happy to send you details or you can use the order form at the back of this book.

138   Argyll & Bute   SELF CATERING

See also Colour Advertisement

At Blarghour, a working hill farm on the shores of lovely Loch Awe, the holiday guest has a choice of high quality, well appointed, centrally heated, double glazed accommodation of individual character, each enjoying its own splendid view over loch and mountain in this highly scenic area.

Barn House sleeps 2, Stable 4, the Bungalow 5, and Upper House sleeps 8. A cot and highchair are available in the bungalow and house, as is a dishwasher. Linen and towels are supplied, also telephone and television. Fitted kitchens have fridge/freezer, washer/dryer, microwave, and electric cooker. Car parking beside each house. Barn and Stable houses are unsuitable for children under 5 years. No pets allowed. Open all year. The area, centrally situated for touring, offers opportunities for walking, bird-watching, boating and fishing. Golf is available at Dalmally.

Colour brochure on request.

Mr & Mrs E. Crawford, Blarghour Farm, Lochaweside, By Dalmally, Argyll PA33 1BW Tel: 01866 833246

Fax: 01866 833338   E-mail: blarghour@aol.com   Website: www.blarghour.com   STB ★★★★ Self-catering   ASSC member

---

1-12   2-5

See also Colour Display Advertisement   APPIN. **Appin Holiday Homes.** Midway between Oban and Fort William in the Scottish Highlands. Fine hill and shoreline walks amid natural beauty. Warm welcoming lodges and lochside caravan, set apart within landscaped park. Fishing (free), boating, cycling, pony-trekking, Sealife Centre, Castle Stalker, licensed inn nearby. Lots to do and see. Price guide £155 to £395 per unit weekly. Sleep two/five. Free colour brochure. **Mr and Mrs I.F. Weir, Appin Holiday Homes, Appin PA38 4BQ (01631 730287).** ASSC MEMBER. STB ★★★★ *SELF-CATERING*
e-mail: info@appinholidayhomes.co.uk
website: www.appinholidayhomes.co.uk

1-12   2-8

See also Colour Display Advertisement   DALMALLY. **Mr & Mrs E. Crawford, Blarghour Farm, Lochaweside, By Dalmally PA33 1BW (01866 833246; Fax: 01866 833338).** At Blarghour, a working hill farm on the shores of lovely Loch Awe, the holiday guest has a choice of high quality, well appointed, centrally heated, double glazed accommodation of individual character, each enjoying its own splendid view over loch and mountain in this highly scenic area. Barn House sleeps two, Stable House accommodates four, Barr-beithe Bungalow sleeps five and Upper Blarghour House sleeps eight. All have fitted kitchens with fridge/freezer, washer/dryer, microwave and electric cooker. The Bungalow and Upper House also include a dishwasher, and a cot and highchair are also available. All houses have a telephone and television. Linen and towels are supplied. Cars may be parked beside each house. Barn and Stable Houses are unsuitable for children under five years. No pets are allowed. Open all year. The area, centrally situated for touring, offers opportunities for walking, bird-watching, boating and fishing. Golf is available at Dalmally and Inveraray. Colour brochure sent on request.
e-mail: blarghour@aol.com
website: www.blarghour.com

1-12 Months open	🐾 Pets welcome	♿ Suitable for disabled	🚗 Car essential
[S] Sporting/special interests provided		〰️ Coast under two miles	🐴 Children welcome
1-6 Number accommodated		🛒 Shops nearby	🛏️ Linen supplied (may be charge)

FREE or REDUCED RATE entry to Holiday Visits and Attractions – see our READERS' OFFER VOUCHERS on pages 35-54

SELF CATERING

Argyll & Bute 139

🐕   🐾   2-6

See also Colour Display Advertisement

OBAN. Cologin Farm Holiday Chalets. All Scottish Glens have their secrets: let us share ours with you – and your pets ! Our cosy holiday chalets, set on an old farm in a peaceful private glen, can sleep from two to six people in comfort. They all have private parking, central heating, colour TV and bed linen.Tranquil country glen, just three miles from Oban. Free fishing and dinghy use on our hill loch. Excellent walks for you and your dogs. Home-cooked food and licensed bar in our converted farm-house byre. A safe haven for pets and children. A friendly, family run complex with a good range of facilities. Call now for our colour brochure and find out more. Open all year round. Rates from £150 to £475 per week. Autumn Gold breaks and mid-week deals also available. **STB ★★ to ★★★★** *SELF CATERING.* ASSC MEMBER. **Mrs Linda Battison, Cologin Farmhouse, Lerags, By Oban PA34 4SE (01631 564501; Fax: 01631 566925).**
e-mail: cologin@west-highland-holidays.co.uk
website: www.west-highland-holidays.co.uk

1-12   🐕   ≋   5-7

See also Colour Display Advertisement   **TARBERT. Dunmore Court, West Loch Tarbert.** Four cottages in architect-designed conversion of home farm on the estate of Dunmore House. Spacious accommodation, all have stone fireplaces for log fires. Bird-watching, sailing, sea fishing and unrestricted walking. Easy access to island ferries. Pets welcome. Open all year. Colour brochure. From £165-£425. **STB ★★** *SELF-CATERING.* Contact: **Amanda Minshall, Dunmore Court, Near Tarbert, Argyll PA29 6XZ (01880 820654)**. *ASSC MEMBER.*
e-mail: dunmorecourt@cs.com

🐕   [S]   ≋

TARBERT. Sophie James, Skipness Castle, By Tarbert, Argyll PA29 6XU (01880 760207; Fax: 01880 760208). This unspoilt, peaceful, West Highland estate with its own historic castle, mediaeval chapel and way-marked walks has traditional cottages to let all year round. Each cottage has an open fire and television; some cottages have a rowing dinghy in summer. Laundry facilities are available alongside the Seafood Cabin at Skipness Castle. Properties sleep 4 – 10. All cottages have magnificent views and beautiful surrounding countryside and coastline. Safe, sandy beaches can be enjoyed on the estate, with fishing, pony trekking and golf nearby. Local ferries to Arran, Gigha, Islay, Jura and Northern Ireland. Pets welcome. Apply for rates and further details. **STB ★** *SELF-CATERING.* FARM HOLIDAY GUIDE DIPLOMA
e-mail: sophie@skipness.freeserve.co.uk

PLEASE NOTE

All the information in this book is given in good faith in the belief that it is correct. However, the publishers cannot guarantee the facts given in these pages, neither are they responsible for changes in policy, ownership or terms that may take place after the date of going to press. Readers should always satisfy themselves that the facilities they require are available and that the terms, if quoted, still apply.

AYRSHIRE & ARRAN

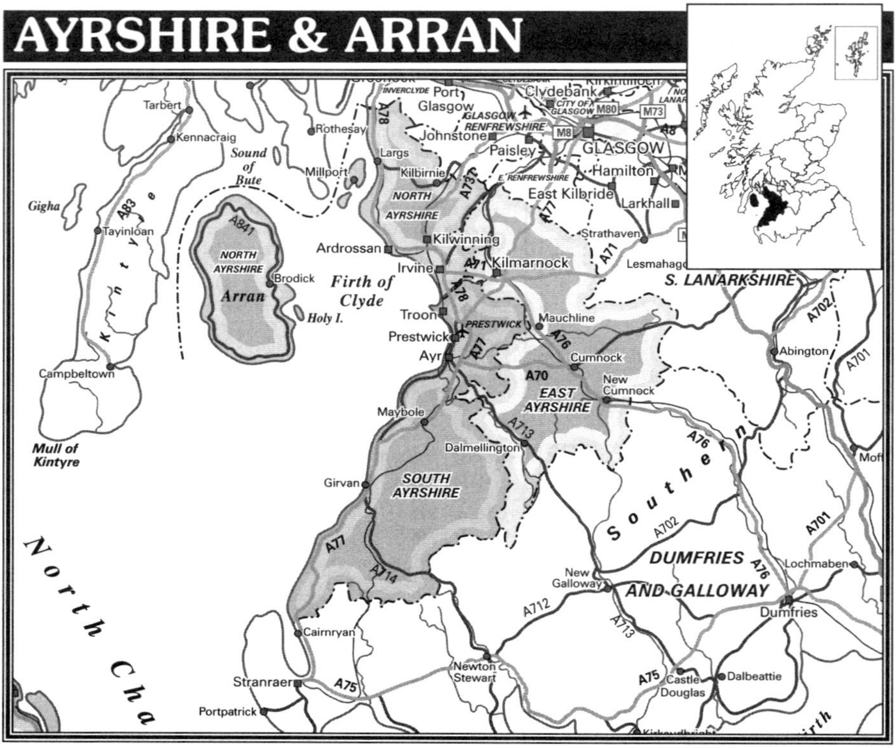

TROON near. Mrs R. Elliott, Old Rome Farmhouse, Gatehead, Kilmarnock KA2 9AJ (01563 850265).

New barn conversion situated in lovely courtyard off the A5759, five miles from Troon. It has three bedrooms (two twin and one double), luxury furniture and fittings including colour TV and video, two bathrooms, fully fitted kitchen with fridge/freezer, microwave, washing machine. Linen and heating included. Pub/restaurant on site. Please telephone for our brochure.

The Island of Arran

1-12

See also Colour Display Advertisement

ARRAN. Arran Holiday Properties, Invercloy House, Brodick, Isle of Arran KA27 8AJ (Office: 01770 302303/302310; Evenings & Weekends: 01770 860556). Choice of properties on the island, available throughout the year. All villages, all dates. Self-catering and bunk house accommodation available. STB Quality Assured. Short breaks available. Major credit cards accepted. Please ask for our brochure. On-line availability. ASSC MEMBER.
e-mail: arran.estateagents@virgin.net
website: www.arranproperties.co.uk

Borders 141

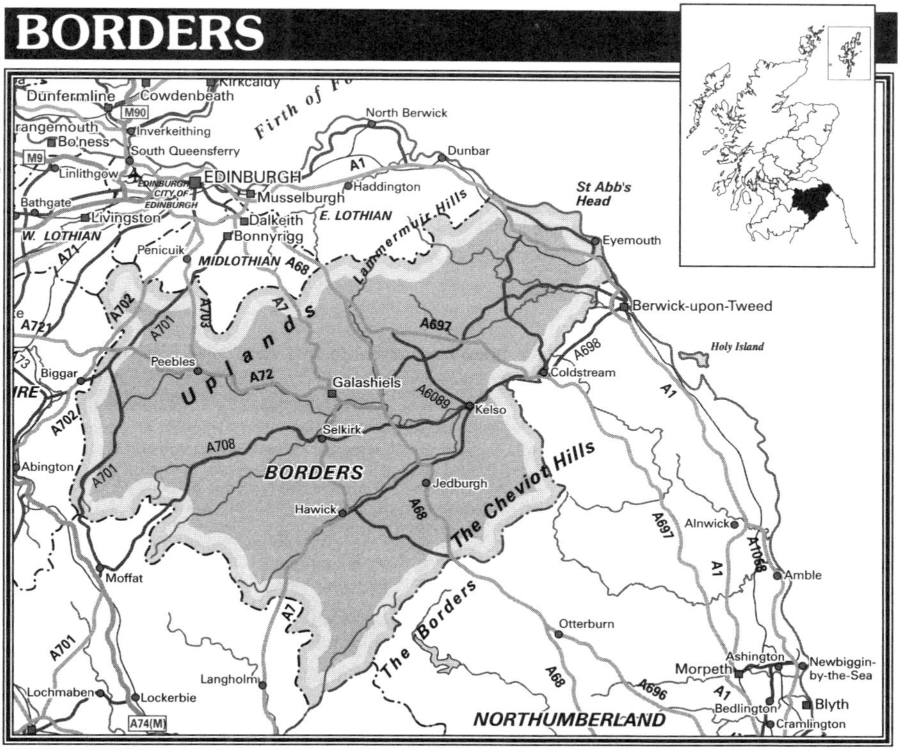

BORDERS

🐴 6 📖

See also Colour Display Advertisement **DUNS. Mrs M. Macfarlane, Quixwood, Abbey St. Bathans, Duns TD11 3RS (01361 840233). Sleeps 6 plus cot.** Come and enjoy a comfortable break in our spacious semi-detached farm cottage. It is conveniently situated on a quiet road with all round views of beautiful rolling farmland, yet only two-and-a-half miles from the A1, giving easy access to North and South and all parts of the Scottish Borders. Edinburgh is less than one hour away by car. The cottage sleeps six people and has a cot and highchair. There are two single bedrooms, one twin and one double bedroom, bathroom with shower, dining kitchen and a large lounge with TV and video. All rooms are on the ground floor level. Linen and towels are provided and central heating is included. There is a large garden to relax in or for children to play. For people who enjoy walking, the Southern Upland Way is just a mile away, or a 15 minute drive takes you to the coast. Prices range from £170 to £250 per week with Short Break terms available on request. ASSC MEMBER

1-12 Months open	🐾 Pets welcome	♿ Suitable for disabled	🚗 Car essential
[S] Sporting/special interests provided	〰️ Coast under two miles	🐕 Children welcome
1-6 Number accommodated	🛒 Shops nearby	🛏️ Linen supplied (may be charge)

Readers are requested to mention this guidebook
when seeking accommodation (and please enclose
a stamped addressed envelope).

1-12

4v8, Jan 2002,

See also Colour Display Advertisement

JEDBURGH. Mill House, Letterbox and Stockman's Cottages. Three recently renovated, quality Cottages, each sleeping four, on a working farm three miles from Jedburgh. Ideal centres for exploring, sporting holidays or getting away from it all. Each cottage has two public rooms (ground floor available). Minimum let two days. Terms £190–£330. Open all year. Bus three miles, airport 54 miles. Green Tourism Business Award – SILVER. **STB ★★★★** *SELF-CATERING*. **Mrs A. Fraser, Overwells, Jedburgh TD8 6LT (01835 863020; Fax: 01835 864334).** ASSC MEMBER.
website: www.overwells.co.uk

See also Colour Display Advertisement

KELSO. Plum Braes Barn & Edmonston. Kelso is two miles away, rich in history, including Floors Castle and the Abbey; interesting shops, Sunday market, Tweed Cycle Way, golf courses and horse racing. Melrose, Jedburgh, Peebles and Selkirk within half-hour's drive. PLUM BRAES BARN has been converted into three cottages, two on the ground floor with two bedrooms (twin and king size beds), the third cottage has gallery bedroom with french windows and a small balcony. All cottages have private gardens with decking and furniture, with wonderful views over the River Eden. The cottages all have wood burners, central heating and kitchens including dishwashers. Laundry. Private parking. EDMONSTON is a large chalet style farmhouse nearby with commanding views in all directions. Five bedrooms, one on ground level. Central heating, log fire, dining room, lounge with panoramic views, kitchen, utility and garage, paddocks, free fishing, wild flower meadow. For brochure and booking form please telephone **Mrs Stewart, Cliftonhill Farm, Ednam, Kelso TD5 7QE (01573 225028).** ASSC MEMBER.
e-mail: archie@sol.co.uk
website: www.plumbraesbarn.freeserve.co.uk or www.edinburghholidaycottages.com

See also Colour Display Advertisement

NEWCASTLETON. Bailey Mill Courtyard, Bailey, Newcastleton, Roxburghshire TD9 0TR (016977 48617; Fax: 016977 48074). A warm welcome awaits you from Pam and Ian on this small farm holiday complex, nestling on the Roxburghshire /Cumbrian border. The rural self-contained apartments create a courtyard setting or enjoy Bed and Breakfast or Full Board riding holidays in the farmhouse. Colour TV and Sky link; heating (oil), electricity and linen included in the rent. On site sauna, solarium, toning table, games room, laundry, babysitting, fully licensed bar and meal service. Enjoy walking or trekking through surrounding forests. Eight horses and six mountain bikes available. Central touring area for Lake District, Hadrian's Wall and Scotland. Colour brochure available. Self catering £78 to £498 weekly, B&B from £20 per person. **ETC ★★/★★★** *SELF-CATERING*.

The **FHG GOLF GUIDE**
Where to Play Where to Stay
2002

Available from most bookshops, the 2002 edition of **THE GOLF GUIDE** covers details of every UK golf course – well over 2800 entries – for holiday or business golf. Hundreds of hotel entries offer convenient accommodation, accompanying details of the courses – the 'pro', par score, length etc.

In association with 'Golf Monthly' and including Holiday Golf in Ireland, France, Portugal, Spain, The USA, South Africa and Thailand.

£9.99 from bookshops or from the publishers (postage charged outside UK) • FHG Publications, Abbey Mill Business Centre, Paisley PAI ITJ

DUMFRIES & GALLOWAY

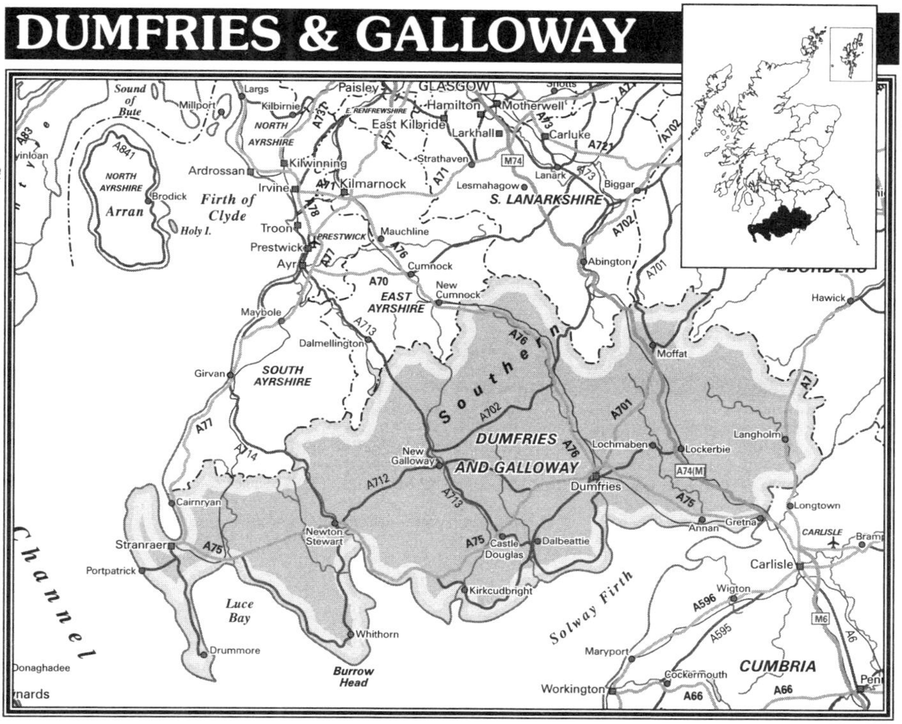

CASTLE DOUGLAS. Kerr and Sheila Steele, Rose Cottage, Gelston, Castle Douglas DG7 1SH (Tel & Fax: 01556 502513). Detached country cottage in village two-and-a-half miles from Castle Douglas, one-and-a-half miles from Threave Gardens and centrally situated for exploring Galloway. The cottage contains four double bedrooms (one en suite), bathroom with bath and shower. Bedrooms have washbasin, TV; bedlinen and towels supplied. Lounge with television and video, dining room/conservatory and large modern kitchen. Facilities include central heating, gas hob, electric oven, fridge, freezer, microwave and washing machine. Large garden with stream and waterfall. Rural views surround property. Private parking for six cars. Weekly terms from £350 to £550. Three night breaks from £200 to £314. Heating included. Electricity £25 extra November - March.

FHG
Visit the FHG website
www.holidayguides.com
for details of the wide choice of accommodation featured in the full range of FHG titles

144 Dumfries & Galloway — SELF CATERING

See also Colour Display Advertisement

DALBEATTIE. Barend Holiday Village, Sandyhills, Dalbeattie DG5 4NU (01387 780663; Fax: 01387 780283). Barend Holiday Village, near Sandyhills, on the beautiful south-west coast of Scotland, with 16 golf courses within a 20 mile drive, yet only one hour's drive from England. Our Scandinavian style log chalets are centrally heated for all year round use and have TV and video. All chalets have decks or verandahs, some overlooking the loch or the adjacent Colvend 18-hole golf course. On-site launderette, bar, restaurant, sauna and indoor heated pool. The two and three bedroomed chalets accommodate up to eight people from £240 to £640 per week including linen, heating and swimming. Short breaks available all year from £145 for four people. Pets welcome. **STB ★★★** *SELF-CATERING* ASSC MEMBER
website: www.barendholidayvillage.co.uk

See also Colour Display Advertisement

GATEHOUSE OF FLEET. Rusko Holidays, Rusko, Gatehouse of Fleet, Castle Douglas DG7 2BS (01557 814215; Fax: 01557 814679). Sleep 2-10. Lovely, spacious farmhouse and cosy comfortable cottages on a beautiful private estate near beaches, hills, forests and golf course. Use of tennis court, loch and river fishing with tuition given, wonderful area for walking, riding and sailing. Rates from £150 to £680. Pets, including horses. TV, telephone, washing machine and enclosed garden. Stabling and grazing available. **STB ★★ to ★★★** *SELF-CATERING. WALKERS AND CYCLISTS WELCOME. DISABLED CATEGORY 3. WELCOME HOST. ASSC MEMBER*
e-mail: gilbey@rusko.demon.co.uk   website: www.ruskoholidays.co.uk

The Mull of Galloway, the most southerly point on the mainland of Scotland

DUNDEE & ANGUS

1-12 See also Colour Display Advertisement 2-4

KIRRIEMUIR. Jenny Scott, Welton Farm, The Welton of Kingoldrum, By Kirriemuir, Angus DD8 5HY (Tel & Fax: 01575 574743). Three luxurious self-catering properties (two with en suite facilities) on a secluded 186 acre working farm. Situated in a spectacular setting with superb panoramic views at the gateway to the glorious Angus Glens. Peaceful and relaxing with an abundance of birds and wildlife. Ideal for hill-walking and bird-watching. An excellent base for outdoor pursuits including fishing, riding, skiing, shooting, golf, and touring the glens, coast and castles (including Glamis). Many visitor attractions in the area. A wide variety of comfortable, high standard accommodation. Central heating, hot water, linen and towels included in rental. Facilities include payphone, laundry and ironing facilities, microwave, electric cooker, fridge and freezer, dishwasher, colour TV, cot, bed setee, electric blankets, radio alarm, hairdryer, garden furniture, parking. Open all year. Short breaks available. Welcome Host. Prices £165 to £350. **STB** ★★★/★★★★ *SELF-CATERING*. ASSC MEMBER.
e-mail: weltonholidays@btinternet.com
website: www.cottageguide.co.uk/thewelton

Terms quoted in this publication may be subject to increase if rises in costs necessitate

EDINBURGH & LOTHIANS

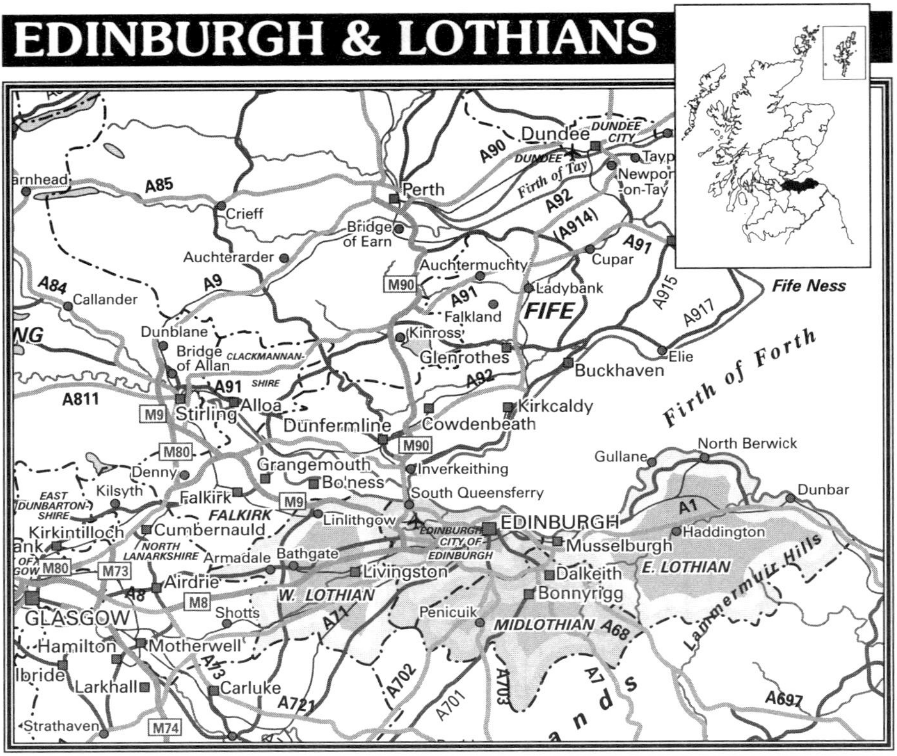

1-12   4-5

EDINBURGH. Elm Place, Leith Links EH6 8AL. Sleeps 4/5. 19th century 'colony', a style of flat unique to Edinburgh, with its own front door and pretty little garden. 10/15 minutes to Princes Street and the city centre. Regular direct buses. Minutes walk to Leith docks, host to Tall Ships and Jazz Festivals, home to Britannia and some great waterside restaurants and bars. Good variety of local shops, park, children's play area and swimming pools. Facilities include living/kitchen, two bedrooms (double bed, two singles, sofa bed), modern kitchen facilities, washing machine, shower room, TV. Children welcome. No Smoking. Terms from £170 per week. Details from **Bridget Webster, 3 Rosevale Place, Edinburgh EH6 8AP (0131 555 4524).**
e-mail: bwebster@supanet.com

FREE or REDUCED RATE entry to Holiday Visits and Attractions — see our READERS' OFFER VOUCHERS on pages 35-54

SELF CATERING

FIFE

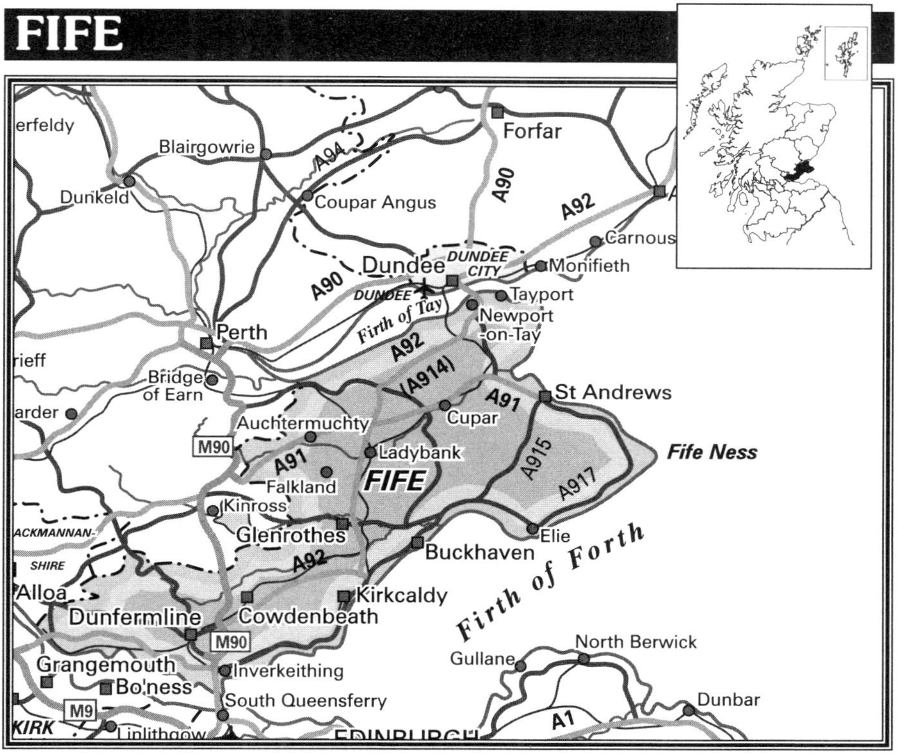

Fife **147**

See also Colour Display Advertisement

ANSTRUTHER. Mr & Mrs R. Sparrow, Old Bank House Restaurant & Apartments, 23-25 High Street East, Anstruther KY10 3DQ (01333 310189/310168). Overlooking its own beach just west of the harbour at Anstruther, the Old Bank House is centrally situated in the heart of the town. Wine and dine in our intimate restaurant or drop in for a drink and a selection of Tapas in the cosy bar; games room with pool table, darts and an inviting log fire. Four letting apartments, all with en suite facilities, central heating, telephone and fully equipped kitchens. All linen and towels are supplied, and a laundry service is available on request. Apartment One sleeps 4-8 and overlooks the garden. Apartment Two is for two people and has twin beds, garden and sea view. Apartment Three has disabled access and facilities and sleeps 2-8. Apartment Four sleeps 4-8 persons. In each apartment one child under seven may stay free of charge. Dogs permitted in apartments One and Two only. Breakfast available on request. Terms from £20 per person per night, based on two sharing. ASSC MEMBER.
e-mail: ricardosrest@hotmail.com
website: www.undiscoveredscotland.co.uk/anstruther/oldbank

2-8

A useful Index of Towns/Villages and Counties appears on page 217 – please also refer to Contents Page 31.

HIGHLANDS

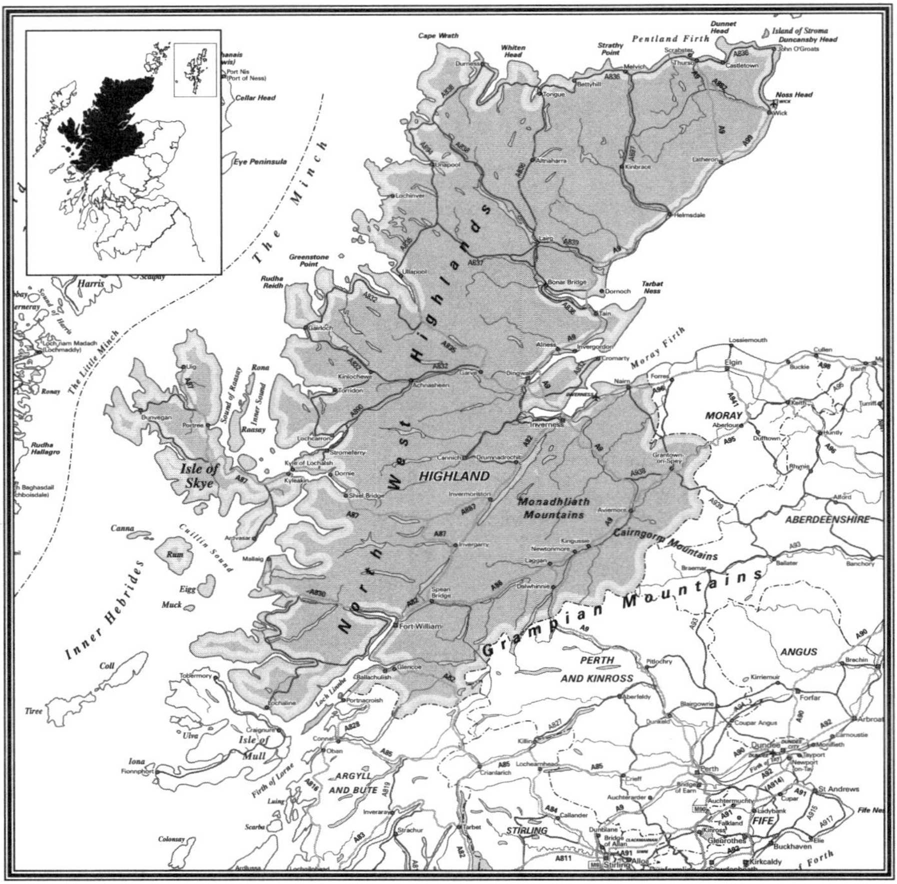

SELF CATERING

PLEASE MENTION THIS GUIDE WHEN YOU WRITE OR PHONE TO ENQUIRE ABOUT ACCOMMODATION

IF YOU ARE WRITING, A STAMPED, ADDRESSED ENVELOPE IS ALWAYS APPRECIATED

HIGHLANDS (NORTH)

4-10

LAIRG. Fernlea, Main Street, Lairg. Sleeps 7. Lovely house with gardens back and front situated in this peaceful village, an ideal centre for touring the North and sailing to the Orkneys and Outer Hebrides; return trips daily. A wonderful place for hill walking, fishing, bird watching, boating; golf course 11 miles away, sandy beaches 18 miles east and 35 miles west. The house is fully equipped including linen. Three bedrooms (three double and one single bed, plus cot); shower room; lounge/dining area with colour TV and video; kitchen with electric cooker, microwave, fridge, automatic washing machine, tumble dryer, immersion heater, electric fires. £1 coin meter for electricity. Free night storage heating in lounge. Parking. The house is double glazed and is available from April to October. Terms from £190 to £240 per week. Free use of rowing boat on Loch Shin. For further information and available dates apply to: **Mrs R. Corbett, An-Airidh, 24 Achfrish, Shinness, Lairg IV27 4DN (01549 402223).**
e-mail: lairg_selfcater@yahoo.co.uk
website: www.uk.geocities.com/lairg_selfcater/hh.html

1-12   2-5

See also Colour Display Advertisement **LOCHINVER. Clashmore Holiday Cottages, Lochinver.** Our three croft cottages at Clashmore are the ideal base for a holiday in the Highlands. They are cosy and fully equipped, with linen provided. Nearby there are sandy beaches, mountains and lochs for wild brown trout fishing. Children welcome, but sorry – no pets. Open all year. Terms from £160 to £330. **STB ★★★** *SELF-CATERING.*
Contact: **Mr and Mrs Mackenzie, Lochview, 216 Clashmore, Stoer, Lochinver, Sutherland IV27 4JQ (Tel & Fax: 01571 855226).** ASSC MEMBER.
e-mail: clashcotts@supanet.com

HIGHLANDS (MID)

6

See also Colour Display Advertisement **POOLEWE. Innes Maree Bungalows, Poolewe IV22 2JU (Tel & Fax: 01445 781454).** Only a few minutes' walk from the world-famous Inverewe Gardens in magnificent Wester Ross. A purpose built complex of six superb modern bungalows, all equipped to the highest standards of luxury and comfort. Each bungalow sleeps six with main bedroom en suite. Children and pets welcome. Terms from £185 to £425 inclusive of bed linen and electricity. Brochure available. **STB ★★★★** *SELF-CATERING.* ASSC MEMBER
e-mail: info@poolewebungalows.com
website: www.poolewebungalows.com

Visit the **FHG** website
www.holidayguides.com
for details of the wide choice of accommodation featured in the full range of FHG titles

HIGHLANDS (SOUTH)

LINNHE LOCHSIDE HOLIDAYS
Corpach, Fort William PH33 7NL
Tel: 01397 772376 • Fax: 01397 772007
e-mail: holidays@linnhe.demon.co.uk
website: www.linnhe-lochside-holidays.co.uk

"Best Park in Scotland 1999 Award"
Almost a botanical garden and stunningly beautiful. Wonderful views and ideal for touring or simply relaxing and soaking up the scenery. Licensed shop, private beach and free fishing. Colour brochure.

★ **De luxe pine chalets** from £56/night (min 3 nights), £315/week.
★ **Luxury holiday caravans** from £31/night (min 2 nights), £180/week.

See also Colour Display Advertisement **CROY. Mrs Strachan, Balblair Cottages, Balblair, Croy IV2 5PH (01667 493 407).** Three cottages, imaginatively created from a stone farm steading, on a small livestock holding, 10 miles east of Inverness. Each cottage has its own south facing garden with patio furniture, double glazing, electric central heating and wood burning stove, making Balblair an ideal all year round base for a Highland holiday. Cawdor Castle, Fort George, Clava Cairns, Inverness and Nairn are all within ten miles, while Loch Ness, the Cairngorms, the Isle of Skye and even John O' Groats can be visited in a day by car. Golf courses are in abundance. Bed linen and towels are provided; telephone. Children and pets welcome. ASSC MEMBER.

See also Colour Display Advertisement **CULLODEN (By Inverness). Blackpark Farm, Westhill, Inverness IV2 5BP (01463 790620; Fax: 01463 794262).** This newly built holiday home is located one mile from Culloden Battlefield with panoramic views over Inverness and beyond. Fully equipped with many extras to make your holiday special, including oil fired central heating to ensure warmth on the coldest of winter days. Ideally based for touring the Highlands including Loch Ness, Skye etc. Extensive information is available on our website. A Highland welcome awaits you. ASSC MEMBER
e-mail: i.alexander@blackpark.co.uk
website: www.blackpark.co.uk

FORT WILLIAM near. Linnhe Lochside Holidays, Corpach, Fort William PH33 7NL (01397 772376; Fax: 01397 772007). "Best Park in Scotland 1999 Award" Almost a botanical garden and stunningly beautiful. Wonderful views and ideal for touring or simply relaxing and soaking up the scenery. Licensed shop, private beach and free fishing. Colour brochure. De luxe pine chalets from £56 per night (minimum three nights), £315 per week. Luxury holiday caravans from £31 per night (minimum two nights), £180 per week. **STB ★★★★ HOLIDAY PARK/★★★★ SELF-CATERING.**

See also Colour Display Advertisement **INVERGARRY. High Garry Lodges, Invergarry.** Four Scandinavian lodges set in an elevated position with superb views. Double glazed, electric central heating. One twin, two double bedrooms, lounge with breakfast bar and well equipped kitchen and bathroom. Terms from £160 to £465. Also one attractively converted cottage nestling at a lower level within the confines of this small working farm. One double and one twin bedroom, tastefully renovated to a high standard. Terms from £190 to £475. Visitors may participate at feeding times on the farm. Ideal for touring the West Highlands. Fishing, walking, golf and bird-watching nearby. Brochure available. **STB ★★★** *SELF-CATERING,* **Cottage STB ★★★★** *SELF-CATERING.* Contact: **Mr and Mrs Wilson (01809 501226; Fax: 01809 501307).** ASSC MEMBER.

SELF CATERING
Highlands (South) 151

 2-12

INVERGARRY. Miss J. Ellice, Taigh-an-Lianach, Aberchalder Estate, Invergarry PH35 4HN (01809 501287). Three self-catering properties, all ideal for hill walkers and country lovers. Salmon and trout fishing available. ABERCHALDER LODGE: traditional Highland shooting lodge extensively modernised to give a high standard of comfort, sleeps 12. TAIGH-AN-LIANACH: modern self-contained bed-sit, secluded and peaceful, sleeps two. LEAC COTTAGE: a secluded cottage which combines old world charm with a high standard of comfort, sleeps three. Please write or telephone for further details.

See also Colour Display Advertisement

KINCRAIG. Loch Insh Log Chalets, Kincraig PH21 1NU (01540 651272; Fax: 01540 651208). Just six miles south of Aviemore these superb log chalets are set in 14 acres of woodland in the magnificent Spey Valley, surrounded on three sides by forest and rolling fields with the fourth side being half a mile of beach frontage. Free watersports hire for guests, 8.30-10am and 4-5.30pm daily. Watersports, salmon fishing, archery, dry ski slope skiing. Hire/instruction available by the hour, day or week mid April to end October. Boathouse Restaurant on the shore of Loch Insh offers coffees, bar meals, children's meals and evening à la carte. Large gift shop and bar. Children's adventure area, interpretation trail, ski slope, mountain bike hire and stocked trout lochan are open all year round. Ski and snow board hire and instruction available December-April. ASSC MEMBER.
e-mail: office@lochinsh.com
website: www.lochinsh.com

See also Colour Display Advertisement

KINGUSSIE. Alvie Holiday Cottages. A secluded and beautiful Highland Estate with breathtaking views over the Spey Valley and the Cairngorm Mountains beyond. Woodland walks, fishing on the River Spey plus many other family activities available nearby. Three traditional farm cottages or two flats in the Estate's Edwardian shooting lodge. All furnished to the most comfortable standards. For further details visit our website or contact: **Alvie Estate Office, Kincraig, Kingussie PH21 1NE (01540 651255; Fax: 01540 651380).** ASSC MEMBER.
e-mail: info@alvie-estate.co.uk
website: www.alvie-estate.co.uk

 4/6

NEWTONMORE. Croft Holidays, Newtonmore PH20 1BA (01540 673504). Thoughtfully renovated cottages in quiet, picturesque surroundings, on outskirts of lovely Highland village in 'Monarch of the Glen' country. Central heating, open fire, TV, fridge/freezer, microwave, washer, drying room, downstairs en suite bedroom, disabled access. Way marked trails, golf course, restaurants, pubs, shops, museums in village. Central for touring, many tourist attractions, great area for walking (guided walk included), bird watching, cycling, pony trekking, water sports. Short breaks or long stays welcome all year. Cottages sleeping four - £140 to £290 per week, sleeping six - £180 to £460 per week, inclusive of heating. Well behaved pets welcome. **STB ★★★** *SELF-CATERING, WALKERS WELCOME, CYCLISTS WELCOME.* ASSC MEMBER.

1-12 Months open	Pets welcome	Suitable for disabled	Car essential
[S] Sporting/special interests provided		Coast under two miles	Children welcome
1-6 Number accommodated		Shops nearby	Linen supplied (may be charge)

Please mention BRITAIN'S BEST HOLIDAYS when enquiring about accommodation

152 Highlands (South)   **SELF CATERING**

See also Colour Display Advertisement   NEWTONMORE. **Crubenbeg Holiday Cottages, Newtonmore PH20 1BE (01540 673566; Fax: 01540 673509).** Rural self-catering cottages in the central Highlands where one can relax and stroll from the doorstep or take part in the choice of many sporting activities in the area. We have a children's play area, a games room, pond stocked with trout for fishing and a barbecue. Pets welcome. **STB ★★★★** *SELF CATERING.*
e-mail: enquiry@crubenbeg.com
website: www.crubenbeg.com

See also Colour Display Advertisement   ONICH. **Cuilcheanna Cottages and Caravans, Onich, Fort William PH33 6SD.** Three cottages and eight caravans situated on a small peaceful site. The cottages are built to the highest standards with electric heating, double glazing and full insulation. Tastefully furnished and fully equipped, each cottage has a large picture window in the main living area which look out over Loch Leven and Glencoe. Adjacent car parking. Laundry room and phone box on site. Only a short walk from the centre of Onich and an ideal base from which to explore the West Highlands. Paradise for hillwalkers. The caravans also have full facilities. Whether your stay with us is a long one, or just a few days, we shall do our best to ensure that it is enjoyable. Weekend Breaks available, winter rates, off season discounts. For further details please telephone **01855 821526** or **01855 821310**. ASSC MEMBER

1-12   1-6

See also Colour Display Advertisement   SPEAN BRIDGE. **Riverside Lodges, Invergloy, Spean Bridge PH34 4DY (Tel & Fax 01397 712684).** Peace and quiet are synonymous with Riverside, where our three identical lodges each sleep up to six people. Accessible from the A82 but totally hidden from it, our 12 acres of woodland garden front on Loch Lochy. Cots, linen, boat, fishing tackle, barbecue, all for hire. Pets welcome. Easy access and assistance to launch boats from our own beach. Fishing from the gorge, loch or private lochan. Brochure provided on request. **STB ★★★** *SELF-CATERING.* ASSC MEMBER.
e-mail: enquiries@riversidelodge.org.uk
website: www.riversidelodge.org.uk

LANARKSHIRE

1-12   2-7

See also Colour Display Advertisement   BIGGAR **(Clyde Valley). Carmichael Country Cottages, Carmichael Estate Office, Westmains, Carmichael, Biggar ML12 6PG (01899 308336; Fax: 01899 308481). Working farm, join in.** These 200-year-old stone cottages nestle among the woods and fields of our 700-year-old family estate. Still managed by the descendants of the original Chief of Carmichael. We guarantee comfort, warmth and a friendly welcome in an accessible, unique, rural and historic time capsule. We farm deer, cattle and sheep and sell meats and tartan - Carmichael of course! Children and pets welcome. Open all year. Terms from £180 to £480. 15 cottages with a total of 32 bedrooms. We have the ideal cottage for you. Private tennis court and fishing loch; cafe, farm shop and visitor centre. Pony trekking. Off-road driving course. **STB ★★/★★★★** *SELF-CATERING.* FHB Member. ASSC MEMBER.
e-mail: chiefcarm@aol.com
website: www.carmichael.co.uk/cottages

PERTH & KINROSS

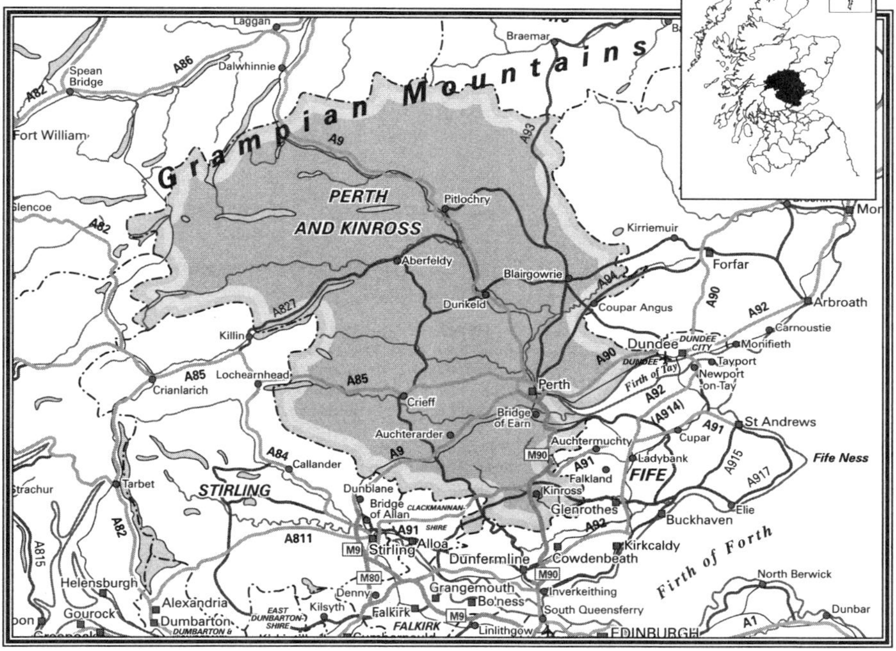

©MAPS IN MINUTES™ 2001. ©Crown Copyright, Ordnance Survey 2001.

1-12 3-5

See also Colour Display Advertisement

ABERFELDY. Mrs Pamela McDiarmid, Mains of Murthly, Aberfeldy PH15 2EA (Tel & Fax: 01887 820427). Two beautifully situated stone-built holiday cottages overlooking Aberfeldy on a working farm, one-and-a-quarter miles from town. Fully equipped for three to five persons. Dining/sittingroom, kitchen, bathroom with shower and bath. Everything supplied except linen. Log fires. Children welcome. Pets accepted. Ample parking. Fishing available on private stretch of River Tay. Golf courses nearby and new recreation centre with swimming pool in Aberfeldy. Available all year, with terms from £180. SAE please for further details.**STB ★★★** *SELF-CATERING.* ASSC MEMBER.

4

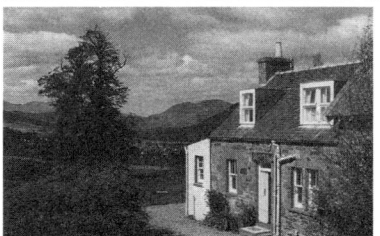

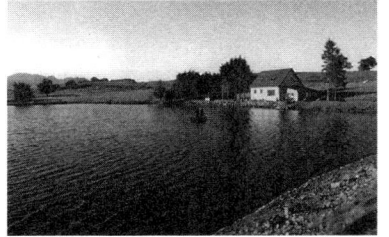

CRIEFF. Mrs Pauline Booth, Loch View Farm, Mill of Fortune, Comrie, Crieff PH6 2JE (Tel & Fax: 01764 670677). There is a south facing lodge and a residential caravan situated separately on the edge of a privately owned loch at Loch View farm, in idyllic surroundings, with beautiful scenery, two miles from the village of Comrie and six miles from the town of Crieff. Ideally situated for a quiet holiday, away from it all, with fishing, walking and birdwatching in abundance. Also centrally situated for touring. Wallace Lodge sleeps up to eight and is equipped to a very high standard. The residential caravan sleeps four. **STB ★★★★** *SELF-CATERING.*

154   Perth & Kinross — SELF CATERING

See also Colour Display Advertisement

[£]   2-8

DUNKELD by. Laighwood Holidays, Butterstone, By Dunkeld PH8 0HB (01350 724241; Fax: 01350 724212). A de luxe detached house, comfortably accommodating eight, created from the West Wing of a 19th century shooting lodge with panoramic views. Two popular cottages sleeping four, situated on our hill farm, with beautiful views. Two well-equipped apartments adjoining Butterglen House near Butterstone Loch. Butterstone lies in magnificent countryside (especially Spring/Autumn), adjacent to Nature Reserve (ospreys). Central for walking, touring, historic houses, golf and fishing. Private squash court and hill loch (wild brown trout) on the farm. Sorry no pets. Terms: House £416 to £648; Cottages and Apartments £160 to £350 per week. **STB** ★★★ to ★★★★ *SELF-CATERING.* ASSC MEMBER.
e-mail: holidays@laighwood.co.uk
website: www.laighwood.co.uk

See also Colour Display Advertisement

LOCH EARN. Riverside Log Cabins. Sitting on the bank of the River Earn, in an Area of Outstanding Natural Beauty, these three-bedroom cabins are ideally situated to explore most of Scotland. Oban and the West Coast (via Glencoe), St Andrews, Stirling and the shopping and cultural Meccas of Glasgow and Edinburgh are all within a 90 minute drive. Many local golf courses, beautiful walks, fishing, sailing, water skiing, riding and country sports nearby. Inverness and Loch Ness (including the monster?) provide an excellent day trip. Colour brochure available on request. **STB** ★★★★ *SELF-CATERING.* ASSC MEMBER. For details contact **Office:- Willoughby, Gordon Road, Crieff PH7 4BL (Tel & Fax: 01764 654048)**
e-mail: riverside@logcabins.demon.co.uk

See also Colour Display Advertisement

[£]   2-6

PITLOCHRY. Vale of Atholl Country Cottages, Blair Atholl, By Pitlochry PH18 5TE (01796 481567; Fax: 01796 481511). Rather nice country cottages converted from former barns, set around a delightfully landscaped garden courtyard, each with private patio and furniture. One to three bedrooms sleeping 2 - 6, all beautifully appointed. The award-winning Loft Restaurant is only across the courtyard. Minutes from Blair Castle and the House of Bruar. Indoor: luxury pool, paddling pool, jacuzzi, steam sauna, gym, standing tan. Outdoor: tennis, private fishing, next to golf course. Sorry no pets. Full colour brochure available. **STB** ★★★ *SELF-CATERING*

4-9   4

STRATHTAY. Carnish, Strathtay. Sleep 4. Modern semi-detached bungalow, comfortably furnished, on edge of small village. Aberfeldy five miles, Pitlochry nine miles; near golf course. Sleeps four in two double bedrooms; electric blankets; duvets; fully equipped except linen; fridge; all-electric; parking. Utility room with washing machine and freezer. No children, no pets. Weekly terms plus electricity. **Mrs Kidd, Eiriostadh, Strathtay, Pitlochry PH9 0PG (01887 840322).**

The **FHG** **Directory of Website Addresses** on pages 182-216 is a useful quick reference guide for holiday accommodation with e-mail and/or website details

WALES
SELF-CATERING

Lake Bala, Gwynedd, a popular sailing centre

THE FHG DIPLOMA

HELP IMPROVE BRITISH TOURIST STANDARDS

You are choosing holiday accommodation from our very popular FHG Publications. Whether it be a hotel, guest house, farmhouse or self-catering accommodation, we think you will find it hospitable, comfortable and clean, and your host and hostess friendly and helpful.

Why not write and tell us about it?

As a recognition of the generally well-run and excellent holiday accommodation reviewed in our publications, we at FHG Publications Ltd. present a diploma to proprietors who receive the highest recommendation from their guests who are also readers of our Guides. If you care to write to us praising the holiday you have booked through FHG Publications Ltd. – whether this be board, self-catering accommodation, a sporting or a caravan holiday, what you say will be evaluated and the proprietors who reach our final list will be contacted.

The winning proprietor will receive an attractive framed diploma to display on his premises as recognition of a high standard of comfort, amenity and hospitality. FHG Publications Ltd. offer this diploma as a contribution towards the improvement of standards in tourist accommodation in Britain. Help your excellent host or hostess to win it!

FHG DIPLOMA

We nominate ....

....

Because

Name ....

Address..

....

Telephone No...

SELF CATERING

Anglesey & Gwynedd 157

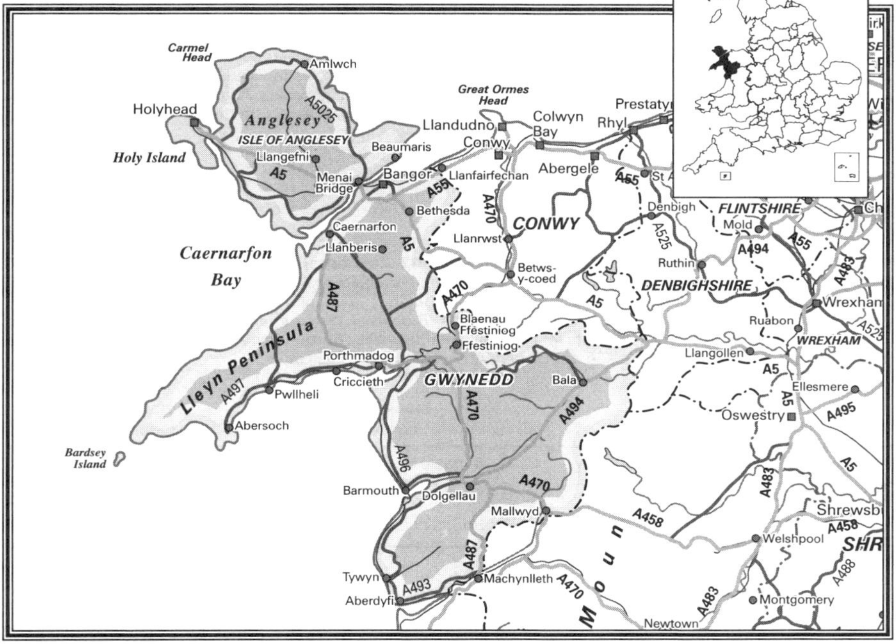

ANGLESEY & GWYNEDD

Seaside Cottages
In Idyllic North Wales

We have a large selection of self-catering seaside and country cottages, bungalows, farmhouses, caravans etc. offering superb, reasonably priced accommodation for owners and their pets. Our brochures contain details of all you need for a wonderful holiday - please telephone for your FREE copies now.

Mann's Holidays, Shaw's Holidays & Snowdonia Tourist Services
01758 701702 (24 hrs)
www.manns-holidays.com www.shaws-holidays.co.uk www.snowdoniatourist.com

BRYN BRAS CASTLE

Welcome to beautiful Bryn Bras Castle – enchanting castle Apartments, elegant Tower-House within unique romantic turreted Regency Castle (Listed Building) in the gentle foothills of Snowdonia. Centrally situated amidst breathtaking scenery, ideal for exploring North Wales' magnificent mountains, beaches, resorts, heritage and history. Near local country inns/restaurants, shops. Each spacious apartment is fully self-contained, gracious, peaceful, clean, with distinctive individual character, comfortable furnishings, generously and conveniently appointed from dishwasher to fresh flowers, etc. Inclusive of VAT, central heating, hot water, linen. All highest WTB grade. 32 acres of tranquil landscaped gardens, sweeping lawns, woodland walks of natural beauty, panoramic hill walks overlooking the sea, Anglesey and Mount Snowdon. Mild climate. Enjoy the comfort, warmth, privacy and relaxation of this castle of timeless charm in truly serene surroundings.

Open all year, including for Short Breaks. Sleep 2-4 persons. No young children. BROCHURE SENT WITH PLEASURE.
Llanrug, Near Caernarfon, North Wales LL55 4RE
Tel & Fax: Llanberis (01286) 870210   E-Mail: holidays@brynbrascastle.co.uk   Website: www.brynbrascastle.co.uk

Anglesey & Gwynedd — SELF CATERING

1-12

See also Colour Display Advertisement — **CAERNARFON near. Brynbras Castle, Llanrug, Near Caernarfon LL55 4RE (01286 870210).** Centrally situated amidst breathtaking scenery, ideal for exploring North Wales' magnificent mountains, beaches, resorts, heritage and history. Near local country inns/restaurants, shops. Each spacious apartment is fully self-contained, gracious, peaceful, clean, with distinctive individual character, comfortable furnishings, generously and conveniently appointed from dishwasher to fresh flowers, etc. Inclusive of VAT, central heating, hot water, linen. All highest WTB grade. 32 acres of tranquil landscaped gardens, sweeping lawns, woodland walks of natural beauty, panoramic hill walks overlooking the sea, Anglesey and Mount Snowdon. Mild climate. Enjoy the comfort, warmth, privacy and relaxation of this castle of timeless charm in truly serene surroundings. Brochure sent with pleasure. **WTB** GRADE 5.
e-mail: holidays@brynbrascastle.co.uk
website: www.brynbrascastle.co.uk

1-12

PWLLHELI. Mann's Holidays, Pwllheli (01758 701 702 24 hours). Seaside cottages. We have a large selection of seaside cottages, farmhouses, bungalows, etc - in excess of 500 - to let on the Lleyn Peninsula, Snowdonia and Anglesey. In the country or in urban surroundings; a country cottage or a flat in a seaside town. Many are near beaches and various sporting attractions. Properties come in all sizes and many are happy to welcome pets, and provision can be made for children. For full details of properties available and prices, telephone or write for our free brochure. Also see our Display Advertisement in this Guide.

1-12 Months open	Pets welcome	Suitable for disabled	Car essential
Sporting/special interests provided		Coast under two miles	Children welcome
1-6 Number accommodated		Shops nearby	Linen supplied (may be charge)

Other specialised

FHG PUBLICATIONS

Published annually: available in all good bookshops
or direct from the publisher.

- Recommended COUNTRY HOTELS OF BRITAIN £5.25
- Recommended WAYSIDE & COUNTRY INNS OF BRITAIN £5.25
- Recommended SHORT BREAK HOLIDAYS IN BRITAIN £5.25
- PETS WELCOME! £6.75
- B&B IN BRITAIN £4.25
- THE GOLF GUIDE Where to Play / Where to Stay £9.99

**FHG PUBLICATIONS LTD
Abbey Mill Business Centre,
Seedhill, Paisley, Renfrewshire PA1 ITJ**

Tel: 0141-887 0428 • Fax: 0141-889 7204
e-mail: fhg@ipcmedia.com • website: www.holidayguides.com

SELF CATERING — Cardiganshire

CARDIGANSHIRE

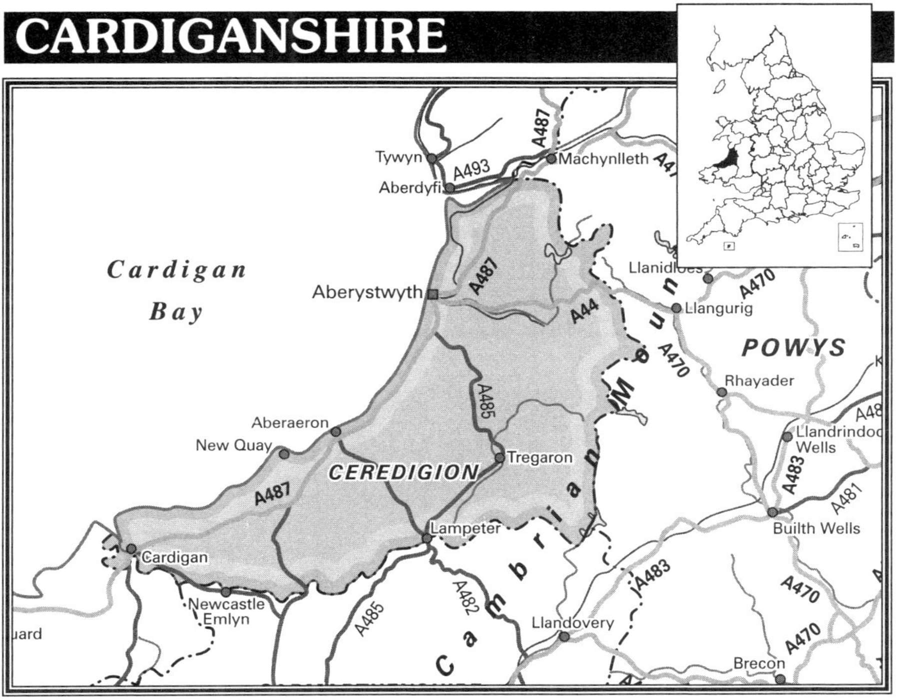

  4-6

CARDIGAN. Nant-y-Croi, Verwig, Cardigan SA43 1PU (01239 614024). Enjoy a holiday on a working farm with extensive sea views over Cardigan Bay and Island. Dolphins and seals are regular visitors to the seas and rocks around the edge of the farm. A footpath from the farmyard leads to the sandy beach at Mwnt. Children are welcome to feed the farm animals and ride the pony. Two cottages, sleeping four and six, have fully equipped kitchens and spacious lounges. Colour TV. Terms from £100 to £450. Electricity and bedlinen included. Midweek and weekend breaks. Bed and Breakfast available. Brochure from Gordon, Mary or Rob Thomas.
website: www.selfcateringholidayswales.net

NOTE

All the information in this book is given in good faith in the belief that it is correct. However, the publishers cannot guarantee the facts given in these pages, neither are they responsible for changes in policy, ownership or terms that may take place after the date of going to press. Readers should always satisfy themselves that the facilities they require are available and that the terms, if quoted, still apply.

Pembrokeshire

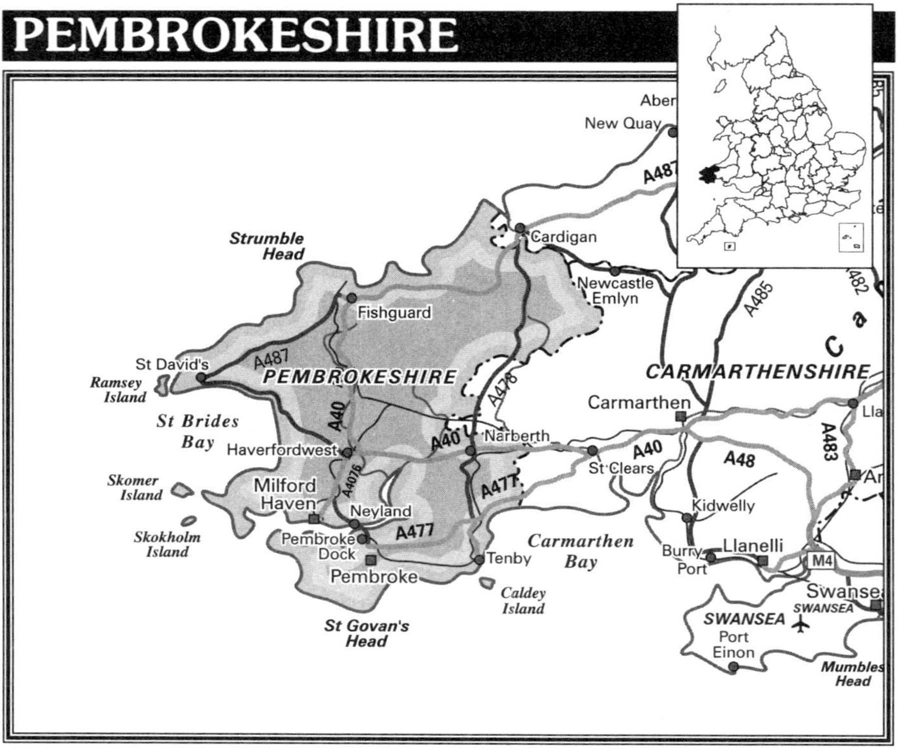

SELF CATERING

PEMBROKESHIRE

LLANTEG. Tony and Jane Baron, Llanteglos Estate, Llanteg, near Amroth SA67 8PU. Sleep up to 6.

Charming self-contained Woodland Lodges set in quiet countryside estate. Views over National Parkland and Carmarthen Bay from balconies. Ideal for holidays or shorter breaks in any season. Safe children's play area. Elsewhere on the property, visit our wonderful rustic clubhouse - 'The Wanderer's Rest Inn', with fully licensed bar, roaring fire, food and entertainment. Miles of sandy beaches, many visitor attractions for all ages and rambling trails close by. A warm welcome awaits you. For further details and colour brochure please telephone: **01834 831677 or 831739. WTB ★★★★** *SELF-CATERING*
e-mail: llanteglosestate@supanet.com

FREE or REDUCED RATE entry to Holiday Visits and Attractions — see our READERS' OFFER VOUCHERS on pages 35-54

CARAVAN & CAMPING HOLIDAYS

A peaceful scene near Stanhope in Weardale, Co. Durham

Ratings You Can Trust

  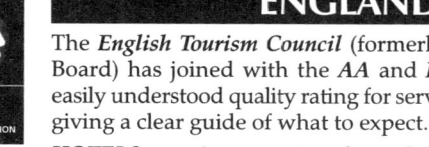

The *English Tourism Council* (formerly the English Tourist Board) has joined with the *AA* and *RAC* to create a new, easily understood quality rating for serviced accommodation, giving a clear guide of what to expect.

HOTELS are given a rating from One to Five *Stars* – the more Stars, the higher the quality and the greater the range of facilities and level of services provided.

GUEST ACCOMMODATION, which includes guest houses, bed and breakfasts, inns and farmhouses, is rated from One to Five *Diamonds*. Progressively higher levels of quality and customer care must be provided for each one of the One to Five Diamond ratings.

HOLIDAY PARKS, TOURING PARKS and CAMPING PARKS are now also assessed using *Stars*. Standards of quality range from a One Star (acceptable) to a Five Star (exceptional) park.

Look out also for the new *SELF-CATERING* Star ratings. The more *Stars* (from One to Five) awarded to an establishment, the higher the levels of quality you can expect. Establishments at higher rating levels also have to meet some additional requirements for facilities.

NB *Some self-catering properties had not been assessed at the time of going to press and in these cases the old-style* **KEY** *symbols will still be shown.*

SCOTLAND

Star Quality Grades will reflect the most important aspects of a visit, such as the warmth of welcome, efficiency and friendliness of service, the quality of the food and the cleanliness and condition of the furnishings, fittings and decor.

THE MORE STARS, THE HIGHER THE STANDARDS.

The description, such as Hotel, Guest House, Bed and Breakfast, Lodge, Holiday Park, Self-catering etc tells you the type of property and style of operation.

WALES

Places which score highly will have an especially welcoming atmosphere and pleasing ambience, high levels of comfort and guest care, and attractive surroundings enhanced by thoughtful design and attention to detail

STAR QUALITY GUIDE FOR

HOTELS, GUEST HOUSES AND FARMHOUSES
SELF-CATERING ACCOMMODATION
(Cottages, Apartments, Houses)
CARAVAN HOLIDAY HOME PARKS
(Holiday Parks, Touring Parks, Camping Parks)

★★★★★ *Exceptional quality*
★★★★ *Excellent quality*
★★★ *Very good quality*
★★ *Good quality*
★ *Fair to good quality*

In England, Scotland and Wales, all graded properties are inspected annually by Tourist Authority trained Assessors.

CARAVANS & CAMPING Cornwall 163

CORNWALL

CORNWALL
ST IVES BAY HOLIDAY PARK

CHALETS CARAVANS AND CAMPING
with private access to a huge sandy beach. With a large indoor pool and two clubs on the Park. Phone us NOW on the toll free number below for your FREE colour brochure.

right on the beach!

Call our 24 hr BROCHURE LINE on 0800 317713

HTC

BODMIN near. Tim and Eileen Zair, Ruthern Valley Holiday Park, Ruthernbridge, Near Bodmin PL30 5LU (01208 831395). No bar, no bingo, no disco. A quiet, sheltered site for thirty caravans/tents within eight acres of mature landscaped grounds. Six electric hook-ups, shower block containing ladies' and gents' showers (free), hot and cold water, flush toilets and laundry facilities. Site shop, Calor gas and Camping Gaz, public telephone, children's play area. Centrally based for beaches, close to the Camel Trail, Saints Way and Eden Project. We also have six fully-equipped and serviced static holiday caravans for hire. Please write or phone for a free brochure. *AA THREE PENNANTS.*

HTC

HAYLE. Mr F. Harvey, St Ives Bay Holiday Park, Upton Towans, Hayle TR27 5BH (24 hr Brochure Line 0800 317713). St Ives Bay Holiday Park has magnificent panoramic views and private access to three miles of sandy beach. There is a choice of licensed premises in the park and also free entertainment, children's rooms and playgrounds, indoor heated pool, supermarket, launderette and hire shop. Choice of accommodation available - chalets, caravans, camping. Pets welcome. See also our Display Advertisement in this Guide.

1-12 Months open	Pets welcome	Suitable for disabled	Car essential
[S] Sporting/special interests provided		Coast under two miles	Hot water and/or showers
Licensed	Shops on site or nearby	HTC Caravans for hire (H) Touring Vans (T) Camp site (C)	

FHG PUBLICATIONS

publish a large range of well-known accommodation guides. We will be happy to send you details or you can use the order form at the back of this book.

CUMBRIA

See also Colour Advertisement

Greenhowe Caravan Park
Great Langdale, English Lakeland.

Greenhowe Caravan Park
Great Langdale, Ambleside,
Cumbria LA22 9JU

Greenhowe is a permanent Caravan Park with Self Contained Holiday Accommodation. Subject to availability Holiday Homes may be rented for short or long periods from 1st March until mid-November. The Park is situated in the Lake District half-a-mile from Dungeon Ghyll at the foot of the Langdale Pikes. It is an ideal centre for Climbing, Fell Walking, Riding, Swimming, Water-Skiing. Please ask about Short Breaks.

Winners of the Rose Award 1983-2000. ETC Grading "Very Good".

For free colour brochure

VERY GOOD

Telephone: (015394) 37231 Fax: (015394) 37464 Freephone: 0800 0717231

ETC ★★★★

Waterside House Campsite

Waterside House, Howtown Road, Pooley Bridge, Penrith CA10 2NA   Tel & Fax: 017684 86332

Farm and campsite situated about one mile from Pooley Bridge. Genuine Lakeside location with beautiful views of Lake Ullswater and Fells. Ideal for windsurfing, canoeing, boating, fell walking and fishing, table tennis, volleyball. Boat, canoe and mountain bike hire on site. Play area, shop and gas exchange also. SAE or telephone for brochure. Open March to October. Directions: M6 Junction 40, A66 follow signs for Ullswater, A592 to Pooley Bridge, one mile along Howtown Road on right - signposted.

e-mail: enquire@watersidefarm-campsite.co.uk
website: www.watersidefarm-campsite.co.uk

AMBLESIDE. Greenhowe Caravan Park, Great Langdale, Ambleside LA22 9JU (015394 37231; Fax: 015394 37464; Freephone: 0800 0717231). Greenhowe is a permanent Caravan Park with self contained holiday accommodation. Subject to availability holiday homes may be rented for short or long periods from 1st March until mid-November. The Park is situated in the Lake District half-a-mile from Dungeon Ghyll at the foot of the Langdale Pikes. It is an ideal centre for climbing, fell walking, riding, swimming, water-skiing. Please ask about Short Breaks. Winners of the Rose Award 1983-2000. **ETC Grading** "Very Good".

3-10   [S]   TC

POOLEY BRIDGE. Waterside House Campsite, Waterside House, Howtown Road, Pooley Bridge, Penrith CA10 2NA (Tel & Fax: 017684 86332). Farm and campsite situated about one mile from Pooley Bridge. Genuine Lakeside location with beautiful views of Lake Ullswater and Fells. Ideal for windsurfing, canoeing, boating, fell walking and fishing, table tennis, volleyball. Boat, canoe and mountain bike hire on site. Play area, shop and gas exchange also. SAE or telephone for brochure. Open March to October. Directions: M6 Junction 40, A66 follow signs for Ullswater, A592 to Pooley Bridge, one mile along Howtown Road on right - signposted. **ETC ★★★★**
e-mail: enquire@watersidefarm-campsite.co.uk
website: www.watersidefarm-campsite.co.uk

POOLEY BRIDGE/LAKE ULLSWATER. Parkfoot Caravan and Camping Park, Howtown Road, Pooley Bridge, Penrith CA10 2NA (017684 86309; Fax: 017684 86041). Family-run park set in magnificent Lakeland scenery. Country Club, licensed bar, restaurant, take-away, games room. Free lake access with boat launching. Car parking. Ideal for watersports, sailing, boating, canoeing, windsurfing and fishing. Tennis court, mountain biking (hire available) and pony trekking from the Park. Private access to Barton Fell for walking. Modern toilets, hot showers, hairdryers, shaver points; fully equipped laundry room. Public telephones. Shop. Adventure playground and children's playgrounds. Camping fields have level and hill sites with views of Lake Ullswater. Grass and hardstanding pitches for touring caravans. Electric hook-ups. Self-catering log cabins and houses for hire, SAE, or telephone. for brochure.
e-mail: park.foot@talk21.com   website: www.parkfootullswater.co.uk

Parkfoot Caravan and Camping Park
Howtown Road, Pooley Bridge, Penrith CA10 2NA Tel: 017684 86309; Fax: 017684 86041

Family-run park set in magnificent Lakeland scenery. Country Club, licensed bar, restaurant, take-away, games room. Free lake access with boat launching. Car parking. Ideal for watersports, sailing, boating, canoeing, windsurfing and fishing. Tennis court, mountain biking (*hire available*) and pony trekking from the Park. Private access to Barton Fell for walking. Modern toilets, hot showers, hairdryers, shaver points; fully equipped laundry room. Public telephones. Shop. Adventure playground and children's playgrounds. Camping fields have level and hill sites with views of Lake Ullswater. Grass and hardstanding pitches for touring caravans. Electric hook-ups. Self-catering log cabins and houses for hire.
SAE, or telephone, for brochure.
e-mail: park.foot@talk21.com   website: www.parkfootullswater.co.uk

COVE CARAVAN & CAMPING PARK
ULLSWATER, WATERMILLOCK, PENRITH CA11 0LS
TEL: 017684 86549

ETC ★★★★★

Cove Park is a peaceful Caravan & Camping Park overlooking Lake Ullswater, surrounded by Fells with beautiful views. The park is very well maintained with a five star and "Excellent" ETC rating. We are ideally situated for walking, watersports and all of the Lake District tourist attractions in the North Lakes. Facilities include clean heated showers and washrooms with hand and hair dryers, washing and drying machines, iron and board, a separate washing up area, hot drinks machine and a freezer for ice packs. We offer electric hook-ups with hardstandings and plenty of sheltered grass for campers.   website: www.cove-park.co.uk

STANWIX PARK HOLIDAY CENTRE
ONE OF CUMBRIA'S PREMIER CARAVAN PARKS

Greenrow, Silloth, Cumbria CA7 4HB
Tel: 016973 32666 • Fax 016973 32555
e-mail: enquiries@stanwix.com
www.stanwix.com
All major credit cards accepted VISA

- Apartments and Caravans for hire sleeping up to six.
Excellent tent and touring park with hook-ups to all pitches.
- FREE Leisure Centre with Swimming pools, Spa, Sauna, Steam Room, Gym, Tenpin bowling, Amusements, Disco, Infant soft-play area and family entertainment Adult cabaret and Dancing.
- Explore the Lake District, Roman Wall and Gretna Green.
○ AA Northern Winner Best Campsite of the Year 1997/98
○ Cumbria for Excellence 1997   *Send for a colour brochure*

Produce this Ad at time of Booking and SAVE 10% on Camping Charges

EXCELLENT FACILITIES AND VALUE FOR MONEY
WHEN MAKING AN ENQUIRY PLEASE QUOTE REFERENCE NO. **FHG**

Church Stile Farm Wasdale, Seascale CA20 1ET

We welcome tents, motor caravans and dormobiles, but not touring caravans, on this quiet, secluded farm park on a working family farm. Situated in excellent walking and climbing area with glorious scenery, one and a half miles from Wastwater and the nearest fells, five miles from Scafell, nine miles to Muncaster Castle and the Ravenglass and Eskdale Railway. Ideal for touring the rest of the Lake District. Children and pets welcome. Facilities include showers, toilets, washbasins, laundry room, hot and cold water and electricity throughout the toilet block. Children's play area. Electric hook-ups. Two country hotels in the village for either food or drink.
For further information please contact **Mrs Ruth Knight: 019467 26252**

166 Cumbria

CARAVANS & CAMPING

3-10   🐕   🚗   ≋   🚿   🍸   HT

SILLOTH-ON-SOLWAY. Mr and Mrs Bowman, Tanglewood Caravan Park, Causeway Head, Silloth-on-Solway CA5 4PE (016973 31253). Tanglewood is a family-run park on the fringes of the Lake District National Park. It is tree-sheltered and situated one mile inland from the small port of Silloth on the Solway Firth, with a beautiful view of the Galloway Hills. Large modern holiday homes are available from March to October, with car parking beside each home. Fully equipped except for bed linen with end bedrooms, electric lighting, hot and cold water, toilet, shower, gas fire, fridge and colour TV, all of which are included in the tariff. Touring pitches also available with electric hook-ups and water/drainage facilities, etc. Play area. Licensed bar with adjoining children's play room. Pets welcome free but must be kept under control at all times. Full colour brochure available. AA 3 PENNANTS. **ETC** ★★★.

[S]   HTC

SILLOTH. Stanwix Park Holiday Centre, Greenrow, Silloth CA7 4HH (016973 32666; Fax: 016973 32555). One of Cumbria's premier caravan parks. Apartments and caravans for hire sleeping up to six. Excellent tent and touring park with hook-ups to all pitches. Free leisure centre with swimming pools, spa, sauna, steam room, gym, tenpin bowling, amusements, disco, infant soft-play area and family entertainment. Adult cabaret and dancing. Explore the Lake District, Roman Wall and Gretna Green. Major credit cards accepted. Send for a brochure. Please quote reference FHG.
ETC ★★★★★ *HOLIDAY PARK*
e-mail: enquiries@stanwix.com
website: www.stanwix.com

3-10   ♿   HTC

ULLSWATER. Cove Caravan and Camping Park, Ullswater, Watermillock, Penrith CA11 0LS (017684 86549). An award-winning park. Peaceful family park sheltered by nearby fells, overlooking Lake Ullswater. Children's playground, launderette, telephone, dishwashing area, super clean toilet block, freezer for ice packs, chemical disposal point, hot and cold drinks machine, hair dryers and shaver sockets, electric hook-up, shop nearby. Suitable for disabled visitors. Convenient for walking, fishing, boating, windsurfing and pony trekking. Leave M6 Junction 40, turn west, follow sign for Ullswater (A592). Turn right at Brackenrigg Inn, park one-and-a-half miles on left. SAE for brochure and booking form. Holiday caravans for sale and to let. Open March to end October.
ETC ★★★★★ *"EXCELLENT"*
website: www.cove-park.co.uk

3-11   🐕   🚿   C

WASDALE. Mrs Ruth Knight, Church Stile Farm, Wasdale, Seascale CA20 1ET (019467 26252). A quiet, secluded farm park on a working family farm welcoming tents, motor caravans and dormobiles, no touring caravans. It is approximately one-and-a-half miles to Wastwater Lake and the nearest fells, Scafell is five miles. This is an excellent walking and climbing area with glorious scenery. Nine miles to Muncaster Castle and The Ravenglass and Eskdale Railway. Ideal for touring the rest of the Lake District. Children and pets welcome. Children's play area. Facilities include showers, toilets, washbasins, laundry room, hot and cold water and electricity throughout the toilet block. Electric hook-ups. Two country hotels in the village for either food or drink. Price list supplied on request. Open March to November.

The FHG Directory of Website Addresses
on pages 182-216 is a useful quick reference guide for holiday accommodation with e-mail and/or website details

---

Terms quoted in this publication may be subject to increase if rises in costs necessitate

DEVON

Parker's Farm Holiday Park
Ashburton TQ13 7LJ
Tel: 01364 652598 • Fax: 01364 654004
e-mail: parkersfarm@btconnect.com website: www.parkersfarm.co.uk

A friendly, family-run farm site set in 400 acres and surrounded by beautiful countryside. 12 miles to the sea and close to Dartmoor National Park; ideal for touring Devon/Cornwall. Perfect for children and pets with all farm animals, play area and plenty of space to roam, also large area for dogs. Holiday cottages and caravans, fully equipped except for linen. Level touring site with some hard standings. Free showers in fully tiled block; laundry room, games room, small family bar, restaurant, shop and phone. Prices start from £90 to £490 High Season. Good discounts for couples. From Exeter, take A38 to Plymouth; when you see sign "25 miles Plymouth", take second left at Alston Cross signposted to Woodland and Denbury.

British Farm Tourist Award, RAC Recommended, AA 4 Pennants, 2000 Gold Award for Quality and Service, Silver David Bellamy Conservation Award, Practical Caravan 1998 - Top 100 Parks, West Country Tourist Board ★★★★

THE SALTER FAMILY WELCOMES YOU
HALDON LODGE FARM
Kennford, Near Exeter, Devon

*20 minutes from Dawlish
and Teignmouth Beaches*

Freedom and safety for all the family

Central for South Devon coast and Exeter in an attractive setting, three modern six-berth holiday caravans and log cabin in a private and friendly park. Excellent facilities including picnic tables and farm shop. Weekly barbecues plus hay-ride, with 'sounds of the sixties' at a friendly country inn nearby, subject to demand during school holidays. Set in glorious rural Devon, the site offers freedom and safety for all the family. Very reasonable prices. Pets accepted/exercising area. Open all year.

Relax and enjoy the scenery or stroll along the many forest lanes. Famous country inns nearby. Three coarse fishing lakes close to the Park and the attraction of ponies and horse riding at a nearby farm.

Large six berth caravans, two bedrooms, lounge with TV, bathroom/toilet (H/C); rates from £70 to £195 High Season.

Personal attention and welcome by David & Betty Salter.
For brochure telephone 01392 832312

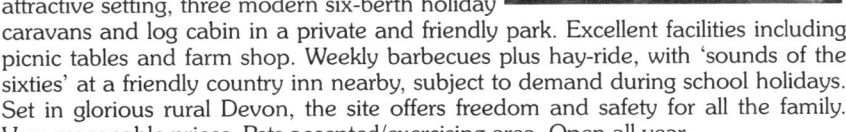
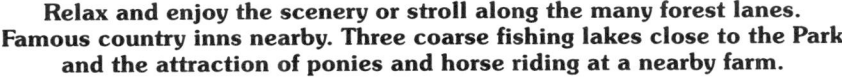

FREE or REDUCED RATE entry to Holiday Visits and Attractions — see our READERS' OFFER VOUCHERS on pages 35-54

168 Devon

CARAVANS & CAMPING

🐕   🚿   ♀   🛒   HTC

ASHBURTON. Parkers Farm Holiday Park, Ashburton TQ13 7LJ (01364 652598; Fax: 01364 654004).
A friendly, family-run farm site set in 400 acres and surrounded by beautiful countryside. 12 miles to the sea and close to Dartmoor National Park; ideal for touring Devon/Cornwall. Perfect for children and pets with all farm animals, play area and plenty of space to roam, also large area for dogs. Holiday cottages and caravans, fully equipped except for linen. Level touring site with some hard standings. Free showers in fully tiled block; laundry room, games room, small family bar, restaurant, shop and phone. Prices start from £90 to £480 High Season. Good discounts for couples. From Exeter, take A38 to Plymouth; when you see sign "26 miles Plymouth", take second left at Alston Cross signposted to Woodland and Denbury). **ETC ★★★★**, **AA** *4 PENNANTS*, **RAC** *RECOMMENDED. 2000 GOLD AWARD FOR QUALITY AND SERVICE. SILVER DAVID BELLAMY CONSERVATION AWARD. PRACTICAL CARAVAN TOP 100 PARKS 1998. BRITISH FARM TOURIST AWARD.*
e-mail: parkersfarm@btconnect.com
website: www.parkersfarm.co.uk

1-12   🐕   [S]   〰   🛒   HTC
See also Colour Display Advertisement

DAWLISH WARREN. Welcome Family Holiday Park, Dawlish Warren EX7 0PH (01626 862070). First rate facilities and friendly personal service provide the perfect family holiday! Stylish Kaleidoscope entertainment centre, superb indoor heated Tropicana Water Leisure Complex with four feature packed pools and spectator viewing area. Cruisers Adult Cocktail Bar with big screen TV, children's Jolly Roger Club with disco and large games arcade. Adventure playground, launderette, three shops, cafe and two takeaways on site. Sports ground, Crazy Golf. Hire service with computer games. Short level walk to the safe, sandy beach. Caravans, villas, apartments and bungalows - accommodation to suit all tastes and pockets - free electricity, linen and colour TV. Please call for your free colour brochure. **ETC ★★★★** *HOLIDAY PARK. ROSE AWARD.*
website: www.welcomefamily.co.uk

1-12   🐕   🚗   [S]   🚿   HTC
EXETER near. Mr D. L. Salter, Haldon Lodge Farm, Kennford, Near Exeter EX6 7YG (01392 832312).

Haldon Lodge Farm is situated in beautiful surroundings near the Teign Valley Forest, only five miles from Exeter and a short drive from the sea. Pony riding is available from the farm nearby, also three private, well stocked coarse fishing lakes close to the park. There are three fully equipped six-berth caravans for hire plus pitches for tourers and tents. The well known Nobody Inn is one of the many country pubs in the vicinity. Pets welcome. Caravans available March to December, pitches available all year. Further details on request. See also our Display Advertisement in this guide.

1-12 Months open	🐕 Pets welcome	⚐ Suitable for disabled
[S] Sporting/special interests provided	〰 Coast under two miles	🚗 Car essential
♀ Licensed	🛒 Shops on site or nearby	🚿 Hot water and/or showers

HTC Caravans for hire (H) Touring Vans (T) Camp site (C)

PLEASE MENTION THIS GUIDE WHEN YOU WRITE OR PHONE TO ENQUIRE ABOUT ACCOMMODATION

IF YOU ARE WRITING, A STAMPED, ADDRESSED ENVELOPE IS ALWAYS APPRECIATED

HAMPSHIRE

One visit is never enough

For a relaxing award winning break
call for a brochure now on:

01425 653042

quoting ref: FHG BB02

Sandy Balls Holiday Centre, Godshill, Fordingbridge, Hants, SP6 2JZ. England.
Fax: +44 (0)1425 653067 e.mail: post@sandy-balls.co.uk www.sandy-balls.co.uk

OPEN ALL YEAR ROUND

See also Colour Advertisement

1-12   HTC

See also Colour Display Advertisement **FORDINGBRIDGE. Sandy Balls Holiday Centre, Godshill, Fordingbridge SP6 2JZ (01425 653042; Fax: 01425 653067).** A New Forest break that's uniquely different. In an idyllic woodland and riverside setting on the edge of the New Forest, Sandy Balls gives you the freedom to enjoy your kind of holiday, any time of year. Spacious touring/camping pitches with electricity, water, drainage and satellite TV. Traditional timber lodges and caravan holiday homes. Heated indoor and outdoor pools, superb leisure centre and fitness suites, solarium, sauna and more. Acres of woodland, adventure playground and games room. Spar store, launderettes and gift shop. Valencio's Italian restaurant and Woodside Inn family pub. Please call for a free colour brochure. ETC ★★★★★ *HOLIDAY PARK*.
e-mail: post@sandy-balls.co.uk
website: www.sandy-balls.co.uk

NORFOLK

4-10   HTC

GREAT YARMOUTH. Mrs B.A. Rawnsley, Scratby Hall Caravan Park, Scratby, Great Yarmouth NR29 3PH (01493 730283). Situated on B1159, five miles from the centre of Great Yarmouth, three-quarters-of-a-mile from the sea and one-and-a-half miles from the Norfolk Broads. Amenities include flush toilets, hot and cold water, free showers, electric hook-ups. Laundry, shop for your needs, games room. Facilities for the disabled visitor. Golf and horse riding nearby. Licences for 108 tourers and tents. Dogs allowed, must be on leads. Open Easter to October. Advance booking advisable at peak times. A quiet, secluded site, level and grassy. ETC ★★★★, *AA THREE PENNANTS, RAC*

FHG PUBLICATIONS LIMITED
publish a large range of well-known accommodation guides. We will be happy to send you details or you can use the order form at the back of this book.

SCOTLAND
CARAVAN & CAMPING HOLIDAYS

ARGYLL & BUTE

CASTLE SWEEN

Around picturesque Castle Sween, the oldest ruined castle in Scotland, and ingeniously placed to take advantage of the natural contours of the ground, are a selection of super luxury and luxury caravans on excellent sites affording magnificent views and first-class amenities. The area is one of the most superb in the West of Scotland, quiet, peaceful and relaxing, and the great attraction of Castle Sween is the freedom to follow your own inclination in the way of holiday pastimes. Walkers will find their paradise. Naturalists will be fascinated by the plentiful wild life, there is sea and loch fishing, bicycles to be hired, boats and dinghies can be launched and sailed in the calm waters of the loch.

The accommodation is in super luxury or in luxury caravans. The manager's house, office and a well-stocked shop are situated in the middle of the complex, as well as a restaurant and bar.

Brochure, full details of accommodation, booking forms etc., can be obtained on application to:

CASTLE SWEEN BAY (HOLIDAYS) LTD, ELLARY, LOCHGILPHEAD, ARGYLL PA31 8PA

Tel: 01880 770232   e-mail: info@ellary.com
website: www.ellary.com

1-12   HTC

LOCHGILPHEAD. Castle Sween Bay (Holidays) Ltd, Ellary, Lochgilphead (01880 770232/770209 or 01546 850223; Fax: 01880 770386). The ground around the old ruined castle falls gently away to the shores of the loch forming different levels at varying heights. The space of these different levels has been used to provide the most beautiful sites for various different units of accommodation. The greatest care has been taken in the siting of chalets, large residential units and static holiday caravans to avoid overcrowding and to leave plenty of space between the units. "Gold" Group Holiday Caravans are the newest being 2000/2001 models and are placed on the best sites with magnificent views. Some have three bedrooms. All have separate bathrooms, kitchens, cooking by gas. "Silver" Group Holiday Caravans are all luxury 2000/01 models sited on spacious pitches with views across Loch Sween. All have two bedrooms, TV, fridge, shower and WC. All electricity, gas and hot water included in the price. Good shop with off-licence on site. See also Display Advertisement in this Guide.
e-mail: info@ellary.com   website: www.ellary.com

GOLF & ACTIVITY HOLIDAYS
INCLUDING NARROWBOAT HOLIDAYS

It's nice to relax and wind down at the start of a holiday, but after a few days our batteries have recharged and we are ready for a bit of action. The following brief section gives an opportunity to stay at accommodation where we can lounge around if we wish, but which is also close to golf courses, or with fishing, sailing, walking, riding and other activities in the vicinity. Many have their own leisure and fitness facilities or swimming pools, some even have tennis courts or children's play areas. You will usually find that the proprietors and staff can also provide lots of information on the best places to visit for a day out.

On the other hand you may wish to try a holiday with a difference. We have included a small selection of Narrowboat Holidays, ideal for all the family and a great way to explore the best of Britain's countryside.

Premier Narrowboat Holidays
Bookings & Administration: 34 Lulworth Park, Kenilworth, Warwickshire CV8 2XG
Tel: 01926 864156/ 07711 589808 • Fax: 01926 863507
We are a family-owned company offering narrowboat holidays from a variety of locations across England and in the South of France. We offer a wide choice of routes and scenery from the various locations – cruise through wonderful Warwickshire countryside, or visit the lovely quiet scenery of the Cotswolds or the Welsh mountains. Our narrowboats are available for holidays all year round – they are well insulated and heated so are suitable for winter breaks. Often length of hire period and start days can be varied off season. Midweek and weekend short breaks available all year.
e-mail: cliffeden315@hotmail.com • website: www.premiernarrowboats.com

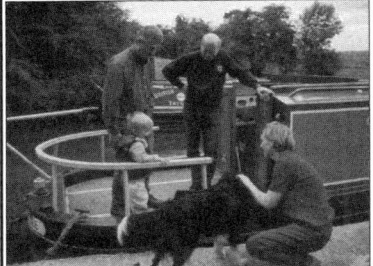

CLAYMOORE NAVIGATION LTD The Wharf, Preston Brook, Cheshire WA4 4BA

Cruise the canals in comfort **more** with Claymoore

With our two new 8 berths and brand new 10 berth, we really do have a fleet to envy.

Beginners are welcome as we provide excellent tuition.

Your pets deserve a holiday too

All our boats are annually inspected by the Tourist Board, why choose a boat that isn't?

www.virtual-canals.com *or* www.claymoore.co.uk
e-mail: FHG@claymoore.co.uk
Tel: (*Lo-Cost*) 08450 900 1800   Fax: 01928 718888

172 ENGLAND **GOLFING & ACTIVITY HOLIDAYS**

CHESHIRE

DISCOVER BRITAIN'S SECRET WORLD!

- Relaxing self-drive cruises on Britain's beautiful canals, in comfortable, fully equipped traditional narrowboats.
- Steering is easy – full tuition included.
- Families, groups, pets all welcome.

Brochure from:
MIDDLEWICH NARROWBOATS
Canal Terrace, Middlewich
Cheshire CW10 9BD
Tel: 01606 832460
website: www.middlewichboats.co.uk

CORNWALL

LANGFIELD MANOR
Broadclose, Bude, Cornwall EX23 8DP

Treat yourself to a special holiday amidst the magnificent splendours of the North Cornwall coastline. Seven quality apartments in this fine Edwardian house with its lovely games room, situated in one-and-a-half acres of delightful, sheltered, south-facing gardens. Come and enjoy the conservatory and the sun terrace set around the 36ft swimming pool. A superb centre for any holiday, out in the country yet only three minutes' walk to the shops and 10 minutes' walk to Bude's sandy beaches. Here we are just across the lane from the Bude and North Cornwall Golf Club. Children welcome. Sorry, no pets

Tel: 01288 352415 • Fax: 01288 353416 • Website: www.langfieldmanor.co.uk
E-mail: info@langfieldmanor.co.uk

See also Colour Advertisement

CORNWALL

Penryn House

A good value, worry-free getaway.

Situated in the tranquil heart of the beautiful fishing village of Polperro, we pride ourselves on providing comfort and excellent service in an informal atmosphere.

Relax in our fireside lounge bar or guest lounge; enjoy the restaurant with fresh home cooking using local produce.

Our comfortable en suite bedrooms have TV, telephones, clock/radios, hairdryers and well-stocked courtesy trays.

Easy access to the coastal paths and a short journey to the Eden Project, National Trust properties and Dartmoor and Bodmin Moor. Also close to golf, riding, fishing and sailing.

AA ♦♦♦ The Coombes, Polperro PL13 2RQ
Tel: 01503 272157

See also Colour Advertisement

CORNWALL

WHITSAND BAY HOTEL
Portwrinkle, By Torpoint, Plymouth, Cornwall PL11 3BU
Tel: 01503 230276 • Fax: 01503 230329   **AA** ★★★ **RAC** ★★ *Recommended by Quality Hotel Guides*
E-mail: earlehotels@btconnect.com • Website: www.cornish-golf-hotels.co.uk

Family-run hotel, spectacularly sited with 100 miles of sea views. Safe sandy beach, vast lawns set in 80 acres. Children of all ages especially welcome. Excellent Rosette standard restaurant. Superb leisure facilities including heated indoor pool, leisure/fitness complex, own 18-hole golf course. Clay pigeon shooting; shark, sea and freshwater fishing; horse riding nearby. Near Eden Project and Lost Gardens of Heligan.

Self-catering accommodation in grounds with full hotel facilities.
Same ownership for over 30 years • Terms on application

See also Inside Front Cover

GOLFING & ACTIVITY HOLIDAYS　　　　　　　　　　　　　ENGLAND　　173

See also Colour Advertisement

No.1 CUDDY'S HALL
CUMBRIA

A self-catering holiday cottage situated on a smallholding in a rural area of North Cumbria. Surrounded by Kershope Forest (part of Kielder Forest Park). Excellent walks & cycle routes. Cosy and spotlessly clean. Sleeping five (one double, one twin and one single bedroom). Open all year. Short breaks available. Central touring area for Cumbria, Northumberland & Scotland.

Full details from:
Mrs Joanna Furness, 2 Cuddy's Hall, Bailey, Newcastleton, Roxburghshire TD9 0TP　　Telephone: 016977 48160

See also Colour Advertisement

HOPE BARTON BARNS
Tel: 01548 561393
★★★★　*Open All Year*

DEVON

Nestling in its own valley close to the sandy cove, Hope Barton Barns is an exclusive group of 17 stone barns in two courtyards and three luxury apartments in the converted farmhouse. Superbly furnished and fully equipped, accommodation ranges from a studio to four bedrooms, sleeping two to 10. Heated indoor pool, sauna, gym, lounge bar, tennis court, trout lake and a children's play barn. We have 35 acres of pastures and streams. Farmhouse meals. Ample parking. Golf, sailing and coastal walking nearby. A perfect setting for family summer holidays, walking in Spring/Autumn or just a "get away from it all" break. Free range children and well behaved dogs welcome. For full colour brochure please contact: *Mike or Judy Tromans*.

Hope Cove – Near Salcombe - South Devon – TQ7 3HT

HAMPSHIRE

Galleon Marine have a range of luxury narrowboats specifically designed to suit the shallow waters of the beautiful Basingstoke Canal.
With tiller steering, a spacious fully fitted galley, full central heating, bathroom, flush toilets, a comfortable lounge/ dining area with doors opening to the bows, these boats really are home from home and a joy to handle while you meander through an environment abundant with plants and wildlife.
For more information contact:
Galleon Marine, Colt Hill, Odiham, Hampshire RG29 1AL
Tel: 01256 703691 • Fax: 01256 703937
Website: www.galleonmarine.co.uk

Fuel, Gas, TV, Bed Linen & Car Parking Charges all included in hire fees

---

See also Colour Advertisement

STOKE by NAYLAND
SUFFOLK

Set in the heart of Dedham Vale, Stoke by Nayland offers some of the finest golfing facilities in East Anglia. Each of the two courses provides an enjoyable experience for all standards of golfers, with trees a feature of both. The multi-purpose clubhouse offers restaurant and bar facilities, along with a spike bar and new leisure facility including gym, indoor pool, sauna and spa. 20-bay covered driving range. There is also a 30-bedroom hotel, with all rooms overlooking the courses and lake.

The Stoke-by-Nayland Club Ltd, Keepers Lane, Leavenheath, Colchester, Essex CO6 4PZ
Tel: 01206 262836　•　Fax: 01206 263356
E-mail: info@golfclub.co.uk　•　Website: www.stokebynaylandclub.co.uk

174 ENGLAND — GOLFING & ACTIVITY HOLIDAYS

WARWICKSHIRE

Clifton Cruisers

– your first choice in Canal Holidays

Clifton Cruisers offer you the freedom of choice in canal cruising. The freedom to boat along some of England's finest waterways: The choice of cruising from misty dawns to spectacular sunsets, or to just linger leisurely in remote and rural places aboard your self-contained floating holiday home. We have one of the most varied choice of boat layouts and accommodation to satisfy the requirements of most family and other holiday group's (sleeping 4-9). Centrally situated on the waterway network for a variety of circular and out-and-return routes. Also a choice of start days for short breaks, weeks or longer holidays. Clifton Cruisers are a friendly, family-owned and run company who specialise in personal service.

We are here to make sure that your choice of a canal holiday with us is the right one.

Clifton Wharf, Vicarage Hill, Clifton-on-Dunsmore, Rugby CV23 0DG.
Tel: 01788 543570 Fax: 01788 579799
website: www.cliftoncruisers.com
e-mail: cliftoncruisers@hotmail.com

VISA / AMERICAN EXPRESS / MasterCard / DELTA

WORCESTERSHIRE

ALVECHURCH
WATERWAY HOLIDAYS

See Britain from a different perspective

Meander through delightfully unspoilt countryside, relaxing on board a high quality, superbly equipped narrowboat. With a fleet of 100 boats, moored at 4 regional marinas, Alvechurch gives access to more than 1500 miles of canals and rivers. 2 to 12 berths available. Pets welcome. Short breaks and weekly rental. Visit our website, or phone for a free colour brochure.

Scarfield Wharf, Alvechurch, Worcestershire B48 7SQ
Telephone: 0121 445 2909 Fax: 0121 447 7120
E-mail: enquiries@alvechurch.com   Website: www.alvechurch.com

---

NORTH YORKSHIRE

The Fox & Hounds Inn

Residential 16th Century Coaching Inn set amidst the beautiful North York Moors.
Freshly prepared dishes served every lunchtime and evening.
Superb en suite accommodation available, with all rooms having glorious views.
Open all year.
Website: www.foxandhounds-ainthorpe.com
ETC ♦♦♦♦   *For bookings please*
Tel: 01287 660218 or Fax: 01287 660030
Ainthorpe, Danby, Yorkshire YO21 2LD

See also Colour Advertisement

The FHG GOLF GUIDE
Where to Play Where to Stay
2002

Available from most bookshops, the 2002 edition of **THE GOLF GUIDE** covers details of every UK golf course – well over 2800 entries – for holiday or business golf. Hundreds of hotel entries offer convenient accommodation, accompanying details of the courses – the 'pro', par score, length etc.

In association with 'Golf Monthly' and including Holiday Golf in Ireland, France, Portugal, Spain, The USA, South Africa and Thailand .

£9.99 from bookshops or from the publishers (postage charged outside UK) • FHG Publications, Abbey Mill Business Centre, Paisley PA1 1TJ

GOLFING & ACTIVITY HOLIDAYS — SCOTLAND

DUMFRIES & GALLOWAY

The Urr Valley Hotel

A privately owned hotel set in 14 acres of mature woodland and gardens within walking distance of Castle Douglas. Galloway is one of the most beautiful and diverse areas of countryside in Britain - offering everything from golden sandy beaches to grouse moors, and picturesque harbour villages to forest walks. Panelled walls, log fires and a cosy Sportsman's bar with over 50 whiskies to offer. 17 en suite rooms, with colour TV, Tea & Coffee making facilities, hair dryers, trouser press and direct dial telephones.

South West Scotland has been blessed with some of the most exciting and varied countryside which plays host to over 20 excellent golf courses. We are familiar and experienced in the organisation of all sporting holidays and would be happy to assist in arranging your sporting break. AA ★★

**The Urr Valley Hotel, Ernespie Road,
Castle Douglas, Kirkcudbrightshire DG7 3JG
Tel: 01556 502188   Fax: 01556 504055**

See also Colour Advertisement

FIFE

Crossford Hotels (Dunfermline) Ltd.
The Pitfirrane Golf Hotel

The hotel is conveniently situated for touring, within easy access of Edinburgh, Glasgow and the M90 motorway. We have 38 comfortable bedrooms, 16 twin, 12 double and 10 single bedded rooms. All rooms have private en suite facilities, colour television, tea/coffee makers, telephone and radio. We have 10 golf courses within 10 miles!

AA ★★★

**CROSSFORD, DUNFERMLINE, FIFE KY12 8NJ
Telephone: 01383 736132   Fax: 01383 621760
E-mail: info@scothotels.com   Website: www.scothotels.com**

See also Colour Advertisement

FIFE

Scotstarvit Farm Cupar KY15 5PA Tel & Fax 01334 653591

Ideally situated in an Area of Outstanding Natural Beauty with breathtaking views, this stone-built cottage is well appointed with colour TV/teletext, microwave, washer/dryer, central heating and optional log fire. Private Parking. Enviably placed for the many golf and leisure activities in the area, Scotstarvit is only 10 minutes' drive from St Andrews and Fife's fishing villages. Edinburgh, Dundee, Perth & Aberdeen are within easy reach. Terms from £140 to £395 per week. 2 person discounts. Short breaks. Open all year. Quality farmhouse B&B also from £16 per night. STB ★★★ Self-Catering.

e-mail: chrisp.scotstarvit@ukgateway.net
website: www.scotstarvitfarm.co.uk

ISLE OF GIGHA

GIGHA HOTEL

Spend a relaxing holiday on the Isle of Gigha (pronounced Gee-a). Meaning "God's Isle", it is surely a little piece of heaven. Explore the sandy bays, lochs, easy walks, cycling, golf, birds and wildlife. But for the jewel in the crown visit Achamore Gardens, with rhododendrons, azaleas and semi-exotic plants. Grass airstrip, 9-hole golf course and a regular ferry service. Holiday Cottages also available.

**Special 3 night Breaks available
Gigha Hotel PA41 7AA   STB ★★★ Hotel
Tel: 01583 505254   Fax: 01583 505244
Website: www.isle-of-gigha.co.uk
E-mail: hotel@isle-of-gigha.co.uk**

See also Colour Advertisement

SOUTH WALES

Castle Narrowboats
The Monmouthshire and Brecon Canal in South Wales.
Discover the beauty of the Brecon Beacons onboard
one of our electric or diesel canal boats.
2-8 berth boats, Short Breaks available. Pets Welcome.

For a FREE colour brochure, call *Castle Narrowboats*
• Tel: 01873 830001 • Fax: 01873 832341
• www.canaljunction.com/castlenarrowboats
• E-mail: castle.narrowboats@btinternet.com
or call in and see us at
Church Road Wharf, Gilwern, Monmouthshire NP7 0EP

Other specialised
FHG PUBLICATIONS
Published annually: available in all good bookshops
or direct from the publisher.

• Recommended COUNTRY HOTELS OF BRITAIN   £5.25
• Recommended WAYSIDE & COUNTRY INNS OF BRITAIN   £5.25
• Recommended SHORT BREAK HOLIDAYS IN BRITAIN   £5.25
• PETS WELCOME!   £6.75
• B&B IN BRITAIN   £4.25
• THE GOLF GUIDE Where to Play / Where to Stay   £9.99

**FHG PUBLICATIONS LTD
Abbey Mill Business Centre,
Seedhill, Paisley, Renfrewshire PA1 1TJ**

Tel: 0141-887 0428 • Fax: 0141-889 7204
e-mail: fhg@ipcmedia.com • website: www.holidayguides.com

Visit the website
www.holidayguides.com
for details of the wide choice of accommodation
featured in the full range of FHG titles

CHANNEL TUNNEL, AIRPORTS AND FERRIES

Accommodation convenient for the Channel Tunnel, Airports and Ferries

The entries which follow provide contact details for overnight accommodation which is convenient for the Channel Tunnel. or for a particular airport or ferry.

Breaking an inward or outward journey has become one of the commonest overnight stops and finding a suitable B&B is often a frustrating experience. Only a brief description is given here, but you will find fuller information for each entry in the appropriate county section preceding this Supplement.

The usual procedures for direct booking apply but with Airports and Ferries it is even more important to make sure that advance bookings are confirmed, that you arrive in good time and that your host knows when you want to leave. Early notice of any cancellation or change in plans is also essential.

In your own interests, you should double-check with the establishment before booking what the distance or average travelling time is from the airport or ferry you are using

FERRIES/CHANNEL TUNNEL/AIRPORTS

FERRIES

The Continent, Isle of Wight, Channel Islands and Scillies

BOURNEMOUTH

FRESHFIELDS HOTEL
55 CHRISTCHURCH ROAD,
BOURNEMOUTH BH1 3PA

Small Licensed Hotel. Close to sandy beach and Bournemouth's attractions. Most rooms en suite, all with colour TV, tea/coffee making. Bargain Breaks September to June.

(01202 394023)

BOURNEMOUTH

MOUNT LODGE HOTEL
19 BEAULIEU ROAD, ALUM CHINE,
BOURNEMOUTH BH4 8HY

Comfortable, friendly, family-run hotel with en suite rooms, TV, coffee/tea making, central heating. Residents' bar, car parking, own keys. Close to Bournemouth and Poole Harbour.
ETC ♦♦♦

(01202 761173)

BOURNEMOUTH

SWEET BRIAR
12 DERBY ROAD
BOURNEMOUTH BH1 3QA

A traditional B&B guest house for non-smokers. Open all year. Full central heating. Ideal for shops, sea and travel interchange.
From £18 per person per night.

(01202 553028)

BRISTOL

TREGONWELL RIVERSIDE
GUEST HOUSE,
1 TORS ROAD, LYNMOUTH,
DEVON EX35 6ET

Elegant riverside Victorian former sea captain's home (the best place to start and finish your holiday) alongside waterfalls, beaches, England's highest clifftops. 'Olde Worlde' smugglers village.

(01598 753369)

DOVER

THE COACH HOUSE
OAKMEAD FARM, BETHERSDEN,
NEAR ASHFORD, KENT TN26 3DU

Comfortable family home. Central for ferries, tunnel, Eurostar, Canterbury, Leeds Castle, Sissinghurst and all tourist attractions.
ETC ♦♦♦

(01233 820583)

DOVER

WYCLIFFE HOTEL
63 BOUVERIE ROAD WEST,
FOLKESTONE, KENT CT20 2RN

Family-run hotel offering excellent choice of home cooked breakfasts. Off-street parking. Near Channel Tunnel/Seacat Terminal, short drive from Dover Ferry.

(01303 252186)

The FHG **Directory of Website Addresses** on pages 182-216 is a useful quick reference guide for holiday accommodation with e-mail and/or website details

FERRIES/CHANNEL TUNNEL/AIRPORTS

⛴ FERRIES

The Continent, Isle of Wight, Channel Islands and Scillies

⛴ FOLKESTONE ⛴
WYCLIFFE HOTEL
63 BOUVERIE ROAD WEST,
FOLKESTONE, KENT CT20 2RN

Family-run hotel offering excellent choice of home cooked breakfasts. Off-street parking. Near Channel Tunnel/Seacat Terminal, short drive from Dover Ferry.

(01303 252186)

⛴ PLYMOUTH ⛴
MRS SUSAN WINZER
HIGHER COARSEWELL FARM,
UGBOROUGH, NEAR IVYBRIDGE,
DEVON PL21 0HP

A3121 turn off from main A38 Exeter to Plymouth Road. Early start - breakfast provided. One family room and one double. Children welcome.

(01548 821560)

⛴ NEWCASTLE ⛴
MRS P. GIBSON
BUSHBLADES FARM, HARPERLEY,
STANLEY, DURHAM DH9 9UA

Comfortable Georgian farmhouse. All rooms tea/coffee facilities, colour TV. En suite available. Easy access to A1(M), Metro Centre, Hadrian's Wall and Northumberland Coast.
ETC ♦♦♦

(01207 232722)

Other specialised FHG PUBLICATIONS
Published annually: available in all good bookshops or direct from the publisher.

- Recommended COUNTRY HOTELS OF BRITAIN   £5.25
- Recommended WAYSIDE & COUNTRY INNS OF BRITAIN   £5.25
- Recommended SHORT BREAK HOLIDAYS IN BRITAIN   £5.25
- PETS WELCOME!   £6.75 • B&B IN BRITAIN   £4.25
- THE GOLF GUIDE Where to Play / Where to Stay   £9.99

FHG PUBLICATIONS LTD, Abbey Mill Business Centre, Seedhill, Paisley, Renfrewshire PA1 1TJ
Tel: 0141-887 0428 • Fax: 0141-889 7204
e-mail: fhg@ipcmedia.com • website: www.holidayguides.com

FERRIES/CHANNEL TUNNEL/AIRPORTS

🚗 CHANNEL TUNNEL

including Eurostar rail links

🚗 BOURNEMOUTH 🚗
FRESHFIELDS HOTEL
55 CHRISTCHURCH ROAD,
BOURNEMOUTH BH1 3PA

Small Licensed Hotel. Close to sandy beach and Bournemouth's attractions. Most rooms en suite, all with colour TV, tea/coffee making. Bargain Breaks September to June.

(01202 394023)

🚗 DOVER 🚗
GREAT BOSSINGTON FARMHOUSE
ADISHAM, CANTERBURY
KENT CT3 3LN

16th Century farmhouse, one double room (second room available for families). Garden surrounded by paddocks. 8 miles from Dover, 12 miles from the Channel Tunnel.

(01227 720921)

🚗 FOLKESTONE 🚗
WYCLIFFE HOTEL
63 BOUVERIE ROAD WEST,
FOLKESTONE, KENT CT20 2RN

Family-run hotel offering excellent choice of home cooked breakfasts. Off-street parking. Near Channel Tunnel/Seacat Terminal, short drive from Dover Ferry.

(01303 252186)

🚗 WINDSOR 🚗
CLARENCE HOTEL
9 CLARENCE ROAD, WINDSOR,
BERKSHIRE SL4 5AE

Town centre location. Licensed bar and steam room. High quality accommodation at guest house prices. All rooms en suite, tea/coffee facilities, TV, radio alarms, hairdryers. Heathrow Airport 25 minutes by car
ETC/AA/RAC Listed.

(01753 864436)

🚗 YORK 🚗
MONT-CLARE GUEST HOUSE
32 CLAREMONT TERRACE,
GILLYGATE, YORK,
NORTH YORKSHIRE YO31 7EJ

City centre accommodation. CCTV parking. All rooms en suite with colour TV (satellite), telephone, tea/coffee tray. B&B from £25.

(01904 627054)

🚗 EDINBURGH 🚗
THE IVY GUEST HOUSE
7 MAYFIELD GARDENS,
EDINBURGH EH9 2AX

Close to City Centre. All rooms with central heating, washbasins, colour TV, tea/coffee making facilities. En suite or standard rooms.
STB ★★★, AA ♦♦♦, RAC ♦♦♦♦

(0131-667 3411)

FHG PUBLICATIONS

publish a large range of well-known accommodation guides. We will be happy to send you details or you can use the order form at the back of this book.

AIRPORTS

BRISTOL
STONEYCROFT HOUSE
STOCK LANE, LANGFORD, BRISTOL,
NORTH SOMERSET BS18 7EX

10 minutes from Bristol Airport with Cheddar Gorge, Wells Cathedral, Bath, Bristol and seaside all nearby. All rooms have TV, tea/coffee facilities and excellent views. Open all year.

(01934 852624)

BRISTOL
FLAXLEY VILLA
9 NEWBRIDGE HILL, BATH,
SOMERSET BA1 3PW

Comfortable Victorian house, 5 minutes from town centre. All rooms have TV, shower, tea/coffee facilities. En suite available. Full English Breakfast. Parking. Terms from £22.
ETC ◆◆◆

(01225 313237)

GATWICK
LYNWOOD GUEST HOUSE
50 LONDON ROAD, REDHILL,
SURREY RH1 1LN

Gatwick Airport 12 minutes by train or car; London 35 minutes by train. Six minutes' walk to Redhill Station and town centre. Comfortable en suite facilities, colour TV and tea/coffee. Car park. AA ◆◆◆.

(01737 766894)

GATWICK
GORSE COTTAGE
66 BALCOMBE ROAD, HORLEY,
SURREY RH6 9AY

Small, friendly, detached accommodation. Two miles Gatwick Airport, five minutes BR station for London and South Coast. £36 double, £25 single.

(01293 784402)

HEATHROW
CLARENCE HOTEL
9 CLARENCE ROAD, WINDSOR,
BERKSHIRE SL4 5AE

Town centre location. Licensed bar and steam room. High quality accommodation at guest house prices. All rooms en suite, tea/coffee facilities, TV, radio alarms, hairdryers. Heathrow Airport 25 minutes by car ETC/AA/RAC Listed.

(01753 864436)

SOUTHAMPTON
FRESHFIELDS HOTEL
55 CHRISTCHURCH ROAD,
BOURNEMOUTH BH1 3PA

Small Licensed Hotel. Close to sandy beach and Bournemouth's attractions. Most rooms en suite, all with colour TV, tea/coffee making. Bargain Breaks September to June.

(01202 394023)

EDINBURGH
THE IVY GUEST HOUSE
7 MAYFIELD GARDENS,
EDINBURGH EH9 2AX

Close to City Centre. All rooms with central heating, washbasins, colour TV, tea/coffee making facilities. En suite or standard rooms.
STB ★★★, AA ◆◆◆, RAC ◆◆◆◆

(0131-667 3411)

EDINBURGH
GRANVILLE GUEST HOUSE
13 GRANVILLE TERRACE,
EDINBURGH EH10 4PQ

Family-run guest house situated close to all amenities including Edinburgh Castle. All rooms have tea/coffee facilities and TV. Limited off-street parking.

(0131-229 1676)

DIRECTORY OF WEBSITE AND E-MAIL ADDRESSES

A quick-reference guide to holiday accommodation with an e-mail address and website, conveniently arranged by country and county, with full contact details

Holiday Parks
GB Holiday Parks, 6 Leylands Park, Nobs Crook, Colden Common, Winchester, Hants SO21 1TH
0870 4429297
• website: www.gbholidayparks.co.uk

• LONDON

Hotel
Mowbray Court Hotel, 30 Penywern Road, Earls Court, KENSINGTON, London SW5 9SU
0207 370 2316 / 370 3690
• e-mail: mowbraycrthot@hotmail.com or mowbraycourthotel@mcmail.com
• website: www.m-c-hotel.mcmail.com

Hotel
Stanley House Hotel, 19-21 Belgrave Road, LONDON SW1V 1RB
020 7834 5042
• e-mail: cmahotel@aol.com
• website: www.londonbudgethotels.co.uk

B & B
Dolphin Hotel, 34 Norfolk Square, Paddington, LONDON W2 1RT
020 7402 4943
• e-mail: info@dolphinhotel.co.uk
• website: www.dolphinhotel.co.uk

Hotel
Dalmacia Hotel, 71 Shepherds Bush Road, Hammersmith, LONDON W6 7LS
020 7603 2887
• e-mail: george@adria.demon.co.uk

Adria Hotel, 44 Glenthorne Road, Hammersmith, LONDON W6 0LS
020 7602 6386
• e-mail: george@adria.demon.co.uk

Hotel
Lincoln House Hotel, 33 Gloucester Place, LONDON W1U 8HY
020 7486 7630
• e-mail: reservations@lincoln-house-hotel.co.uk
• website: www.lincoln-house-hotel.co.uk

Hotel
The Elysee Hotel, 25/26 Craven Terrace, London W2 3EL
020 7402 7633
• e-mail: information@elyseehotel-london.co.uk
• website: www.elyseehotel-london.co.uk

B & B
St Athans Hotel, 20 Tavistock Place, Russell Square, LONDON WC1H 9RE
020 7837 9627
• website: www.stathanshotel.com

• BERKSHIRE

Guest House
Mrs Sue Chapman, Lyndrick House, The Avenue, ASCOT, Berkshire SL5 7ND
01344 883520
• e-mail: mail@lyndrick.com
• website: www.lyndrick.com

Hotel
Netherton Hotel, 96 St Leonards Road, WINDSOR, Berkshire SL4 3DA
01753 855508
• e-mail: netherton@btconnect.com
• website: www.nethertonhotel.co.uk

• BUCKINGHAMSHIRE

Guest House
Mr Ben Dickinson, Beacon House, 113 Maxwell Road, BEACONSFIELD, Buckinghamshire HP9 1RF
01494 672923
• e-mail: ben.dickinson@tesco.net
• website: www.beaconhouse.org.uk

• CAMBRIDGESHIRE

Guest House
Dykelands Guest House, 157 Mowbray Road, CAMBRIDGE, Cambridgeshire CB1 7SP
01223 244300
• e-mail: dykelands@fsbdial.co.uk
• website: www.dykelands.com

WEBSITE DIRECTORY 183

Guest House
Mrs Julie Webb, Redby Lodge, 15 Queen Ediths Way, CAMBRIDGE, Cambridgeshire CB1 4PH
01223 566686
- e-mail:redbylodge@15qewcb.freeserve.co.uk
- website: www.cambridge-bedandbreakfast.co.uk

B & B
J & R Farndale, Cathedral House, 17 St Mary's Street, ELY, Cambridgeshire CB7 4ER
01353 662124
- e-mail: farndale@cathedralhouse.co.uk
- website: www.cathedralhouse.co.uk

•CHESHIRE

Hotel
Oasis Hotel (UK) Ltd, 46-48 Barrington Road, ALTRINCHAM, Cheshire WA14 1HN
0161 9284523
- e-mail: enquiries@oasishotel.co.uk
- website: www.oasishotel.co.uk

Guest House / Self-Catering
Mrs Angela Smith, Mill House and Granary, Higher Wych, MALPAS, Cheshire SY14 7JR
01948 780362
- e-mail: angela@videoactive.co.uk
- website: www.millhouseandgranary.co.uk

•CORNWALL

Self-Catering / Caravan & Camping
Ruthern Valley Holidays, Ruthernbridge BODMIN, Cornwall PL30 5LU
01208 831395
- e-mail: ruthernvalley@hotmail.com
- website: www.self-catering-ruthern.co.uk

B & B / Self-Catering
Mrs S. Perry, Polgrain Holiday Cottages, Higher Polgrain, St Wenn, BODMIN, Cornwall PL30 5PR
01637 880637 / 881944
- e-mail: polgrainholidaycottages@ukgateway.net
- website: www.selfcateringcornwall.uk.com

Self-Catering
Cornish Traditional Cottages, Blisland, BODMIN, Cornwall PL30 4HS
01208 821666
- e-mail: info@corncott.com
- website: www.corncott.com

Self-Catering
Angela Clark, Darrynane Cottages, Darrynane, St Breward, BODMIN MOOR, Cornwall PL30 4LZ
01208 850885
- e-mail: darrynane@eclipse.co.uk
- website: www.darrynane.co.uk

Self-Catering
Mrs Aileen Feasey, Mellon Farm, St Breward, Bodmin Moor
Cornwall PL30 4PL
01208 851497
- e-mail: feaseymellon@aol.com
- website: www.mellonfarm.co.uk

Self Catering
Mr Charles Tippet, Mineshop Holiday Cottages, Crackington Haven, BUDE, Cornwall EX23 0NR
01840 230338
- website: www.cornwall-online.co.uk/mineshop

Caravan Park
Keywood Caravan Park, Whitstone, Near BUDE, Cornwall EX22 6TW
01288 341338
- e-mail: info@keywoodholidays.co.uk
- website: www.keywoodholidays.co.uk

Self-Catering / Caravan & Camping
Hentervene Caravan & Camping Park, Crackington Haven, Near BUDE, Cornwall EX23 0LF
01840 230365
- e-mail: contact@hentervene.co.uk
- website: www.hentervene.co.uk

Self-Catering
Keith Freestone, Langfield Manor, Broadclose, BUDE, Cornwall EX23 8DP
01288 352415
- e-mail: info@langfieldmanor.co.uk
- website: www.langfieldmanor.co.uk

Guest House
Harvey Jay, Wringford Down Motel, CAWSAND, Cornwall PL10 1LE
01752 822287
- e-mail: ramehols@aol.com
- website: www.cornwallholidays.co.uk

Guest House
Mrs Anna Machin-Weaver, Colan Barton, COLAN, Near Newquay, Cornwall TR8 4NB
01637 874395
- e-mail: colanbarton.hotmail.com@barclays.net

184 WEBSITE DIRECTORY

Guest House
Mrs C. Carruthers, The Clearwater,
59 Melvill Road, FALMOUTH,
Cornwall TR11 4DF
01326 311344
- e-mail: clearwater@lineone.net
- website: www.clearwaterhotel.co.uk

Guest House
Trevaylor Hotel, 8 Pennance Road,
FALMOUTH, Cornwall TR11 4EA
01326 313041
- e-mail: stay@trevaylor.co.uk
- website: www.trevaylor.co.uk

Self-Catering
Fowey Harbour Cottages, 3 Fore Street,
FOWEY, Cornwall PL23 1AH
01726 832211
- e-mail: hillandson@talk21.com

Self-Catering / Caravan Park
Mr Christopher Harvey, St Ives Bay Chalet &
Caravan Park, HAYLE, Cornwall TR27 5BH
01736 752274
- e-mail: stivesbay@dial.pipex.com
- website: www.stivesbay.co.uk

Self-Catering
Mrs Sue Cox, The Old Dairy,
Hollington Lane, Ednaston, HELSTON,
Cornwall DE6 3AE
01335 361325
- website:
  www.zyworld.com/suecox/information.htm

Self-Catering
Mrs K. Chapman, Well Meadow Cottage,
Coldrinnick Farm, Duloe, Near LISKEARD,
Cornwall PL14 4QF
01503 220251
- e-mail: kaye@coldrinnick.fsnet.co.uk

B & B
Mrs S. Rowe, Tregondale Farm, Menheniot,
LISKEARD, Cornwall PL14 3RG
01579 342407
- e-mail: tregondale@connectfree.co.uk
- website: www.tregondalefarm.co.uk

Self-Catering
Mr & Mrs Cotter, Trewalla Farm, Minions,
LISKEARD, Cornwall PL14 6ED
01579 342385
- e-mail: cotter.trewalla@virgin.net
- website: http://uk.geocities.com/trewalla/

Self-Catering
Cutkive Wood Holiday Lodges, St Ives,
LISKEARD, Cornwall PL14 3ND
01579 362216
- e-mail: cutkwood@hotmail.com
- website: www.cutkivewood.co.uk

Guest House
Linda Brookes, Parc Brawse House,
Penmenner Road, THE LIZARD, Helston,
Cornwall TR12 7NR
01326 290466
- e-mail: parcbrawsehouse@netscapeonline.co.uk
- website:
  www.cornwall-online.co.uk/parcbrawsehouse

Self-Catering
Mr J.G. Spreckley, Tremaine Green Country
Cottages, Pelynt, Near LOOE,
Cornwall PL13 2LT
01503 220333
- e-mail: stay@tremainegreen.co.uk
- website: www.tremainegreen.co.uk

Self-Catering
Mr & Mrs Chapman, Trenant Park Cottages,
Trenant Lodge, Sandplace, LOOE,
Cornwall PL13 1PH
01503 263639
- e-mail: liz@holidaycottage.com
- website: www.holiday-cottage.com

Hotel
Malcolm Ward, Malmar Hotel, Trenance,
MAWGAN PORTH, Cornwall TR8 4DA
01637 860324
- e-mail: malmarhotel@supanet.com
- website: www.malmarhotel.com

Hotel
White Lodge Hotel, Mawgan Porth Bay,
Near NEWQUAY, Cornwall TR8 4BN
01637 860512
- e-mail: dogfriendlyhotel@redhotant.com
- website: www.dogfriendlyhotel.co.uk

Self-Catering
The Old Vicarage, Church Street, St Columb
Minor, NEWQUAY, Cornwall TR7 3ET
01637 872625
- e-mail: paul.gardner4@btinternet.com
- website: www.theoldvicarage-newquay.co.uk

FREE or REDUCED RATE
entry to Holiday Visits
and Attractions
see our
READERS' OFFER
VOUCHERS
on pages 35-54

WEBSITE DIRECTORY

Guest House
Trewerry Mill Guest House, Trewerry Mill,
Trerice, St Newlyn East, NEWQUAY,
Cornwall TR8 5GS
01872 510345
- e-mail: trewerry.mill@which.net
- website: www.connexions.co.uk/trewerry.mill

Self-Catering
Jenny Bertoli, The Granary, Retorrick Mill,
St Mawgan, NEWQUAY, Cornwall TR8 4BH
01637 860460
- website:
  www.selfcateringbungalowscornwall.com

Hotel
Mrs M.G. Waldron, Golden Bay Hotel,
Pentire Avenue, Pentire, NEWQUAY,
Cornwall TR7 1PD
01637 873318
- e-mail: enquiries@goldenbayhotel.co.uk
- website: www.goldenbayhotel.co.uk

Self-Catering
Cornish Horizons Holiday Cottages, Higher
Trehemborne, St Merryn, PADSTOW,
Cornwall PL28 8JU
01841 521333
- e-mail: cottages@cornishhorizons.co.uk
- website:www.cornishhorizons.co.uk

Self-Catering
Raintree House Holidays, Whistlers,
Treyarnon Bay, PADSTOW,
Cornwall PL28 8JR
01841 520228
- e-mail: gill@raintreehouse.co.uk
- website: www.raintreehouse.co.uk

Guest House
Mr Clive Whittington, Ednovean House,
Perranuthnoe, PENZANCE,
Cornwall TR20 9LZ
01736 711071
- e-mail: clive@ednoveanhouse.co.uk
- website: www.ednoveanhouse.co.uk

Farm/ B & B
Mrs P.M. Hall, Treen Farmhouse, Treen,
St Levan, PENZANCE, Cornwall TR19 6LF
01736 810253
- e-mail: paulachrishall@treenfarmfsnet.co.uk

Guest House
Mr & Mrs J.A. Leggatt, Cornerways Guest
House, 5 Leskinnick Street, PENZANCE,
Cornwall TR18 2HA
01736 364645
- e-mail: enquiries@cornerways-penzance.co.uk
- website: www.penzance.co.uk/cornerways

B & B
Mr Keith Richards, Con Amore, 38 Morrab
Road, PENZANCE, Cornwall TR18 4EX
01736 363423
- website: www.con-amore.co.uk

Hotel
Boscean Country Hotel, St Just,
PENZANCE, Cornwall TR19 7QP
01736 788748
- e-mail: Boscean@aol.com
- website: www.bosceancountryhotel.co.uk

Farmhouse B & B
Mrs Penny Lally, Rose Farm, Chyanhal,
Buryas Bridge, PENZANCE,
Cornwall TR19 6AN
01736 731808
- e-mail: lally@rosefarm.co.uk
- website: www.rosefarmcornwall.co.uk

Guest House
Homefields Guest House, Sennen,
Near PENZANCE, Cornwall TR19 7AD
01736 871418
- e-mail: homefields1BandB@aol.com
- website: www.homefieldsguesthouse.co.uk

Self-Catering
Mr Jon Mansfield, Sandbay Holiday Flats,
St Pirans Road, PERRANPORTH,
Cornwall TR6 0BH
01872 572081
- e-mail: enquiries@sand-bay.co.uk
- website: www.sand-bay.co.uk

Self-Catering Cottage
Cottage in POLPERRO, c/o Mrs T. Cornish,
8 The Queensway, Gerrards Cross,
Buckinghamshire SL9 8NF
01753 882482
- e-mail: tefan@cornish-cottage.com
- website: www.cornish-cottage.com

Caravan & Camping
Lanyon Holiday Park, Fourlanes, REDRUTH,
Cornwall TR16 6LP
01209 313474
- e-mail: jamierielly@supanet.com
- website:
  www.lanyoncaravanandcampingpark.co.uk

Please mention
Britain's Best Holidays
*when enquiring about
accommodation*

WEBSITE DIRECTORY

Caravan & Camping
Globe Vale Holiday Park, Radnor, REDRUTH, Cornwall TR16 4BH
01209 891183
• e-mail: globe@ukgo.com
• website: www.globe.ukgo.com

Inn
Gordon & Jill Treleaven & Family, Driftwood Spars Hotel, Trevaunance Cove, ST AGNES, Cornwall TR5 0RT
01872 552428
• e-mail: driftwoodspars@hotmail.com
• website: www.driftwoodspars.com

Country House Hotel
Mr & Mrs I. Jefferies, The Sunholme Hotel, Goonvrea Road, ST AGNES, Cornwall TR5 0NW
01872 552318
• e-mail: jefferies@sunholme.co.uk
• website: www.sunholme.co.uk

Self-Catering
Mr C.W. Pestell, Hockadays, Tregenna, Near Blisland, ST TUDY, Cornwall PL30 4QJ
01208 850146
• website: www.hockadaysholidaycottages.co.uk

Self-Catering
Mrs Sandy Wilson, Salutations, Atlantic Road, TINTAGEL, Cornwall PL34 0DE
01840 770287
• e-mail: sandyanddave@tinyworld.co.uk

Caravan Park
C.R. Simpkins, Summer Valley Touring Park, Shortlanesend, TRURO, Cornwall TR4 9DW
01872 277878
• e-mail: res@summervalley.co.uk
• website: www.summervalley.co.uk

Inn
J.B. Gayton, The New Inn, Veryan, TRURO, Cornwall TR2 5QA
01872 501362
• e-mail: jack@veryan44.freeserve.co.uk
• website: www.veryan44.freeserve.co.uk

Self-Catering
Mrs Pamela Carbis, Trenona Farm, Ruan High Lanes, TRURO, Cornwall TR2 5JS
01872 501339
• e-mail: pcarbis@compuserve.com
• website: www.connexions.co.uk/trenona

•CUMBRIA

Hotel
Ivy House Hotel, Hawkshead, Near AMBLESIDE, Cumbria LA22 0NS
015394 36204
• e-mail: david@ivyhousehotel.com
• website: www.ivyhousehotel.com

Guest House / Self-Catering
Anthony J Marsden, Betty Fold, Hawkshead Hill, AMBLESIDE, Cumbria LA22 0PS
015394 36611
• e-mail: holidays@bettyfold.freeserve.co.uk
• website: www.bettyfold.freeserve.co.uk

Small Hotel
Lyndhurst Hotel, Wansfell Road, AMBLESIDE, Cumbria LA22 0EG
015394 32421
• e-mail: lyndhurst@amblesidehotels.co.uk
• website: www.amblesidehotels.co.uk

Guest House
Mary Adamson, Wanslea Guest House, Lake Road, AMBLESIDE, Cumbria LA22 0DB
015394 33884
• e-mail: wanslea.guesthouse@virgin.net
• website: www.wansleaguesthouse.co.uk

Guest House
Mr & Mrs B & A Jeffrey, The Anchorage, Rydal Road, AMBLESIDE, Cumbria LA22 9AY
015394 32046
• e-mail:info@anchorageguesthouse.ltd.uk
• website: www.anchorageguesthouse.ltd.uk

Board / Self-Catering
Mr & Mrs P. Hart, Bracken Fell, Outgate, AMBLESIDE, Cumbria LA22 0NH
015394 36289
• e-mail: hart.brackenfell@virgin.net
• website: www.brackenfell.com

Guest House
Anne & Malcolm Dayson, Bongate House, APPLEBY, Cumbria CA16 6UE
017683 51245 / 0703
• e-mail: information@bongatehouse.com
• website: www.bongatehouse.co.uk

Visit the FHG website
www.holidayguides.com
for details of the wide choice of accommodation featured in the full range of FHG titles

WEBSITE DIRECTORY 187

Self-Catering
J.F. Cobson, Dyke Nook, BASSENTHWAITE,
Keswick, Cumbria CA12 4QG
017687 76263
- e-mail: dykenook@lineone.net
- website: www.lakesandsea.addr.com
  or: www.keswick.org

Self-Catering
Lakelovers, Belmont House, Lake Road,
BOWNESS-ON-WINDERMERE,
Cumbria LA23 3BJ
015394 88855
- e-mail: bookings@lakelovers.co.uk
- website: www.lakelovers.co.uk

Hotel / Self-Catering
Bridge Hotel & Self-Catering, Bridge Hotel,
BUTTERMERE, Lake District,
Cumbria CA13 9UZ
017687 70252
- e-mail: enquiries@bridge-hotel.com
- website: www.bridge-hotel.com

Farmhouse / Hotel
Hazel Thompson, New House Farm, Lorton,
BUTTERMERE, Near Cockermouth,
Cumbria CA13 9UU
01900 85404
- e-mail: hazel@newhouse-farm.co.uk
- website: www.newhouse-farm.co.uk

Self-Catering
Mrs J.M. Almond, Irton House Farm, Isel,
COCKERMOUTH, Cumbria CA13 9ST
017687 76380
- e-mail: almond@farmersweekly.net
- website: www.almondirtonhousefarm.com

Self-Catering
Mr P. Johnston, The Coppermines at
Coniston, The Estate Office, The Bridge,
CONISTON, Cumbria LA21 8HX
015394 41765
- e-mail: bookings@coppermines.co.uk
- website: www.coppermines.co.uk

Self-Catering
Alan Jefferson, Thurson House,
Tilberthwaite Avenue, CONISTON,
Cumbria
01204 419261
- e-mail: alan@jefferson99.freeserve.co.uk
- website: www.jefferson99.freeserve.co.uk

Self-Catering
Mrs J. Hall, Fisherground Farm Cottages,
Fisherground, ESKDALE,
Cumbria, CA19 1TF
01946 723319
- e-mail: holidays@fisherground.co.uk
- website: www.fisherground.co.uk

Guest House
T. Bulcock, Dunmail House, Keswick Road,
GRASMERE, Ambleside, Cumbria LA22 9RE
015394 35256
- e-mail: enquiries@dunmailhouse.freeserve.co.uk
- website: www.dunmailhouse.com

Guest House
Mrs J. Welch, Braemar, 21 Eskin Street
KESWICK, Cumbria CA12 4DQ
017687 73743
- e-mail: enquiries@braemar-guesthouse.co.uk
- website: www.braemar-guesthouse.co.uk

B & B
Mrs Deborah Mawson, Dalton Cottage,
Bassenthwaite, KESWICK,
Cumbria CA12 4QG
01768 776952
- e-mail: deborah@daltoncottage.co.uk
- website:www.daltoncottage.co.uk

Self-Catering
Manesty Holiday Cottages, Youdale Knot,
Manesty, KESWICK, Cumbria CA12 5UG
017687 77216
- e-mail: alan.t.leyland@talk21.com
- website: www.manesty.co.uk

Hotel
Rickerby Grange Country House Hotel,
Portinscale, KESWICK, Cumbria CA12 5RH
017687 72344
- e-mail: val@ricor.co.uk
- website: www.ricor.co.uk

Self-Catering / B & B
Mrs A.M. Trafford, Bassenthwaite Hall Farm,
Near KESWICK, Cumbria CA12 4QP
017687 76393
- website: www.holidaycottageslakedistrict.co.uk

Hotel
Swan Hotel, Thornthwaite, KESWICK,
Cumbria CA12 5SQ
017687 78100
- e-mail: bestswan@aol.com
- website: www.swan-hotel-keswick.co.uk

Self-Catering
Lakeland Character Cottages,
The Kings Head, Thirlspot, Near KESWICK,
Cumbria CA12 4TN
017687 72393
- website: www.lakelandinns.com

Guest House
Tony & Ann Atkin, Glencoe Guest House,
21 Helvellyn Street, KESWICK,
Cumbria CA12 4EN
017687 71016
- e-mail: enquiries@glencoeguesthouse.co.uk
- website: www.glencoeguesthouse.co.uk

188 WEBSITE DIRECTORY

Self-Catering
Midtown Cottages, KESWICK,
c/o Mr Mick Burrell, 20 Hillside, Abbotts
Ann, Andover, Hampshire SP11 7DF
01264 710165
- e-mail: info@midtowncottages.co.uk
- website: www.midtowncottages.co.uk

Self-Catering
The Bungalows c/o Mr Paul Sunley,
Sunnyside, Threlkeld, KESWICK,
Cumbria CA12 4SD
017687 79679
- e-mail: paulsunley@msn.com
- website: www.thebungalows.co.uk

Self-Catering
Liz Webster, Howscales, KIRKOSWALD,
Penrith, Cumbria CA10 1JG
01768 898666
- e-mail: liz@howscales.fsbusiness.co.uk
- website: www.eden-in-cumbria.co.uk/howscales

Guest House / B & B
Mr & Mrs C. Smith, Mosedale House,
MOSEDALE, Mungrisdale,
Cumbria CA11 0XQ
01768 779371
- e-mail: mosedale@northlakes.co.uk
- website: www.northlakes.co.uk/mosedalehouse

Self-Catering
Stephen Foxall, Patterdale Hall Estate,
Glenridding, PENRITH, Cumbria CA11 0PJ
017684 82308
- e-mail: welcome@phel.co.uk
- website: www.phel.co.uk

Guest House
Geoff Mason, Knotts Mill Country Lodge,
Ullswater, Watermillock, PENRITH,
Cumbria CA11 0JN
017684 86699
- e-mail: knottsmill@cwcom.net
- website: www.knottsmill.cwc.net

B & B
Marion Barritt, Elm Tree Barn, Culgaith,
PENRITH, Cumbria CA10 1QW
01768 88789
- e-mail: marion@elmtreebarn.co.uk
- website: www.elmtreebarn.co.uk

Self-Catering
Mr & Mrs Dodsworth, Birthwaite Edge,
Birthwaite Road, WINDERMERE,
Cumbria LA23 1BS
015394 42861
- e-mail: lakedge@lakedge.com
- website: www.lakedge.com

Self-Catering
J.R. Benson, High Sett, Sun Hill Lane,
Troutbeck Bridge, WINDERMERE,
Cumbria LA23 1HJ
015394 42731
- e-mail: info@accommodationlakedistrict.com
- website: www.accommodationlakedistrict.com

Guest House / Self-Catering
Neil Cox, Kirkwood Guest House, Prince's
Road, WINDERMERE, Cumbria LA23 2DD
015394 43907
- e-mail: info@kirkwood51.co.uk
- website: www.kirkwood51.co.uk

Guest House
Mr & Mrs M. Rooney, Villa Lodge, Cross
Street, WINDERMERE, Cumbria LA23 1AE
015394 43318
- e-mail: rooneym@btconnect.com
- website: www.villa-lodge.co.uk

Guest House
Mr Brian Fear, Cambridge House, 9 Oak
Street, WINDERMERE, Cumbria LA23 1EN
015394 43846
- e-mail: reservations@cambridge-house.fsbusiness.co.uk
- website: www.cambridge-house.fsbusiness.co.uk

•DERBYSHIRE

Inn
Mrs Stelfox, The Dog & Partridge Country
Inn, Swinscoe, ASHBOURNE,
Derbyshire DE6 2HS
01335 343183
- e-mail: dogpart@fsbdial.co.uk
- website: www.dogandpartridge.co.uk

Farmhouse B & B / Self-Catering
Mrs M.A. Richardson, Throwley Hall Farm,
Ilam, ASHBOURNE, Derbyshire DE6 2BB
01538 308202
- e-mail: throwleyhall@talk21.com
- website: www.throwleyhallfarm.co.uk

Farm / Board
New House Organic Farm, Kniveton,
ASHBOURNE, Derbyshire DE6 1JL
01335 342429
- e-mail: b&b@newhousefarm.co.uk

Self-Catering
Mill Farm, BARLOW, Derbyshire S18 7TJ
0114 2890543
- e-mail: barfish@fsnet.co.uk
- website: www.barlowlakes.co.uk

WEBSITE DIRECTORY 189

Guest House
Mr & Mrs Hyde, Braemar,10 Compton Road, BUXTON, Derbyshire SK17 9DN
01298 78050
- e-mail: buxtonbraemar@supanet.com
- website: www.cressbrook.co.uk/buxton/braemar

Self-Catering
R.D. Hollands, Wheeldon Trees Farm, Earl, Sterndale, BUXTON, Derbyshire SK17 0AA
01298 83219
- e-mail: hollands@earlsterndale.fsnet.co.uk
- website: www.wheeldontreesfarm.co.uk

Hotel
Biggin Hall Hotel, Biggin-by-Hartington, BUXTON, Derbyshire SK17 0DH
01298 84451
- e-mail: bigginhall@compuserve.com
- website: www.bigginhall.co.uk

Farm / Self Catering
Angela Kellie, Shatton Hall Farm, Bamford, HOPE VALLEY, Derbyshire S33 0BG
01433 620635
- e-mail: ahk@peakfarmholidays.co.uk
- website: www.peakfarmholidays.co.uk

•DEVON

Guest House
Mr C.D. Moore, Gages Mill, Buckfastleigh Road, ASHBURTON, Devon TQ13 7JW
01364 652391
- e-mail: moore@gagesmill.co.uk
- website: www.gagesmill.co.uk

Farm / Self-Catering / Caravan
Parkers Farm Holiday Park, Higher Mead Farm, ASHBURTON, Newton Abbot, Devon TQ13 7LJ
01364 652598
- e-mail: parkersfarm@btconnect.com
- website: www.parkersfarm.co.uk

Caravan Park
Hunters Moon Park, Hawkchurch, AXMINSTER, Devon EX13 5UL
01297 678402
- website: www.ukparks.co.uk/huntersmoon

Self-Catering
G.E Ridge, Braddon Cottages, Ashwater, BEAWORTHY, Devon EX21 5EP
01409 211350
- website: www.braddoncottages.co.uk

Self-Catering Lodges
Watermouth Lodges, Watermouth, BERRYNARBOR, North Devon EX34 9SJ
01271 865361
- e-mail: cajhill39@aol.co.uk
- website: www.watermouth.co.uk

B & B
Mrs Thompson, Rosewood, Knotty Corner, BIDEFORD, North Devon EX39 5BT
01737 451514
- e-mail: christhompson81@hotmail.com

Self-Catering / B & B
Peter & Lesley Lewin, Lake House Cottages and B&B, Lake Villa, BRADWORTHY, Devon EX22 7SQ
01409 241962
- e-mail: info@lakevilla.co.uk
- website: www.lakevilla.co.uk

Self-Catering
Marsdens Cottage Holidays, 2 The Square, BRAUNTON, Devon EX33 2JB
01271 813777
- e-mail: holidays@marsdens.co.uk
- website: www.marsdens.co.uk

B & B
Mrs Roselyn Bradford, St Merryn, Higher Park Road, BRAUNTON, Devon EX33 2LG
01271 813805
- e-mail: ros@st-merryn.co.uk
- website: www.st-merryn.co.uk

Guest House
Mr John Parry, Woodlands Guest House, Parkham Road, BRIXHAM, South Devon TQ5 9BU
01803 852040
- e-mail: Diparry@aol.com
- website: www.dogfriendlyguesthouse.co.uk

Hotel
The Smugglers Haunt, Church Hill, BRIXHAM, Devon TQ5 8HH
01803 853050
- e-mail: enquiries@smugglershaunt-hotel-devon.co.uk
- website: www.smugglershaunt-hotel-devon.co.uk

Please mention BRITAIN'S BEST HOLIDAYS when enquiring about accommodation

WEBSITE DIRECTORY

Self-Catering
John & Christine Robertson, Wheel Farm Country Cottages, Berry Down, COMBE MARTIN, North Devon EX34 0NT
01271 882100
• e-mail: holidays@wheelfarmcottages.co.uk
• website: www.wheelfarmcottages.co.uk

Caravans & Chalets
M.J. Hughes, Manleigh Holiday Park, Rectory Road, COMBE MARTIN, North Devon EX34 0NS
01271 883353
• e-mail: info@manleighpark.co.uk
• website: www.manleighpark.co.uk

Self-Catering
Mr & Mrs Simpson, Middle Garland, CHULMLEIGH, Devon EX18 7DU
01769 580461
• e-mail: deercott@sosi.net
• website: www.sosi.net/users/deercott

Self-Catering
Mrs S. Charman, South Farm, Blackborough, CULLOMPTON, Devon EX15 2JE
01823 681078
• e-mail: chapmans@southfarm.co.uk
• website: www.southfarm.co.uk

Self-Catering
Swan Holidays (Westward) Ltd, Welcome Family Holiday Park, Warren Road, DAWLISH WARREN, Devon EX7 0PH
01626 862070
• e-mail: fun@welcomefamily.co.uk
• website: www.welcomefamily.co.uk

Farm / B & B
Mrs Karen Williams, Stile Farm, Starcross, EXETER, Devon EX6 8PD
01626 890268
• e-mail: info@stile-farm.co.uk
• website: www.stile-farm.co.uk

Self-Catering Flats
Mrs C.G. Duncan, Raleigh Holiday Homes, EXMOUTH, Devon EX8 2SB
01395 266967
• e-mail: ceduncan@amserve.net

Farm B & B
Mrs Elizabeth Tucker, Lower Luxton Farm, Upottery, HONITON, Devon EX14 9PB
01823 601269
• e-mail: lwrluxtonfm@hotmail.com
• website: www.SmoothHound.co.uk/hotels/devonfarmh.html

Self-Catering
Mr F. Wigram, Riggles Farm, Upottery, HONITON, Devon EX14 4SP
01404 891229
• e-mail: rigglesfarm@farming.co.uk
• website: www.braggscottage.co.uk

Self-Catering
Mr Tromans, Hope Barton Barns, HOPE COVE, Devon TQ7 3HT
01548 561393
• e-mail: info@hopebarton.co.uk
• website: www.hopebarton.co.uk

Farm / Self-Catering
Mrs E. Sanson, Widmouth Farm, Watermouth, Near ILFRACOMBE, Devon EX34 9RX
01271 863743
• e-mail: holiday@widmouthfarmcottages.co.uk
• website: www.widmouthfarmcottages.co.uk

Touring & Camping Park
Hidden Valley Touring & Camping Park, West Down, Near ILFRACOMBE, Devon EX34 8NU
01271 813637
• e-mail: hvpdevon@aol.com
• website: www.hiddenvalleypark.com

Guest House
David & Marianna Holdsworth, Lyncott House, 56 St Brannock's Road, ILFRACOMBE, North Devon EX34 8EQ
01271 862425
• e-mail: david@ukhotels.com
• website: www.lyncottdevon.com

B & B
Mrs M. Newsham, Marsh Mills, Aveton Gifford, KINGSBRIDGE, Devon TQ7 4JW
01548 550549
• e-mail: Newsham@Marshmills.co.uk
• website: www.Marshmills.co.uk

FHG PUBLICATIONS LTD publish a large range of well-known accommodation guides. We will be happy to send you details or you can use the order form at the back of this book.

WEBSITE DIRECTORY 191

Self-Catering
Mr A. Lubrani, West Charleton Grange, West Charleton, KINGSBRIDGE,
Devon TQ7 2AD
01548 531779
- e-mail: colbet@globalnet.co.uk
- website: www.users.globalnet.co.uk/
  colbetusealtvista/inforseek

Self-Catering
Dittiscombe Holiday Cottages, Slapton,
Near KINGSBRIDGE, Devon
01548 521272
- e-mail: dittiscombe@lineone.net
- website: www.dittiscombe.co.uk

Farm / Caravan & Camping
Alston Farm, Malborough, KINGSBRIDGE,
Devon TQ7 3BJ
01548 561260
- e-mail: alston.campsite@ukgateway.net
- website: www.welcome.to/alstonfarm

Guest House
Tricia & Alan Francis, Glenville House,
2 Tors Road, LYNMOUTH,
North Devon EX35 6ET
01598 752202
- e-mail: tricia@glenvillelynmouth.co.uk
- website: www.glenvillelynmouth.co.uk

Hotel
Alford House Hotel, Alford Terrace,
LYNTON, North Devon EX35 6AT
01598 752359
- e-mail: enquiries@alfordhouse.co.uk
- website: www.alfordhouse.co.uk

Farm / B & B
Great Sloncombe Farm,
MORETONHAMPSTEAD,
Newton Abbot, Devon TQ13 8QF
01647 440595
- e-mail: hmerchant@sloncombe.freeserve.co.uk
- website: www.greatsloncombefarm.co.uk

Self-Catering
Helen Griffiths, Look Weep Farm Cottages,
Liverton, NEWTON ABBOT,
Devon TQ12 6HT
01626 833277
- e-mail: holidays@lookweep.co.uk
- website: www.lookweep.co.uk

Self-Catering
Simon Whale, Roselands Holiday Chalets,
Totnes Road, Ipplepen, NEWTON ABBOT,
Devon TQ12 5TD
01803 812701
- e-mail: enquiries@roselands.net
- website: www.roselands.net

Guest House
The Lamplighter Hotel, 103 Citadel Road,
The Hoe, PLYMOUTH, Devon PL1 2RN
01752 663855
- e-mail: lamplighterhotel@ukonline.co.uk

Hotel / Inn
The Port Light, Bolberry Down,
Near SALCOMBE, South Devon TQ7 3DY
01548 561384
- e-mail: info@portlight-salcombe.co.uk
- website: www.portlight-salcombe.co.uk

Caravan Park
Mr Thomas, Axevale Caravan Park,
SEATON, Devon EX12 2DF
0800 0688816
- e-mail: info@axevale.co.uk
- website: www.axevale.co.uk

Farm / Self-Catering
Mr & Mrs Baxter, Lower Knapp Farm
Holidays, SIDMOUTH, Devon EX10 0QN
01404 871438
- website: www.knappfarm-holidays.co.uk

Self-Catering
Boswell Farm Cottages, Boswell Farm,
SIDFORD, Devon EX10 0PP
01395 514162
- e-mail: dillon@boswell-farm.co.uk
- website: www.boswell-farm.co.uk

Farm / Board
Mrs Hilary Tucker, Beera Farm, Milton
Abbot, TAVISTOCK, Devon PL19 8PL
01822 870216
- website: www.beera-farm.co.uk

Hotel
Mr Stevens, The Coach House Hotel, Ottery,
Near TAVISTOCK, Devon PL19 8NS
01822 617515
- e-mail: eddie@coachhouse1.supanet.com
- website: www.the-coachouse.co.uk

Self-Catering
South Sands Apartments, Torbay Road,
TORQUAY, Devon TQ2 6RG
01803 293521
- e-mail: southsands.torquay@virgin.net
- website: www.southsands.co.uk

Hotel / Guest House
Rowan & Carole Ward, Green Park Hotel, 25
Morgan Avenue, TORQUAY,
Devon TQ2 5RR
01803 293618
- website: www.greenpark.eclipse.co.uk

Self-Catering
Jane Cromey-Hawke, Collacott Farm,
Kings Nympton, UMBERLEIGH,
North Devon EX37 9TP
01791 572491
• e-mail: jane@collacott.co.uk
• website: www.collacott.co.uk

B & B
Mrs G. Swann, Springfield-Garden,
Atherington, UMBERLEIGH,
North Devon EX37 9JA
01769 560034
• e-mail: broadgdn@eurobell.co.uk
• website: www.broadgdn.eurobell.co.uk

Hotel
Woolacombe Bay Hotel, WOOLACOMBE,
Devon EX34 7BN
01271 870388
• e-mail: woolacombe.bayhotel@btinternet.com
• website: www.woolacombe-bay-hotel.co.uk

Guest House
Lynda Hunt, Sunnymeade Country Hotel,
Dean Cross, West Down, WOOLACOMBE,
Devon EX34 8NT
01271 863668
• e-mail: info@sunnymeade.co.uk
• website: www.sunnymeade.co.uk

Hotel
Crossways Hotel, The Seafront,
WOOLACOMBE, Devon EX34 7DJ
01271 870395
• website:
www.s-h-systems.co.uk/hotels/crossway.html

Farm B & B
Justine Colton, Peek Hill Farm, Donsland,
YELVERTON, Devon PL20 6PD
01822 854808
• e-mail: colton@peekhill.freeserve.co.uk
• website: www.peekhill.freeserve.co.uk

•DORSET

Guest House
Mrs M.E. Jones, Cashmoor House,
Cashmoor, BLANDFORD, Dorset DT11 8DN
01725 552339
• e-mail: spencer.jones@ukonline.co.uk
• website: www.cashmoorhouse.cjb.net

Hotel
The Anvil Hotel, Salisbury Road, Pimperne,
BLANDFORD, Dorset DT11 8UQ
01258 453431
• e-mail: theanvil@euphony.net
• website: www.anvilhotel.co.uk

Farm / Self-Catering
Mr M. Kayll, Luccombe Farm, Luccombe,
Milton Abbas, BLANDFORD FORUM,
Dorset DT11 0BE
01258 880558
• e-mail: mkayll@aol.com
• website: www.Luccombeholidays.co.uk

Guest House
Mr Stevenson, Amitie Guest House,
1247 Christchurch Road, BOURNEMOUTH,
Dorset BH7 6BP
01202 427255
• e-mail: B&B@amitie.co.uk
• website: www.amitie.co.uk

Guest House
S. Barling, Mayfield, 46 Frances Road,
BOURNEMOUTH, Dorset BH1 3SA
01202 551839
• e-mail: accom@may-field.co.uk
• website: www.may-field.co.uk

Hotel
Heathlands Hotel, Grove Road, East Cliff,
BOURNEMOUTH, Dorset BH1 3AY
01202 553336
• e-mail: info@heathlandshotel.com
• website: www.heathlandshotel.com

Guest House
K. Mackie, St Antoine, 2 Guildhill Road,
Southbourne, BOURNEMOUTH,
Dorset BH6 3EY
01202 433043
• e-mail: kathden@kathden.fsnet.co.uk

Guest House
Cherry View Hotel, 66 Alum Chine Road,
BOURNEMOUTH, Dorset BH4 8DZ
01202 760910
• e-mail: enquiries@cherryview.co.uk
• website: www.cherryview.co.uk

Self-Catering
Mrs Bryan, Court Farm Cottages,
Askerswell, Dorchester, Near BRIDPORT,
Dorset DT2 9EJ
01308 485668
• e-mail: courtfarmcottages@eclipse.co.uk
• website:
www.eclipse.co.uk/CourtFarmCottages/WEBPG2

Farm / Self-Catering
Westover Farm Cottages, Wootton
Fitzpaine, BRIDPORT, Dorset DT6 6NE
01297 560451
• e-mail: wfcottages@aol.com
• website:
www.lymeregis.com/westover-farm-cottages

Caravan Park
Manor Farm Holiday Centre, Charmouth,
BRIDPORT, Dorset DT6 6QL
01297 560226
• website: www.manorfarmholidaycentre.co.uk

Self-Catering Cottages
Mrs C. Mansfield, Lancombes House, West Milton, BRIDPORT, Dorset DT6 3TN
01308 485375
• e-mail: mail@lancombeshouse.co.uk
• website: www.lancombeshouse.co.uk

B & B / Self-Catering
Mrs S.M. Johnson, Cardsmill Farm Holidays, Whitchurch Canonicorum, CHARMOUTH, Bridport, Dorset DT6 6RP
01297 489375
• e-mail: cardsmill@aol.com
• website:www.farmhousedorset.com

Self-Catering
Paddlegrade Ltd, Riverside Park, Willow Way, CHRISTCHURCH, Dorset BH23 1JJ
01202 471090
• e-mail: riversidepark@cwcom.net
• website: www.riversidepark@cwc.net

Self-Catering / Chalets / Caravans
Mrs L.M. Bowling, Owlpen Caravans,
148 Burley Road, Bransgore,
Near CHRISTCHURCH, Dorset BH23 8DB
01425 672875
• e-mail: holidays@owlpen.freeserve.co.uk

Inn
Mr A. Forster, The Fleur De Lys, CRANBORNE, Near Wimborne Minster, Dorset BH21 5PP
01725 517282
• e-mail: fleurdelys@btinternet.com
• website:www.fleurdelys-cranborne.com

B & B
Mrs J. Langley, The Stables, Hyde Crook, Frampton, DORCHESTER, Dorset DT2 9NW
01300 320075
• e-mail: dudleylang@aol.com

Guesthouse
Churchview Guest House, Winterbourne Abbas, DORCHESTER, Dorset DT2 9LS
01305 889296
• e-mail: stay@churchview.co.uk
• website: www.churchview.co.uk

Country House B&B
Mrs Martine Tree, The Old Rectory, Winterbourne Steepleton, DORCHESTER, Dorset DT2 9LG
01305 889468
• e-mail: trees@eurobell.co.uk
• website: www.trees.eurobell.co.uk

Self-Catering
Mr Terry Dunn, Little Hewish Barn, MILTON ABBAS, Blandford Forum, Dorset DT11 0DP
01258 881235
• e-mail: terry@littlehewish.co.uk

Touring Park
Mrs Bond, Beacon Hill Touring Park, Blandford Road North, POOLE, Dorset BH16 6AB
01202 631631
• website: www.beaconhilltouringpark.co.uk

Farm / Caravan & Camping
Mrs Scrimgeour, Huntick Farm, Lytchett Matravers, POOLE, Dorset BH16 6BB
01202 622222 / 631876
• e-mail: john@huntick.fsnet.co.uk

Inn
Mrs Penny, Three Horseshoes, POWERSTOCK, Dorset DT6 3TP
01308 485328
• website: www.threehorseshoespowerstock.com

Guest House / Self-Catering
White Horse Farm, Middlemarsh, SHERBOURNE, Dorset DT9 5QN
01963 210222
• e-mail: enquiries@whitehorsefarm.co.uk
• website: www.whitehorsefarm.co.uk

Hotel / Guest House
The Limes Hotel, 48 Park Road, SWANAGE, Dorset BH19 2AE
01929 422664
• e-mail: info@limeshotel.demon.co.uk
• website: www.limeshotel.demon.co.uk

Farm / Bed & Breakfast
Mrs Justine Pike, Downshay Farm, Haycrafts Lane, Harmans Cross, SWANAGE, Dorset BH19 3EB
01929 480316
• e-mail: downshay.pike/@farmersweekly.net

Self-Catering
Dorset Holiday Cottages, 11 Tyneham Close, Sandford, WAREHAM, Dorset BH20 7BE
01929 553443
• e-mail: holidaycottages@hotmail.com
• website: www.dhcottages.co.uk

Farm B & B / Caravan & Camping
Mrs L.S. Barnes, Luckford Wood House, East Stoke, WAREHAM, Dorset BH20 6AW
01929 463098
• e-mail: info@luckfordleisure.co.uk
• website: www.luckfordleisure.co.uk

194 WEBSITE DIRECTORY

B & B / Touring Caravan Site
Mrs G.A. Topp, Manor Farm Caravan Park,
East Stoke, WAREHAM, Dorset.BH20 6AW
01929 462870
- e-mail: info@manorfarmcp.co.uk
- website: www.manorfarmcp.co.uk
  or: www.caravan-sitefinder.co.uk

Self-Catering on Working Farm
Josephine Pearse, Tamarisk Farm Cottages,
WEST BEXINGTON, Dorchester,
Dorset DT2 9DF
01308 897784
- e-mail: tamarisk@eurolink.ltd.net
- website: www.tamariskfarm.co.uk

Guest House
Mrs Harvey, Florian, 59 Abbotsbury Road,
WEYMOUTH, Dorset DT4 0AQ
01305 773836
- e-mail: clare@florian-guesthouse.co.uk
- website: www.florian-guesthouse.co.uk

B & B
Mrs Tory, Hemsworth Farm, Witchampton,
Near WIMBORNE, Dorset BH21 5BN
01258 840216
- website: www.ruraldorset.org.uk/bed

• DURHAM

Self-Catering
Kay Elliot, Derwent Grange Farm,
Castleside, CONSETT, Durham DH8 9BN
01207 508358
- e-mail: ekelliot@aol.com

• ESSEX

Self-Catering
Jan Hollingsbee, Fairacre Cottage, French
Road, NORTH FAMBRIDGE, Essex
01621 742100
- e-mail: RHollings@aol.com

Hotel / Country Club
Five Lakes Hotel, Golf, Country Club & Spa,
Colchester Road, Tollesunt Knights,
MALDON, Essex CM9 8HX
01621 868888
- e-mail: enquiries@fivelakes.co.uk
- website: www.fivelakes.co.uk

•GLOUCESTERSHIRE

B & B
Mrs Carter, Beechmount, BIRDLIP,
Gloucestershire GL4 8JH
01452 862262
- e-mail: thebeechmount@breathemail.net
- website: www.the beechmount.co.uk

Hotel
Chester House Hotel, Victoria Street,
BOURTON-ON-THE-WATER,
Gloucestershire GL54 2BU
01451 820286
- e-mail: juliand@chesterhouse.u-net.com
- website: www.chesterhouse.u-net.com

B & B / Self-Catering
Marilyn & Bob Downes, Box Hedge Farm
(B & B and Self-Catering), Coalpit Heath,
BRISTOL, Gloucestershire BS36 2UN
01454 250786
- e-mail: marilyn@boxhedgefarmbandb.co.uk
- website: www.boxhedgefarmb&b.co.uk

Hotel / Guest House
Beechworth Lawn Hotel, 133 Hales Road,
CHELTENHAM, Gloucestershire GL52 6ST
01242 522583
- e-mail: beechworth.lawn@dial.pipex.com
- website: www.beechworthlawnhotel.co.uk

Guest House / Self-Catering
Dorothy Brook, Tod Cot, Noel Court,
Calf Lane, CHIPPING CAMPDEN,
Gloucestershire GL55 6BS
01386 841127
- e-mail: dotbrook@easicom.com
- website:
  www.stratford-upon-avon.co.uk/honeypat.htm

B & B
Mrs C. Hutsby, Holly House, Ebrington,
CHIPPING CAMPDEN,
Gloucestershire GL55 6NL
01386 593213
- e-mail: hutsby@talk21.com
- website:
  www.stratford-upon-avon.co.uk/hollyhouse.htm

Farm / B & B
Mrs D. Gwilliam, Dryslade Farm,
English Bicknor, COLEFORD,
Gloucestershire, GL16 7PA
01594 860259
- e-mail: dryslade@agriplus.net
- website: www.fweb.org.uk/dryslade

Please mention BRITAIN'S BEST HOLIDAYS when equiring about accommodation

WEBSITE DIRECTORY 195

Hotel
Speech House Hotel, COLEFORD,
Forest of Dean, Gloucestershire GL16 7EL
01594 822607
- e-mail: relax@thespeechhouse.co.uk
- website: www.thespeechhouse.co.uk

B & B
Mr Rackley, Burrows Court, Nibley Green,
North Nibley, DURSLEY,
Gloucestershire GL11 6AZ
01453 546230
- e-mail: burrowscourt@tesco.net
- website: www.burrowscourt.co.uk

Guest House
Mrs E. Hayward, Hyde Wood House,
Cirencester Road, MINCHINHAMPTON,
Gloucestershire GL6 8PE
01453 885504
- e-mail: info@hydewoodhouse.co.uk
- website: www.hydewoodhouse.co.uk

Guest House
Mrs C.A. Anderson, Gunn Mill Guest House,
Lower Spout Lane, MITCHELDEAN,
Gloucestershire GL17 0EA
01594 827577
- e-mail: info@gunnmillhouse.co.uk
- website: www.gunnmillhouse.co.uk

B & B
Mrs F.J. Adams, Aston House,
Broadwell, MORETON-IN-MARSH,
Gloucestershire GL56 0TJ
01451 830475
- e-mail: fja@netcomuk.co.uk
- website:
www.netcomuk.co.uk/~nmfa/aston_house.html

Inn
J.A. Johnston, The Falcon Inn, PAINSWICK,
Gloucestershire GL6 6UN
01452 814222
- e-mail: bleninns@clara.net
- website: www.falconinn.com

B & B
Mrs Sheila Barnfield, Kilmorie, Gloucester
Road, Corse, STAUNTON,
Gloucestershire GL19 3RQ
01452 840224
- e-mail: sheila-barnfield@supanet.com

B & B
Anthea Rhoton, Hyde Crest, Cirencester
Road, Minchinhampton, Near STROUD,
Gloucestershire GL6 8PE
01453 731631
- e-mail: hydecrest@compuserve.com
- website: www.hydecrest.co.uk

Motel style accommodation
Cathie Korn, Symonds Yat Rock Lodge,
Hillersland, Near Coleford, SYMONDS YAT
Gloucestershire GL16 7NY
01594 836191
- e-mail: info@rocklodge.co.uk
- website: www.rocklodge.co.uk

Farmhouse B & B
B. Williams, Abbots Court, Church End,
Twyning, TEWKESBURY,
Gloucestershire GL20 6DA
- e-mail: bernie@abbotscourt.fsbusiness.co.uk

B & B
Mrs Wendy Swait, Inschdene, Atcombe
Road, SOUTH WOODCHESTER, Stroud,
Gloucestershire GL5 5EW
01453 873254
- e-mail: malcolm.swait@repp.co.uk
- website: www.inschdene.co.uk

•HAMPSHIRE

B & B
Mrs Arnold-Brown, Hilden B&B,
Southampton Road, Boldre,
BROCKENHURST, Hampshire SO41 8PT
01590 623682
- website: www.newforestbandb-hilden.co.uk

Campsites
Hayling Island Campsites, Copse Lane,
HAYLING ISLAND, Hampshire PO11 0QB
023 9246 2479
- e-mail: lowertye@euphony.net
- website: www.haylingcampsites.co.uk

Guest House
The Penny Farthing Hotel, Romsey Road,
LYNDHURST, Hampshire SO43 7AA
023 8028 4422
- e-mail: stay@pennyfarthinghotel.co.uk
- website: www.pennyfarthinghotel.co.uk

Guest House
M. Sullivan, Lyndhurst House, 35 Romsey
Road, LYNDHURST, Hampshire SO43 7AR
023 8028 2230
- website: www.lyndhursthouse@aol.com

Guest House
Mrs Tee, Gorse Meadow Guest House,
Sway Road, LYMINGTON,
Hampshire SO41 8LR
01590 673354
- e-mail:
gorse.meadow.guesthouse@wildmushrooms.co.uk
- website: www.wildmushrooms.co.uk

WEBSITE DIRECTORY

B & B
Mrs Thelma Rowe, Tiverton, 9 Cruse Close,
Sway, Near LYMINGTON,
Hampshire SO41 6AY
01590 683092
• e-mail: ronrowe@talk21.com

Farm / B & B
John & Penny Harkinson, Fritham Farm,
Fritham, LYNDHURST,
Hampshire SO43 7HH
023 8081 2333
• e-mail: frithamfarm@supanet.com

Hotel / Guest House
Mr Paul Ames, Ormonde House Hotel,
Southampton Road, LYNDHURST,
Hampshire SO43 7BT
023 8028 2806
• e-mail: info@ormondehouse.co.uk
• website: www.ormondehouse.co.uk

Hotel
Woodlands Lodge Hotel, Bartley Road,
Woodlands, NEW FOREST,
Hampshire SO40 7GN
023 8029 2257
• e-mail: woodlands@nortels.ltd.uk
• website: www.nortels.ltd.uk

Hotel / Guest House
Mr Rennie Law, Whitley Ridge Hotel,
Beaulieu Road, Brockenhurst,
NEW FOREST, Hampshire SO42 7QL
01590 622354
• e-mail: whitleyridge@brockenhurst.co.uk
• website: www.whitleyridge.co.uk

B & B
Graham & Sandra Tubb, Hamilton House,
95 Victoria Road North, Southsea,
PORTSMOUTH, Hampshire PO5 1PS
023 9282 3502
• e-mail: sandra@hamiltonhouse.co.uk
• website: www.hamiltonhouse.co.uk

Hotel
Seacrest Hotel, 11/12 South Parade,
SOUTHSEA, Hampshire PO5 2JB
023 9273 3192
• e-mail: seacrest@mcmail.com
• website: www.seacresthotel.co.uk

Hotel
The Winchester Royal, St Peter Street,
WINCHESTER, Hampshire SO23 8BS
01962 840840
• e-mail: royal@marstonhotels.com
• website: www.marstonhotels.com

•HEREFORDSHIRE

Guest House
Brian Roby, Felton House, FELTON,
Herefordshire HR1 3PH
01432 820366
• e-mail: bandb@ereal.net
• website:
www.SmoothHound.co.uk/hotels/felton.html
or: www.bandbherefordshire.co.uk

Hotel
Mrs J. Williams, Leadon House Hotel, Ross
Road, LEDBURY, Herefordshire HR8 2LP
01531 631199
• e-mail: leadon.house@amserve.net
• website: www.leadonhouse.co.uk

Farmhouse / B & B
Jane West, Church Farm, Coddington,
LEDBURY, Herefordshire HR8 1JJ
01531 640271
• e-mail: jane@dexta.co.uk
• website: www.dexta.co.uk

Farm / Self-Catering
Mrs Elizabeth M. Thomas, Woonton Court,
Leysters, LEOMINSTER,
Herefordshire HR6 0HL
01568 750232
• e-mail:
thomas.woontoncourt@farmersweekly.net

Farm / B & B
Ivy Pritchard, Olchon Cottage Farm,
LONGTOWN, Herefordshire HR2 0NS
01873 860233
• website: www.golden-valley.co.uk/olchon

Hotel
Mrs Alison Curtis, Woodlea Hotel,
Symonds Yat West, ROSS-ON-WYE,
Herefordshire HR9 6BL
01600 890206
• website: www.woodleahotel.com

**FREE or REDUCED RATE
entry to Holiday Visits
and Attractions
see our
READERS' OFFER
VOUCHERS
on pages 35-54**

WEBSITE DIRECTORY 197

•ISLE OF WIGHT

Caravan Park / Self-Catering
Mrs A.J. Coleman, Sunnycott Caravan Park, Rew Street, Gurnard, COWES, Isle of Wight PO31 8NN
01983 292859
• e-mail: sunnycott2000@sunnycott2000.freeserve.co.uk
• website: www.sunnycott.co.uk

Hotel / Self-Catering
Old Park Hotel, Old Park Road, St Lawrence, VENTNOR, Isle of Wight PO38 1XS
01983 852583
• e-mail: admin@oldpark-hotel.co.uk
• website: www.oldpark-hotel.co.uk

Caravan Site
Castlehaven Caravan Site, Mr L.F. Wayman-Hales, Mews Cottage, 93 High Street, VENTNOR, Isle of Wight PL38 1LU
01983 855567
• e-mail: caravans@castlehaven.co.uk
• website: www.castlehaven.co.uk

•KENT

Hotel
Carol Jones, Warren Cottage Hotel, 136 The Street, Willesborough, ASHFORD, Kent TN24 0NB
01233 621905
• e-mail: general@warrencottage.co.uk
• website: warrencottage.co.uk

Hotel
Mrs J. Webb, Hanson Hotel, 41 Belvedere Road, BROADSTAIRS, Kent CT10 1PF
01843 868936
• e-mail: hotelhanson@aol.com

Farm
Mrs Lewana Castle, Great Field Farm, Misling Lane, Stelling Minnis, CANTERBURY, Kent CT4 6DE
01227 709223
• e-mail: greatfieldfarm@aol.com

Farm
Bower Farm House, Stelling Minnis, CANTERBURY, Kent CT4 6BB
01227 709430
• e-mail: book@bowerbb.freeserve.co.uk
• website: www.kentac.co.uk/bowerfm

Guest House
Mr R.D. Linch, Upper Ansdore, Duckpit Lane, Petham, CANTERBURY, Kent CT4 5QB
01227 700672
• e-mail: upperansdore@hotels.activebooking.com
• website: www.SmoothHound.co.uk/hotels/upperans.html

Guest House
Penny Farthing Guest House, 109 Maison Dieu Road, DOVER, Kent CT16 1RT
01304 205563
• e-mail: pennyfarthing@doverbtinternet.com
• website: www.pennyfarthingdover.com

Hotel
Mrs M.A. Shorland, Wycliffe Hotel, 63 Bouverie Road West, FOLKESTONE, Kent CT20 2RN
01303 252186
• e-mail: shorland@wycliffehotel.freeserve.co.uk
• website: www.visitus.co.uk/bnbhtm/wycliffe.htm

Country House Guest House
Mrs S.M. Woodard, Southgate, Rye Road, HAWKHURST, Kent TN18 5DA
01580 752526
• e-mail: Susan.Woodard@southgate.uk.net
• website: www.southgate.uk.net/

Hotel
Stade Court, West Parade, HYTHE, Kent CT21 6DT
01303 268263
• e-mail: stadecourt@marstonhotels.com
• website: www.marstonhotels.com

B & B / Self-Catering
Mrs Diane Leat, Bramley Knowle Farm, Eastwood Road, Ulcombe, MAIDSTONE, Kent
01622 858878
• e-mail: diane@bramleyknowlefarm.co.uk
• website: www.bramleyknowlefarm.co.uk

B & B
Mr D. Bage, Forge Cottage, Lynstead, SITTINGBOURNE, Kent ME9 0RH
01795 521273
• website: www.s-h-systems.co.uk/hotels/forge.html

Self-Catering
Charles Foulkes, 3 Great Pagehurst Farm Cottages, Pagehurst Road, STAPLEHURST, Kent TN12 0JD
07790 675994
• e-mail: chasfoulkes@madasafish.com
• website: www.mill-cottage.com

Please mention BRITAINS BEST HOLIDAYS when enquiring about accommodation

198 WEBSITE DIRECTORY

•LANCASHIRE

B & B
Mr & Mrs M. Smith, The Old Coach House,
50 Dean St, BLACKPOOL,
Lancashire FY4 1BP
01253 349195
- e-mail: blackpool@theoldcoachhouse.freeserve.co.uk
- website: www.theoldcoachhouse.freeserve.co.uk

B & B
Mrs Melanie Smith, Capernwray House,
Capernwray, CARNFORTH,
Lancashire LA6 1AE
01524 732363
- e-mail: thesmiths@capernwrayhouse.com
- website: www.capernwrayhouse.com

Hotel
New England Inn, 314 Clifton Drive North,
LYTHAM ST ANNES, Lancashire FY8 2PB
01253 722355
- e-mail: Anthony.Duggan@btinternet.com
- website: www.hotel-lythamstannes.co.uk

Hotel
Dalmeny Hotel, 19-33 South Promenade, ST ANNES ON SEA, Lancashire FY8 1LX
01253 712236
- e-mail: reservations@dalmeny.demon.co.uk
- website: www.dalmenyhotel.com

•LEICESTERSHIRE

Guest House
Mrs Indge, The Highbury Guest House,
146 Leicester Road, LOUGHBOROUGH,
Leicestershire LE11 2AQ
01509 230545
- e-mail: emkhighbury@supanet.com
- website: www.SmoothHound.co.uk/highbury.html

•LINCOLNSHIRE

Guest House
Edward King House, The Old Palace,
LINCOLN, Lincolnshire LN2 1PU
01522 528778
- e-mail: enjoy@ekhs.org.uk
- website: www.ekhs.org.uk

Guest House
J. & V. Rosling, Savill Guest House,
203 Yarnborough Road, LINCOLN,
Lincolnshire LN1 3NQ
01522 523261
- e-mail: vvn@themail.co.uk
- website: www.savillhouse.co.uk

Self-Catering
E. Mary Cooper, 18 St Mary's Lane,
LOUTH, Lincolnshire LN11 0DT
01507 604408
- e-mail: uehydon@thisvillage.com
- website: www.thisvillage.com/uwghydon

Hotel
Mrs S.J. Doe, The Priory Hotel, Eastgate,
LOUTH, Lincolnshire, LN5 8EN
01507 602930
- website: www.theprioryhotel.com

Farm / B & B / Caravan
Mrs Cave, Sycamore Farm, 6 Station Road,
Gedney Hill, SPALDING,
Lincolnshire PE12 0NP
01406 330445
- e-mail: sycamore.farm@virgin.net
- website: www.bedandbreakfast.freeserve.co.uk

Farm / Board
Mrs Evans, Willow Farm, THORPE
FENDYKES, Wainfleet, Skegness,
Lincolnshire PE24 4QH
01754 830316
- website: www.willowfarmholidays.fsnet.co.uk

•NORFOLK

Self-Catering
Mrs Enid Parry, Beechwood, Goose Lane,
ALBY, Norfolk NR11 7PS
01263 768606
- e-mail: beechwoodcottage@talk21.com
- website: www.beechwoodcottages.co.uk

Self-Catering / Caravans & Pine Lodges
Castaways Holiday Park, Paston Road,
BACTON, Norfolk NR12 0JB
01692 650436
- e-mail: castaways.bacton@ic24.net
- website: www.castawaysholidaypark.co.uk

Self-Catering
Blue Riband Holidays, CAISTER-ON-SEA,
Great Yarmouth, Norfolk NR29 4HA
01493 730445
- website: www.blue-riband.com

Guest House
Mr David Alexander, The Hedges Guest
House, Tunstead Road, COLTISHALL,
Norfolk NR12 7AL
01603 738361
- e-mail: thehedges@msn.com
- website: www.hedgesbandb.co.uk

WEBSITE DIRECTORY 199

Farmhouse B & B
Mrs J.A. Bell, Peacock House, Peacock Lane, Old Beetley, DEREHAM, Norfolk NR20 4DG
01362 860371
- e-mail: peackh@aol.com
- website: www.SmoothHound.co.uk/hotels/peacockh.html

Farm B & B
Mrs S.A. Kellett, Park Farm, Gressenhall, DEREHAM, Norfolk NR19 2QL
01362 860245
- e-mail: personaltouch@3wa.co.uk
- website: www.parkfarmnorfolk.co.uk

B & B
Jeanne Partridge, Shillingstone, Church Road, Old Beetley, DEREHAM, Norfolk NR20 4AD
01362 861099
- e-mail: jeannepartridge@ukgateway.net
- website: www.norfolkshillingstone.co.uk

Self-Catering
Moor Farm Stable Cottages, Moor Farm, FOXLEY, Dereham, Norfolk NR20 4QN
01362 688523
- e-mail: moorfarm@aol.com
- website: www.moorfarmstablecottages.co.uk

Self-Catering Chalets
Mrs June Hudson, 42 Lark Way, Bradwell, GREAT YARMOUTH, Norfolk NR31 8SB
01493 444700
- e-mail: wintertonholiday@aol.com
- website: www.wintertonholidays.co.uk

Self-Catering
Cathy Saxelby, Silver Birches Holidays, Grebe Island, Lower Street, HORNING, Norfolk
01692 630858
- e-mail: cathy.saxelby@virgin.net
- website: www.silverbirchesholidays.co.uk

Guest House / Self-Catering
L.D. Poore, 3 Wodehouse Road, OLD HUNSTANTON, Norfolk PE36 6JD
01485 534206
- e-mail: st.crispins@dial.pipex.com
  or: cobblers.cottage@dial.pipex.com

Self-Catering
Peter & Fionna Harnett, The Cottage, Crossbeck Close, ILKNEY LS29 9JW
01943 601743
- e-mail: fylfot@dialstart.net
- website: www.rosycot.co.uk

Farm / Board
Mrs Davidson, Holmdene Farm, Beeston, KING'S LYNN, Norfolk, PE32 2NJ
01328 701284
- e-mail: holmdenefarm@farmersweekly.net
- website: www.northnorfolk.co.uk/holmdenefarm

Guest House
Colin & Fiona Goodhead, White House Farm, KNAPTON, Norfolk NR28 0RX
01263 721344
- e-mail: GOODHEAD@whfarm.swinternet.co.uk
- website: www.geocities.com/whitehousefarmnorfolk

Farm / B & B
Joanna Douglas, Greenacres Farm, Woodgreen, LONG STRATTON, Norfolk NR15 2RR
01508 530261
- e-mail: greenacresfarm@hugworld.co.uk

Guest House B & B
Mrs Christine Lilah Thrower, Whincliff, Cromer Road, MUNDESLEY-ON-SEA, Norfolk NR11 8DU
01263 721554
- e-mail: whincliff@freeuk.com
- website: http:/whincliff.freeuk.com

Guest House / Farm / Self-Catering
Tadorna Holdings Ltd, Church Farm, NARBOROUGH, Kings Lynn, Norfolk PE32 1TE
01760 337696
- e-mail: nickystlawrence@ouvip.com
- website: www.churchfarmholidayhomes.com

Guest House
Mrs D. Curtis, Rosedale, 145 Earlhay Road, NORWICH, Norfolk NR2 3RG
01603 453743
- e-mail: drebae@aol.com
- website: www.http://members.aol.com/drebae.

Board
Mrs J. Read, George's House, The Nurseries, WOODTON, Near Bungay, Norfolk NR35 2LZ
01508 482214
- website: www.rossmag.com/georges/

Please mention
Britain's Best Holidays
when enquiring about accommodation

•NORTHUMBERLAND

B & B
Eileen Finn, Thornley House, ALLENDALE, Northumberland NE47 9NH
01434 683255
• e-mail: e.finn@ukonline.co.uk
• website: www.web.ukonline.co.uk/e.finn

Self-Catering
Mrs Vicki Taylor, Quality Self Catering, Letton Lodge, ALNMOUTH, Northumberland NE66 2RJ
01665 830633
• e-mail: lettonlodge@aol.com
• website: www.alnmouth.co.uk

Hotel
Mr Orde, The Famous Schooner Hotel, Northumberland Street, ALNMOUTH, Northumberland NE66 2RS
01665 830216
• e-mail: ghost@schooner.sagehost.co.uk
• website: www.schooner.sagehost.co.uk

B & B
Marilyn Davidson, 7 Benthall, BEADNELL, Northumberland NE67 5BQ
01665 720900
• e-mail: stay@7benthall.co.uk
• website: www.7benthall.co.uk

B & B
S. Newington-Bridges, High Steads, Lowick, BERWICK-UPON-TWEED, Northumberland TD15 2QE
01289 388689
• e-mail: highstead@aol.com
• website: www.lindisfarne.org.uk

Guest House / Self-Catering / Caravan
C.T. & M.J. Matthews, The Hayes, CORBRIDGE, Northumberland NE45 5LP
01434 632010
• e-mail: mjct@mmatthews.fsbusiness.co.uk
• website: www.hayes-corbridge

Guest House
John & Edith Howliston, North Cottage, Birling, WARKWORTH, Morpeth, Northumberland NE65 0XS
01665 711263
• e-mail: edithandjohn@another.com
• website: www.accta.co.uk/north

•NOTTINGHAMSHIRE

Hotel
C.A. Pike, Old England Hotel, Sutton-on-Trent, NEWARK, Nottinghamshire NG23 6QA
01636 821216
• e-mail: theoldenglandhotel@ukonline.co.uk
• website: www.theoldenglandhotel.co.uk

•OXFORDSHIRE

Guest House
Mrs Elizabeth Reay, Apple Tree Guest House, Buscot Village, Faringdon, LECHLADE, Oxfordshire SN7 8DA
01367 252592
• e-mail: emreay@aol.com
• website: www.geocities.com/elizabeth.reay

Farm / Board
Mrs Katherine Brown, Hill Grove Farm, Crawley Road, MINSTER LOVELL, Oxfordshire OX29 ONA
01993 703120
• e-mail: kbrown@eggconnect.net

B & B / Guest House
Diana & Richard Mitchell, Highfield West, 188 Cumnor Hill, OXFORD, Oxfordshire OX2 9PJ
01865 863007
• e-mail: highfieldwest@email.msn.com
• website: www.oxfordcity.co.uk/accom/highfield-west/

Guest House
Mrs Elizabeth Simpson, Field View, Wood Green, WITNEY, Oxfordshire OX28 1DE
01993 705485
• e-mail: jsimpson@netcomuk.co.uk
• website: www.netcomuk.co.uk/~kearse/index.html

Inn
Killingworth Castle Inn, Glympton Road, Wootton, By WOODSTOCK, Oxfordshire OX20 1EJ
01993 811401
• e-mail: wiggiscastle@aol.com
• website: www.oxlink.co.uk/woodstock/kilcastle

Visit the FHG website
www.holidayguides.com
for details of the wide choice of accommodation
featured in the full range of FHG titles

•SHROPSHIRE

Farm / B & B
Mrs Brereton, Brereton's Farm, Woolston, CHURCH STRETTON, Shropshire SY6 6QD
01694 781201
- e-mail: brereton @tao2000.net
- website: www.tao2000.net/~brereton/

Farm B & B
Mrs M. Jones, Acton Scott Farm, Acton Scott, CHURCH STRETTON, Shropshire SY6 6QN
01694 781260
- e-mail: edandm@clara.co.uk
- website: http://welcome.to/acton-scott-b&b

Inn
The Crown Inn, Hopton Wafers, CLEOBURY MORTIMER, Kidderminster, Shropshire DY14 0NB
01299 270372
- e-mail: desk@crownathopton.co.uk
- website: www.crownathopton.co.uk

Inn
Mr Richard Arnold, The Crown Country Inn, MUNSLOW, Near Craven Arms, Shropshire SY7 9ET
01584 841205
- e-mail: crown.country.inn@ntlworld.com
- website: www.crowncountryinn.co.uk

Hotel
Miles Hunter, Pen-y-Dyffryn Country Hotel, OSWESTRY, Shropshire SY10 7JD
01691 653700
- e-mail: stay@peny.co.uk
- website: www.peny.co.uk

Guest House B & B
P.A. Morrissey, Top Farm House, Knockin, Near OSWESTRY, Shropshire SY10 8HN
- e-mail: p.a.m.@knockin.freeserve.co.uk
- website: www.topfarmknockin.co.uk

Guest House
Judie McCoy, The Stiperstones Guest House, 18 Coton Crescent, Coton Hill, SHREWSBURY, Shropshire SY1 2NZ
01743 246720
- e-mail: Thestiperstones@aol.com
- website: www.Thestiperstones.com

Self-Catering
Mrs Ann Cartwright, Ryton Farm, Ryton, Dorrington, SHREWSBURY, Shropshire SY5 7LY
01743 718449
- website: www.rytonfarm.co.uk

•SOMERSET

B & B / Self-Catering
Jackie & David Bishop, Toghill House Farm, Wick, BATH, Somerset BS30 5RT
01225 891261
- website: www.toghillhousefarm

Hotel
Elaine Sexton, Bailbrook Lodge Hotel, 35-37 London Road West, BATH, Somerset BA1 7HZ
01225 859090
- e-mail: hotel@bailbrooklodge.co.uk
- website: www.bailbrooklodge.co.uk

Guest House
Jan Wotley, The Albany Guest House, 24 Crescent Gardens, BATH, Somerset BA1 2NB
01225 313339
- e-mail: the_albany@lineone.net
- website: www.bath.org/hotel/albany.htm

Guest House
Mrs C. Bryson, Walton Villa, 3 Newbridge Hill, BATH, Somerset BA1 3PW
01225 482792
- e-mail: walton.villa@virgin.net
- website: www.walton.izest.com

B & B
Mrs Chrissie Besley, The Old Red House, 37 Newbridge Road, BATH, Somerset BA1 3HE
01225 330464
- website: www.oldredhouse.co.uk

Self-Catering
Mrs V. Beale, Brean Sands Holiday Flats, 43 Hillview, South Road, BREAN. Somerset TA8 2RD
07000 789334
- e-mail: valbeale@easicom.com

Self-Catering
T.M. Hicks, Diamond Farm, Weston Road, BREAN, Nr Burnham-on-Sea, Somerset TA8 2RL
01278 751263
- e-mail: trevor@diamondfarm42.freeserve.co.uk
- website: www.diamondfarm.co.uk

Caravan Holiday Homes
Beachside Holiday Park, Coast Road, BREAN SANDS, Somerset TA8 2QZ
01278 751346
- e-mail: beachside@breansands.fsnet.co.uk
- website: www.beachsideholidaypark.co.uk

WEBSITE DIRECTORY

B & B
Mrs Alexander, Priors Mead, 23 Rectory Road, BURNHAM-ON-SEA, Somerset TA8 2BZ
01278 782116
• e-mail: priorsmead@aol.com
• website: www.SmoothHound.co.uk/hotels/priors.html

B & B
Barry Harvey, Butcombe Farm, Aldwick Lane, BUTCOMBE, North Somerset BS40 7UW
01761 462380
• e-mail: info@butcombe-farm.demon.co.uk
• website: www.butcombe-farm.demon.co.uk

Caravan & Camping Park
Broadway House Holiday Touring Caravan & Camping Park, CHEDDAR, Somerset BS27 3DB
01934 742610
• e-mail: enquiries@broadwayhouse.uk.com
• website: www.broadwayhouse.uk.com

Self-Catering Cottages
Buckland, Spring Cottage, Venns Gate, CHEDDAR, Somerset BS27 3LW
01934 742493
• e-mail: buckland@springcottages.co.uk
• website: www.springcottages.co.uk

Farm / Board
Mrs Humphrey, Highercombe Farm, DULVERTON, Exmoor, Somerset TA22 9PT
01398 323616
• e-mail: abigail@highercombe.demon.co.uk
• website: www.highercombe.demon.co.uk

Farm / Self-Catering
Mrs Styles, Wintershead Farm, Simonsbath, EXMOOR, Somerset TA24 7LF
01643 831222
• website: www.wintershead.co.uk

Self-Catering
Draydon Cottages, EXMOOR, c/o Karen Bennett, 12 St Anthony's Close, Ottery St Mary, Devon EX11 1EN
01404 812859
• e-mail: karen@draydon.fsnet.co.uk
• website: www.escapetoexmoor.co.uk

B & B
Gaye Phillips, Hermitage, Station Road, ILMINSTER, Somerset TA19 9BE
01460 53028
• website: www.home.freeuk.net/hermitage

Self-Catering
Mrs N. Hanson, Woodcombe Lodges, Bratton, MINEHEAD, Somerset TA24 8SQ
01643 702789
• e-mail: nicola@woodcombelodge.co.uk
• website: www.woodcombelodge.co.uk

Guest House
Gordon Wright, Clements Cottage, Tivington, Near MINEHEAD, Somerset TA24 8SU
01643 703970
• e-mail: clementscottage@exmoorbandb.co.uk
• website: www.exmoorbandb.co.uk

Caravan / Self-Catering
Mr G. Daniel, Beeches Holiday Park, Blue Anchor Bay, MINEHEAD, Somerset TA24 6JW
01984 640391
• e-mail: info@beeches-park.co.uk
• website: www.beeches-park.co.uk

Self-Catering
Mrs Joan Atkins, 2 Edgcott Cottage, Exford, MINEHEAD, Somerset TA24 7QG
01643 831564
• e-mail: info@stilemoorexmoor.co.uk
• website: www.stilemoorexmoor.co.uk

Self-Catering / B & B
Joy Thorne, Gothic House, MUCHELNEY, Langport, Somerset TA10 0DW
01458 250624
• e-mail: joy-thorne@totalserve.co.uk

Guest House
Mr Wade, Ashlea House, High Street, NORTH CADBURY, Somerset BA22 7DP
01963 440891
• website: www.ashleahouse.co.uk

Hotel
Mrs Murphy, Farthings Hotel & Restaurant, Hatch Beauchamp, TAUNTON, Somerset TA3 6SG
01823 480664
• website: www.farthingshotel.com

FREE or REDUCED RATE entry to Holiday Visits and Attractions — see our READERS' OFFER VOUCHERS on pages 35-54

WEBSITE DIRECTORY 203

Self-Catering
Croft Holiday Cottages, Anchor Street,
WATCHET, Somerset TA23 0BY
01984 631121
- e-mail: croftcottages@talk21.com
- website:
  www.cottageguide.co.uk/croft-cottages

Holiday Caravans
Westbay Caravan Park, Cleeve Hill,
WATCHET, Somerset TA23 0BJ
01984 631261
- e-mail: alistair@westbay2000.freeserve.co.uk
- website: www.westbaycaravanpark.co.uk

•STAFFORDSHIRE

Farm
Mrs M. Hiscoe-James, Offley Grove Farm,
Adbaston, ECCLESHALL,
Staffordshire ST20 0QB
01785 280205
- e-mail: accom@offleygrovefarm.freeserve.co.uk
- website: www.offleygrovefarm.co.uk

Guest House
Mrs Griffiths, Prospect House Guest House,
334 Cheadle Road, Cheddleton, LEEK,
Staffordshire ST13 7BW
01782 550639
- e-mail: prospect@talk21.com
- website:
  www.touristnetuk.com/wm/prospect/index.htm

•SUFFOLK

Hotel
Chris Knight, Ravenwoodhall, Rougham,
BURY ST EDMUNDS, Suffolk IP30 9JA
01359 271542
- e-mail: enquiries@ravenwoodhall.co.uk
- website: www.ravenwoodhall.co.uk

Self-Catering
Maltings Holiday Accommodation,
c/o Ivy House Farm Hotel, Ivy Lane,
Oulton Broad, LOWESTOFT,
Suffolk NR33 8HY
01502 501353
- e-mail: maltings@ivyhousefarm.co.uk
- website: www.ivyhousefarm.co.uk

Farm House / Self-Catering
Mrs Sarah Kindred, High House Farm,
Cransford, WOODBRIDGE, Suffolk IP13 9PD
01728 663431
- e-mail: bed&breakfast@highhousefarm.co.uk
- website: www.highhousefarm.co.uk

•SURREY

Hotel
Chase Lodge Hotel, 10 Park Road, Hampton
Wick, KINGSTON-UPON-THAMES,
Surrey KT1 4AS
020 8943 1862
- e-mail: info@chaselodgehotel.com
- website: www.chaselodgehotel.com

Self-Catering
Mr I.R.V. Langford, 1 Fleetway,
THORPE, Surrey TW20 8UA
01932 560503
- e-mail: rod@irvl.freeserve.co.uk
- website: www.irvl.freeserve.co.uk

•EAST SUSSEX

Hotel
Lansdowne Hotel, King Edward's Parade,
EASTBOURNE, East Sussex, BN21 1EE
01323 725174
- e-mail: the.lansdowne@btinternet.com
- website: www.the.lansdowne.btinternet.co.uk

Country Hotel
Cleavers Lyng Country Hotel, Church Road,
HERSTMONCEUX, Near Hailsham,
East Sussex BN27 1QJ
01323 833131
- e-mail: scil@supanet.com
- website: www.cleaverslyng.co.uk

Guest House
Mrs J. P. Hadfield, Jeake's House, Mermaid
Street, RYE, East Sussex TN31 7ET
01797 222828
- e-mail: jeakeshouse@btinternet.com
- website: www.jeakeshouse.com

•WEST SUSSEX

B & B
Deborah S. Collinson, The Old Priory,
80 North Bersted Street, BOGNOR REGIS,
West Sussex PO22 9AQ
01243 863580
- e-mail: old.priory@mcmail.com
- website: www.old.priory.mcmail.com

B & B
Lady M.R. Milton, Beacon Lodge B&B,
London Road, Watersfield,
West Sussex RH20 1NH
01798 831026
- e-mail: beaconlodge@freeuk.com
- website: www.beaconlodge.co.uk

•WARWICKSHIRE

Guest House
Mr J. Worboys, Broadlands Guest House,
23 Evesham Place, STRATFORD-UPON-
AVON, Warwickshire CV37 6HT
01789 299181
- e-mail: broadlands.com@virgin.net
- website:
  www.stratford-upon-avon.co.uk/broadlands.htm

Self-Catering
Karen Cauvin, 34 Evesham Place,
STRATFORD-UPON-AVON,
Warwickshire CV37 6HT
01789 550197
- e-mail: karen.cauvin@ntlworld.com
- website: www.anneshouse.com

Guest House
Mr Carr, Penryn Guest House,
126 Alcester Road, STRATFORD-UPON-
AVON, Warwickshire CV37 9DP
01789 293718
- e-mail: penrynhouse@btinternet.com
- website:
  www.SmoothHound.co.uk/hotels/penryn.html

Guest House
Julia Downie, Holly Tree Cottage, Pathlow,
STRATFORD-UPON-AVON,
Warwickshire CV37 0ES
01789 204461
- e-mail:
  john@hollytree-cottage.co.uk
- website: www.hollytree-cottage.co.uk

Guest House / Self-Catering
Mrs Elizabeth Draisey, Forth House, 44 High
Street, WARWICK, Warwickshire CV34 4AX
01926 401512
- e-mail: info@forthhouseuk.co.uk
- website: www.forthhouseuk.co.uk

•WEST MIDLANDS

Guest House
P.J. Hiley, Box Trees Farm, Stratford Road,
Hockley Heath, SOLIHULL,
West Midlands B94 6EA
01564 782039
- e-mail: bandb@boxtrees.co.uk
- website: www.boxtrees.co.uk

Please mention this guide when enquiring about accommodation

•WILTSHIRE

Self-Catering
The Cyder House & The Cheese House,
c/o Mrs Sue King, Wick Farm, Lacock,
CHIPPENHAM, Wiltshire SN15 2LU
01249 730244
- e-mail: kingsilverlands2@btinternet.com

Farmhouse / Board
Mrs D. Robinson, Boyds Farm, Gastard,
Near Corsham, Wiltshire SN13 9PT
01249 713146
- e-mail:
  dorothyrobinson@boyds.farm.freeserve.co.uk

Farmhouse / Board
Susan Barnes, Lovett Farm,
Little Somerford, Near MALMESBURY,
Wiltshire SN14 8RP
01666 823268
- e-mail: lovettfarm@btinternet.com
- website:
  www.SmoothHound.co.uk/hotels/lovett

Farm Guest House
J.W. Lanham, Newton Farmhouse,
Southampton Road, Whiteparish,
SALISBURY, Wiltshire SP5 2QL
01794 884416
- e-mail: enquiries@newtonfarmhouse.co.uk
- website: www.newtonfarmhouse.co.uk

Self-Catering
Mr G. Gould, The Old Stables, Bridge Farm,
Lower Road, Britford, SALISBURY,
Wiltshire SP5 4DY
01722 349002
- e-mail: mail@old-stables.co.uk
- website: www.old-stables.co.uk

Guest House
Alan & Dawn Curnow, Hayburn Wyke Guest
House, 72 Castle Road, SALISBURY,
Wiltshire SP1 3RL
01722 412627
- e-mail: hayburn.wyke@tinyonline.co.uk
- website: www.hayburnwykeguesthouse.co.uk

Farmhouse B & B
A. Shering, Swaynes Firs Farm, Grimsdyke,
Coombe Bissett, SALISBURY,
Wiltshire SP5 5RF
01725 519240
- e-mail: swaynes.firs@virgin.net
- website: www.swaynesfirs.co.uk

•WORCESTERSHIRE

Farm B & B
Pam Hutcheon, Burhill Farm, Buckland, Nea BROADWAY, Worcestershire WR12 7LY
01386 858171
• e-mail: burhillfarm@yahoo.co.uk
• website: www.burhillfarm.co.uk

Farmhouse B & B
Mrs Jane Hill, Lowerfield Farm, Willersey, BROADWAY, Worcestershire WR11 5HF
01386 858273
• e-mail: info@lowerfield-farm.co.uk
• website: www.lowerfield-farm.co.uk

B & B
The Crown & Sandys, Main Road, Ombersley, DROITWICH, Worcestershire WR9 9AQ
01905 620252
• e-mail: crown&sandys@evertons.co.uk

Hotel
Mrs Julie Josey, Mount Pleasant Hotel, Belle Vue Terrace, GREAT MALVERN, Worcestershire WR14 4PZ
01684 561837
• e-mail: mountpleasant@btinternet.com
• website: www.mountpleasanthotel.co.uk

Guest House
Mrs S.A. Wynn, The Old Smithy, Pirton, WORCESTER, Worcestershire WR8 9EJ
01905 820482
• e-mail: Welcome@TheOldSmithy.co.uk
• website: www.SmoothHound.com/hotels/oldsmith.html

•EAST YORKSHIRE

B & B
Paws-a-While, KILNWICK PERCY, East Yorkshire YO42 1UF
01759 301168
• e-mail: paws.a.while@lineone.net
• website: www.pawsawhile.net

Farm B & B
Mrs G. Bowden, Eastgate Farm Cottage, RUDSTON, East Yorkshire YO25 4UX
01262 420150
• website: www.eastgatefarmcottage.com

•NORTH YORKSHIRE

Guest House
Mr Kingsley, Arbutus Guest House, Riverside, CLAPHAM, Near Settle, North Yorkshire LA2 8DS
01524 251240
• e-mail: info@arbutus.co.uk
• website: www.arbutus.co.uk

Inn
Foresters Arms, 20 Main Street, GRASSINGTON, Near Skipton, North Yorkshire BD23 5AA
01756 752349
• e-mail: theforesters@totalise.co.uk

Self-Catering
Mrs A.M. Durance, Harrogate Holiday Cottages, The Old Post Office, Kettlesing, HARROGATE, North Yorkshire HG3 2LB
01423 772700
• e-mail: bookings@harrogateholidays.co.uk
• website: www.harrogateholidays.co.uk

B & B
Mr & Mrs C. Richardson, The Coppice, 9 Studley Road, HARROGATE, North Yorkshire HG1 5JU
01423 569626
• e-mail: coppice@harrogate.com
• website: www.harrogate.com/coppice

Farm B & B / Self-Catering
John & Felicity Wiles, Sinnington Common Farm, KIRKBY MOORSIDE, York, North Yorkshire YO62 6NX
01751 431719
• e-mail: felicity@scfarm.demon.co.uk
• website: www.scfarm.demon.co.uk

Hotel
Mrs Ella Bowes, Banavie, Roxby Road, Thornton-Le-Dale, PICKERING, North Yorkshire YO18 7SX
01751 474616
• e-mail: ella@banavie-fsbusiness.co.uk
• website: www.SmoothHound.co.uk/hotels/banavie

Visit the FHG website
www.holidayguides.com
for details of the wide choice of accommodation featured in the full range of FHG titles

Guest House
Sue & Tony Hewitt, Harmony Country Lodge, 80 Limestone Road, Burniston, SCARBOROUGH,
North Yorkshire YO13 0DG
0800 2985840
- e-mail: harmonylodge@cwcom.net
- website: www.spiderweb.co.uk/harmony

Farm B & B
Valerie Green, Killerby Cottage Farm, Killerby Lane, Cayton, SCARBOROUGH, North Yorkshire YO11 3TP
01723 581236
- e-mail:valgreen@killerbycottagefarm.fsnet.co.uk
- website: www.killerbycottagefarm.fsnet.co.uk

Hotel / Guest House
D.B. Hurrell, The Anchor, 61 Northstead, Manor Drive, SCARBOROUGH,
North Yorkshire YO12 6AF
01723 364518
- e-mail: theanchorhotel@hotmail.com

Hotel
Mrs M.M Abbott, Howdale Hotel,
121 Queen's Parade, SCARBOROUGH, North Yorkshire YO12 7HU
0500 400478
- e-mail: maria_keith_howdalehotel@yahoo.co.uk
- website: www.howdalehotel.moonfruit.com

Conference, Education & Holiday Centre
Cober Hill Conference, Education & Holiday Centre, Newlands Road, Cloughton, SCARBOROUGH, North Yorkshire YO13 0AR
01723 870310
- e-mail: enquiries@coberhill.co.uk
- website: www.coberhill.co.uk

Self-Catering
Peter & Maggie Martin, Gowland Farm, Gowland Lane, Cloughton, SCARBOROUGH,
North Yorkshire YO13 0DU
01723 870924
- e-mail: gowlandfarm@hotmail.com
- website: www.gowlandfarm.co.uk

Hotel
Ganton Grey Hound, Main Street, Ganton, Near SCARBOROUGH,
North Yorkshire YO12 4NX
01944 710116
- e-mail: gantongreyhound@supanet.com
- website: www.gantongreyhound.com

Self-Catering
Brenda Jones, New Close Farm, Kirkby Malham, SKIPTON,
North Yorkshire BD23 4DP
01729 830240
- e-mail: newclose@farmersweekly.net

Guest House
Sharon Barker, Fourways Guest House, Townend, THIRSK, North Yorkshire YO7 1PY
01845 522601
- e-mail: fairways@nyorks.fsbusiness.com.uk

Inn
Mr Anderson, Long Ashes Inn,
THRESHFIELD, Near Skipton,
North Yorkshire BD23 5PN
01756 752434
- e-mail: info@longashesinn.co.uk
- website: www.longashesinn.co.uk

Self-Catering
June Roberts, White Rose Holiday Cottages, 5 Brook Park, Sleighs, Nr WHITBY,
North Yorkshire YO21 1RT
01947 810763
- e-mail: enquiries@whiterosecottages.com
- website: www.whiterosecottages.com

B & B / Self-Catering / Holiday Caravans
Mr & Mrs Tyerman, Partridge Nest Farm, Eskdaleside, Sleights, WHITBY,
North Yorkshire YO22 5ES
01947 810450
- e-mail: pnfarm@aol.com
- website: www.tmis.uk.com/partridge-nest/

Self-Catering
Mrs O. Hepworth, Land of Nod Farm, Ugthorpe, Near WHITBY,
North Yorkshire YO21 2BL
01947 840325
- e-mail: colin@thecottage-ugthorpe.freeserve.co.uk
- website: www.thecottage-ugthorpe.freeserve.co.uk

Hotel
Seacliffe Hotel, North Promenade,
West Cliff, WHITBY,
North Yorkshire YO21 3JX
01947 603139
- e-mail: julie@seacliffe.fsnet.co.uk
- website: www.seacliffe.co.uk

Self-Catering
Mr Eddleston, Greenhouses Farm Cottages Lealholm, NEAR WHITBY, North Yorkshire YO21 2AD
01947 897486
- e-mail: n_eddleston@yahoo.com
- website: www.greenhouses-farm-cottages.co.uk

Self-Catering
York Lakeside Lodges, Moor Lane, YORK, North Yorkshire YO24 2QU
01904 702346
- e-mail: neil@yorklakesidelodges.co.uk
- website: www.yorklakesidelodges.co.uk

Guest House
Mr Gary Hudson, Orillia House,
89 The Village, Stockton on Forest,
YORK, North Yorkshire YO3 9UP
01904 400600
- e-mail: orillia@globalnet.co.uk
- website: www.orilliahouse.co.uk

Guest House
Mont Clare Guest House, 32 Claremont Terrace, Gillygate, YORK,
North Yorkshire YO31 7EJ
01904 627054
- e-mail: montclarey@aol.com
- website: www.mont-clare.co.uk

Farm / Self-Catering
Mrs Robinson, Valley View Farm,
Old Byland, Helmsley, YORK,
North Yorkshire YO6 5LG
01439 798221
- e-mail: sally@valleyviewfarm.com
- website: www.valleyviewfarm.com

Farmhouse B & B
High Gaterley Farmhouse, Castle Howard Estate, YORK, North Yorkshire YO60 7HT
01653 694636
- e-mail: relax@highgaterley.com
- website: www.highgaterley.com

•WEST YORKSHIRE

Farm B & B / Self-Catering
H.H. Brown, Currer Laithe Farm, Long Lee, KEIGHLEY, West Yorkshire BD21 4SL
01535 604387
- website:
www.edgey8843.free-online.co.uk/currer/index.htm

•ISLE OF MAN

Hotel
Port Erin Hotels, Wilson House, Promenade, PORT ERIN, Isle of Man IM9 6LH
44 1624 833558
- e-mail: fhg@porterinhotels.com
- website: www.porterinhotels.com

•CHANNEL ISLANDS

Self-Catering
Mark Hesse, Swallow Apartments,
Les Clotures, L'Ancresse, GUERNSEY,
Channel Islands
01481 249633
- e-mail: swallowapt@aol.com
- website: www.swallowapartments.com

•SCOTLAND

•ABERDEEN, BANFF & MORAY

Self-Catering
Willie Bremner, Bremners of Foggie, Old School, ABERCHIRDER, Huntly,
Aberdeenshire AB54 7XS
01466 780260
- website: www.bremnersoffoggie.co.uk

Guest House
E. Robertson, Aberdeen Springbank Guesthouse, 6 Springbank Terrace,
ABERDEEN, Aberdeenshire AB11 6LS
01224 592048
- e-mail: betty@springbank6.fsnet.co.uk
- website:
www.aberdeenspringbankguesthouse.co.uk
or: www.aberdeen-guesthouse.co.uk

Guest House
M.F. Franklin, Callater Lodge, 9 Glenshee Road, BRAEMAR, Aberdeenshire AB35 5YQ
073397 41275
- e-mail: maria@hotel-braemar.co.uk
- website: www.hotel-braemar.co.uk

Self-Catering Chalet
Mrs J.M. Shaw, North East Farm Chalet, Sheriffston, ELGIN, Moray IV30 8LA
01343 842695
- e-mail: jennifer.shaw@moray.gov.uk

•ARGYLL & BUTE

Self-Catering / Caravan Lodges
Mr & Mrs I. Weir, Appin Holiday Homes,
APPIN, Argyll PA38 4BQ
01631 730287
- e-mail: info@appinholidayhomes.co.uk
- website: www.appinholidayhomes.co.uk

B & B
Mrs D. MacCormick, Mains Farm,
CARRADALE, Campbeltown,
Argyll PA28 6QG
01583 431216
- e-mail:
maccormick@mainsfarm.freeserve.co.uk

Self-Catering
Mrs Isabella Crawford, Blarghour Farm, Loch Awe-side, By DALMALLY,
Argyll PA33 1BW
01866 833246
- e-mail: blarghour@aol.com
- website: www.blarghour.com
or: www.self-catering-argyll.co.uk

Guest House
Mr J. Scott, Caladhsona, 53 Frederick
Crescent, Port Ellen, ISLAY, Argyll PA42 7BD
01496 302694
- e-mail: hamish.scott@lineone.net
- website: www.isle-of-islay.com/caladhsona

Self-Catering
B. & M. Phillips, Kilbride Croft, Balvicar,
ISLE OF SEIL, Argyll PA34 4RD
01852 300475
- e-mail: kilbridecroft@aol.com
- website: www.kilbridecroft.fsnet.co.uk

Self-Catering Cottage
East Shore, LOCH FYNE,
c/o J.F.A. Rankin, 12 Hamilton Place,
Perth PH1 1BB
01738 632580
- e-mail: john@claddie.co.uk
- website: www.claddie.co.uk

Self-Catering
Castle Sween Bay (Holidays) Ltd,
Ellery, LOCHGILPHEAD, Argyll PA31 8PA
01880 770232
- e-mail: info@ellary.com
- website: www.ellary.com

Hotel
Willowburn Hotel, Clachan Seil,
By OBAN, Argyll PA34 4TJ
01852 300276
 e-mail: willowburnhotel@virgin.net
- website: www.willowburn.co.uk

Self-Catering
Melfort Pier & Harbour, Kilmelford,
OBAN PA34 4XD
01852 200333
- e-mail: melharbour@aol.com
- website: www.scotland2000.com/melfort

Farm / Self-Catering
Mrs McCorkindale, Scammadale Farm,
Kilninver, By OBAN, PA34 4UU
01852 316282
- e-mail: scammadale@hotmail.com
- website: www.scammadale.co.uk

Self-Catering
Mr J. Hanna, Seaview Grazings Holidays,
STRONTIAN, Argyll, PH36 4HZ
01967 402191
- e-mail: seaviewgrazings@amserve.net
- website: www.ardnamurchan.com

Inn
George & Claire Primrose, Kilberry Inn,
Kilberry, By TARBERT, Argyll PA29 6YD
01880 770223
- e-mail: relax@kilberryinn.com
- website: www.kilberryinn.com

•AYRSHIRE & ARRAN

Farm B & B
Mary Watson, South Whittlieburn Farm,
Brisbane Glen, LARGS, Ayrshire, KA30 8SN
01475 675881
- e-mail: largsbandb@southwhittlieburnfarm.freeserve.co.uk
- website: www.SmoothHound.co.uk/hotels/whittlie.html

•BORDERS

Guest House
Mrs Ewen Kenworthy, St Albans, Clouds,
DUNS, Berwickshire TD11 3BB
01361 883285
- e-mail: st–albans@email.msn.com
- website: www.scotlandbordersbandb.co.uk

Self-Catering
Mrs Sarah Longland, Whitmuir Hall,
Whitmuir, SELKIRK, Borders TD7 4PZ
01750 20118
- e-mail: sarah.longland@tesco.net

Self-Catering
The Lodge Cottage, Tweed Flat & Garden
Flat, c/o Mr Michael Stephen, Woll House,
Woll Estate, Ashkirk, SELKIRK,
Borders TD7 4NY
01750 32381
- e-mail: accom@thewoll.com
- website: www.thewoll.com

Self-Catering
Slipperfield House, WEST LINTON,
Peeblesshire EH46 7AA
01968 660401
- e-mail: cottages@slipperfield.com
- website: www.slipperfield.com

**FREE or REDUCED RATE
entry to Holiday Visits
and Attractions
see our
READERS' OFFER
VOUCHERS
on pages 35-54**

•DUMFRIES & GALLOWAY

Self-Catering
Mr Ball, Barncrosh Leisure Co Ltd,
Barncrosh, CASTLE DOUGLAS,
Dumfries & Galloway DG7 1TX
01556 680216
- e-mail: enq@barncros.demon.co.uk
- website:
  www.aboutscotland.com/south/barncrosh.html

Hotel / Guest House
Mrs Nicki Proudlock, Mabie House Hotel,
Mabie, DUMFRIES,
Dumfries & Galloway DG2 8HB
01387 263188
- e-mail: niki@mabiehouse.co.uk
- website: www.mabiehouse.co.uk

Chalets, Caravans & Bunkhouses
Barnsoul Farm, Shawhead, DUMFRIES,
Dumfries & Galloway DG2 9SQ
01387 730249
- e-mail: barnsoul@aol.com
- website: www.barnsoulfarm.co.uk

Self-Catering
Mrs B. Gilbey, Rusko,
GATEHOUSE OF FLEET, Castle Douglas,
Dumfries & Galloway DG7 2BS
01557 814215
- e-mail: gilbey@rusko.demon.co.uk
- website: www.ruskoholidays.co.uk

Self-Catering
1 Ford View, Roughfirth, KIPPFORD,
Dumfries, c/o J.F. Copson, Dyke Nook,
Bassenthwaite, Cumbria.
- e-mail: fordview@lineone.net
- website: www.lakesandsea.addr.com
  or: www.dumfriesandgalloway.co.uk

Self-Catering
Mrs S.M. Finlay, Manor Cottage,
Ross Bay, KIRKCUDBRIGHT,
Kirkcudbrightshire DG6 4TR
01557 870381
- e-mail: finlay.baycottage@btinternet.com

•DUNDEE & ANGUS

B & B on a Farm
Rosemary Beatty, Brathinch Farm,
By BRECHIN, Angus DD9 7QX
01356 648292
- e-mail: adam.brathinch@btinternet.com

Hotel
Panmure Arms Hotel, 52 High Street,
EDZELL, Dundee & Angus DD9 7TA
01356 648950
- e-mail: david@panmurearmshotel.co.uk
- website: www.panmurearmshotel.co.uk

Self-Catering
Jenny Scott, Welton Farm, The Welton of
Kingoldrum, KIRRIEMUIR, Angus DD8 5HY
01575 574743
- e-mail: weltonholidays@btinternet.com
- website: www.cottageguide.co.uk/thewelton

•EDINBURGH & LOTHIANS

Guest House
Mr David Martin, Spylaw Bank House,
2 Spylaw Ave, Colinton, EDINBURGH,
Lothians EH13 0LR
0131 441 5022
- e-mail: angela@spylawbank.freeserve.co.uk
- website: www.spylawbank.freeserve.co.uk

Guest House
D. Green, Ivy Guest House, 7 Mayfield
Gardens, EDINBURGH, Lothians EH9 2AX
0131 667 3411
- e-mail: don@ivyguesthouse.com
- website: www.ivyguesthouse.com

Guest House
Dorothy Vidler, Kenvie Guest House,
16 Kilmaurs Road, EDINBURGH,
Lothians EH16 5DA
0131 668 1964
- e-mail: dorothy@kenvie.co.uk
- website: www.kenvie.co.uk

Guest House
McWilliams, Ben Craig Guest House,
3 Craigmillar Park, EDINBURGH,
Lothians EH16 5PG
0131 667 2593
- e-mail: bencraighouse@dial.pipex.com
- website: www.bencraighouse.co.uk

Self-Catering & Campus Accommodation
Edinburgh First, 18 Holyrood Park Road,
EDINBURGH, Lothians EH16 5AY
0800 0287118
- e-mail: edinburgh.first@ed.ac.uk
- website: www.edinburghfirst.com

Guest House
International Guest House, 31 Mayfield
Gardens, EDINBURGH, Lothians EH9 2BX
0131 667 2511
- e-mail: intergh@easynet.co.uk
- website: www.accommodation-edinburgh.com

WEBSITE DIRECTORY

B & B
McCrae's B&B, 44 East Claremont Street,
EDINBURGH, Lothians EH7 4JR
0131 556 2610
- e-mail: mccraes.bandb@lineone.net
- website:
  http://website.lineone.net/~mccraes.bandb

Guest House
M.F. Sandilands, 25 Queensferry Road,
EDINBURGH, Lothians EH4 3HB
0131 332 2057
- e-mail: SandilandsHouse@aol.com
- website: www.guesthouse-sandilands.com

•FIFE

Self-Catering & Farmhouse B & B
Morna H. Chrisp, Scotstarvit Farm,
CUPAR, Fife KY15 5PA
01334 653591
- e-mail: chrisp.scotstarvit@ukgateway.net
- website: www.scotstarvitfarm.co.uk

Guest House
Mrs MacDonald, Dunclutha Guest House,
16 Victoria Road, LEVEN, Fife KY8 4EX
01333 425515
- e-mail:
  pam.leven@dunclutha-accomm.demon.co.uk
- website:
  www.dunclutha-accomm.demon.co.uk

Self-Catering
Mrs Anne Scrimgeour, Woodland Holidays,
Kincaple Lodge, Kincaple, ST ANDREWS,
Fife KY16 9SH
01334 850217
- e-mail: jim@woodlandholidays.co.uk
- website: www.woodlandholidays.co.uk

•GLASGOW

Hotel
Argyll Hotel, 973 Sauchiehall Street,
GLASGOW, G3 7TQ
0141 337 3313
- e-mail: info@argyllhotelglasgow.co.uk
- website: www.argyllhotelglasgow.co.uk

Guest House
Kirkland House, 42 St Vincent Crescent,
GLASGOW, G3 8NG
0141 248 3458
- e-mail: admin@kirkland.gispnet.com
- website:
  www.s-h-systems.co.uk/hotels/kirkland.html

•HIGHLANDS

Self-Catering
Mrs Murray, Cairngorm Highland
Bungalows, Glen Einich, 29 Grampian View,
AVIEMORE, Inverness-shire PH22 1TF
01479 810653
- e-mail: linda.murray@virgin.net
- website: www.cairngorm-bungalows.co.uk

B & B / Self-Catering
Gill Kirkpatrick, Kerrow House, Cannich,
By BEAULY, Inverness-shire IV4 7NA
01456 415243
- e-mail: gill@kerrow-house.demon.co.uk
- website: www.kerrow-house.demon.co.uk

Hotel
The Boat Hotel, BOAT OF GARTEN,
Inverness-shire IV25 3SD
01479 831258
- e-mail: holidays@boathotel.co.uk
- website: www.boathotel.co.uk

Guest House
Mrs Lynn Benge, The Pines Country House,
Duthil, CARRBRIDGE,
Inverness-shire PH23 3ND
01479 841220
- e-mail: lynnfhg@thepines-duthil.fsnet.co.uk
- website: www.thepines-duthil.fsnet.co.uk

Self-Catering
Agnes Strachan, Balblair Cottages, CROY,
Inverness-shire IV2 5PH
01667 493407
- e-mail: b.strachan@virgin.net
- website: www.balblaircottages.co.uk

Self-Catering / Guest House
Mr A. Allan, Torguish Self-Catering & B&B,
DAVIOT, Inverness-shire IV2 5XQ
01463 772208
- e-mail: torguish@torguish.com
- website: www.torguish.com

Guest House B & B
Mrs Sandra Silke, Westwood,
Lower Balmacaan, DRUMNADROCHIT,
Inverness-shire IV63 6WU
01456 450826
- e-mail: sandra@westwoodbb.freeserve.co.uk
- website: www.westwoodbb.freeserve.co.uk

Hotel
Clan Macduff Hotel, Achintore Road,
FORT WILLIAM, Inverness-shire PH33 6RW
01397 702341
- e-mail: reception@clanmacduff.co.uk
- website: www.clanmacduff.co.uk

WEBSITE DIRECTORY 211

Farm
Mrs H. Gunn, Achintee Farm, Glen Nevis,
FORT WILLIAM, Inverness-shire PH33 6TE
01397 705899
- e-mail: achintee.accom@glennevis.com
- website: www.glennevis.com

Self-Catering
Mr & Mrs W. Murray, Springwell Holiday
Homes, Onich, FORT WILLIAM,
Inverness-shire PH33 6RY
01855 821257
- e-mail: info@springwellholidayhomes.co.uk
- website: www.springwellholidayhomes.co.uk

Guest House
Norma E. McCallum, The Neuk, Corpach,
FORT WILLIAM, Inverness-shire PH33 7LR
01397 772244
- e-mail: normamccallum@theneuk.fsbusiness.co.uk
- website: www.fortwilliamguesthouse.com

Guest House
Mrs M. Matheson, Thistle Cottage, Torlundy,
FORT WILLIAM, Inverness-shire PH33 6SN
01397 702428
- website: www.thistlescotland.co.uk

Guest House
Mr & Mrs McQueen, Stronchreggan View
Guest House, Achintore Road, FORT
WILLIAM, Inverness-shire PH33 6RW
01397 704644
- e-mail: patricia@apmac.freeserve.co.uk
- website: www.stronchreggan.co.uk

Self-Catering
Alvie Estate Office, Kincraig,
KINGUSSIE PH21 1NE
01540 651255
- e-mail: info@alvie-estate.co.uk
- website: www.alvie-estate.co.uk

Self-Catering
Fernlea, Main Street, LAIRG, c/o H. Corbett,
24 Achfrish, Shinness, LAIRG,
Sutherland IV27 4DN
01549 402223
- e-mail: lairg_selfcater@yahoo.co.uk
- website: www.uk.geocities.com/lairg_selfcater/hh.html

Self-Catering
A.G. MacKenzie, Stromecarronach,
LOCHCARRON WEST, Strathcarron,
Ross-shire
01520 722289
- website: www.wester-ross.com

Guest House
Gary Clulow, Sunset Guest House, MORAR,
by Mallaig, Inverness-shire PH40 4PA
01687 462259
- e-mail: sunsetgh@aol.com
- website: www.sunsetguesthouse.co.uk

Self-Catering
Birchfield Cottages, Birchfield,
NETHYBRIDGE, Inverness-shire PH25 3DD
01479 821613
- e-mail: collins@birchcot.freeserve.co.uk
- website: www.nethybridge.com/birchfield.htm

Self-Catering
Mr A. Urquhart, Crofters Cottages,
15 Croft, POOLEWE, Ross-shire IV22 2SY
01445 781268
- e-mail: croftcottage@faxvia.net
- website: www.scotia-sc.com/335a.htm

Self-Catering
Mr Hughes, Innes Maree Bungalows,
POOLEWE, Ross-shire IV22 2JU
01445 781454
- e-mail: info@poolewebungalows.com
- website: www.poolewebungalows.com

Hotel
Mrs Helen Fish, Rhiconich Hotel,
RHICONICH, Sutherland IV27 4RN
01971 521224
- e-mail: helen&ray@rhiconichhotel.co.uk
- website: www.rhiconichhotel.co.uk

Self-Catering
Mr Foley, Bunroy Holiday Park, ROYBRIDGE,
Inverness-shire PH31 4AG
01397 712332
- e-mail: bunroy@btinternet.com
- website: www.bunroy.co.uk

Holiday Caravans / B & B
Mrs M.H. Cairns, Invergloy House,
SPEAN BRIDGE, Inverness-shire PH34 4DY
01397 712681
- e-mail: cairns@invergloy-house.co.uk
- website: www.invergloy-house.co.uk

Self-Catering
Riverside Lodges, Invergloy,
SPEAN BRIDGE,
Inverness-shire PH34 4DY
01397 712684
- e-mail: enquiries@riversidelodge.org.uk
- website: www.riversidelodge.org.uk

Hotel
Mansfield House Hotel, Scotsburn Road,
TAIN, Ross-shire IV19 1PR
01862 892052
- e-mail: mansfield@cali.co.uk
- website: www.mansfield-house.co.uk

212 WEBSITE DIRECTORY

Self-Catering
David & Sheila Green, Stac Pollaidh
Self-Catering, Achnahaird, Achiltibuie,
ULLAPOOL IV26 2YT
01854 622340
• e-mail: sheilagreen@hotmail.com
• website: www.stacpollaidh.com

Self-Catering
Taigh a' Bhraoin, Loch Broom, ULLAPOOL,
c/o Mrs McKenzie, 1 Hillhouse Place,
Stewarton Ayrshire KA3 3HT
01560 484003
• e-mail: mary@taighabhraoin.freeserve.co.uk
• website: www.taighabhraoin.freeserve.co.uk

•LANARKSHIRE

Guest House / Farm
Mrs Heather Stephens, Blairmains Farm,
HARTHILL, Shotts, Lanarkshire ML7 5TJ
01501 751278
• e-mail: heather@blairmains.freeserve.co.uk
• website: www.blairmains.co.uk

•PERTH & KINROSS

Self-Catering / Caravan / Farm
Kenmore Caravan & Camping Park & Mains
of Taymouth Cottages,
Mains of Taymouth, Kenmore, ABERFELDY,
Perthshire PH15 2HN
01887 830226
• e-mail: info@taymouth.co.uk
• website: www.taymouth.co.uk

Self-Catering
A & J Duncan Millar, Loch Tay Lodges,
Remony, ABERFELDY,
Perthshire PH15 2HR
01887 830209
• e-mail: remony@btinternet.com
• website: www.lochtaylodges.co.uk

Hotel / Self-Catering
Dalmunzie House Hotel, Glenshee,
BLAIRGOWRIE, Perthshire PH10 7QG
01250 885224
• e-mail: dalmunzie@aol.com
• website: www.welcome.to/dalmunzie

Self-Catering
Laighwood Holidays, Laighwood,
Butterstone, By DUNKELD,
Perthshire PH8 0HB
01350 724241
• e-mail: holidays@laighwood.co.uk
• website: www.laighwood.co.uk

Self Catering
Mrs Hunt, Wester Lix Holiday Cottages,
Wester Lix, KILLIN, Perthshire FK21 8RD
01567 820990
• e-mail: gill@westerlix.co.uk
• website: www.westerlix.co.uk

Self-Catering
The Luggie, KIRKMICHAEL, c/o George &
Andrea Hay, 3 Rosemount Place, PERTH,
Perthshire PH2 7EH
01738 625240
• e-mail: andrea.hay@cableinet.co.uk
• website: www.assc.co.uk/luggie

Self-Catering
Pamela & Lawrence Hopkins, Earnknowe,
LOCHEARNHEAD, Perthshire FK19 8PY
01567 830238
• e-mail: enquiries@earnknowe.co.uk
• website: www.earnknowe.co.uk

Guest House
Jacky Catterall, Tulloch Enochdhu,
By PITLOCHRY, Perthshire PH10 7PW
01250 881404
• e-mail: maljac@tulloch83.freeserve.co.uk
• website: www.econet.org.uk/tulloch

Hotel
Killiecrankie Hotel, Pass of Killiecrankie,
By PITLOCHRY, Perthshire PH16 5LG
01796 473220
• e-mail: enquiries@killiecrankiehotel.co.uk
• website: www.killiecrankiehotel.co.uk

Hotel / Apartment
Balrobin Hotel, Higher Oakfield,
PITLOCHRY, Pethshire PH16 5HT
01796 472901
• e-mail: info@balrobin.co.uk
• website: www.balrobin.co.uk

B & B / Self-Catering
Ian & Christine, Oakbank, 20 Lower Oakfield,
PITLOCHRY, Perthshire PH16 5DS
01796 472080
• e-mail: ian@oakburn.clara.co.uk
• website:
www.SmoothHound.co.uk/hotels/oakburn

Guest House / Self-Catering
Yvonne & John Howes, Ardoch Lodge,
STRATHYRE, Perthshire FK18 8NF
01877 384666
• e-mail: ardoch@btinternet.com
• website: www.ardochlodge.co.uk

Please mention
Britain's Best Holidays
when enquiring about accommodation

WEBSITE DIRECTORY

•STIRLING & TROSSACHS

B & B / Self-Catering

Mrs A.J. Heaney, Invertrossachs Country House, CALLANDER, Perthshire FK17 8HG
01877 331126
- e-mail: reservations@invertrossachs.co.uk
- website: www.invertrossachs.co.uk

Guest House / Farm

Mrs Jennifer Steel, The Topps Farm, DENNY, Stirlingshire FK6 5JF
01324 822471
- e-mail: 2lambs@onetel.net.uk
- website: www.thetopps.com

•ISLE OF SKYE

Self-Catering

Cottage in HARLOSH, c/o Mrs I. MacDiarmid, 21 Dunrobin Avenue, ELDERSLIE, Renfrewshire PA5 9NW
01505 324460
- website: www.self-catering-homes.com/skyeweb

Guest House / B & B

Fiona Scott, Blairdhu House, Old Kyle Farm Road, KYLEAKIN, Isle of Skye IV41 8PR
01599 534760
- e-mail: blairdhuskye@compuserve.com
- website: http://ourworld.compuserve.com/homepages/blairdhuskye

Self-Catering

Islands & Highlands Cottages, Bridge Road, PORTREE, Isle of Skye IV51 9ER
01478 612123
- website: www.ihc.ndirect.co.uk

•ORKNEY ISLES

Self-Catering

Jean Craigie, Hall of Clestrain, STROMNESS, Orkney
01856 850 365
- e-mail: jeancraigie@compuserve.com
- website: www.hallofclestrain.com

Readers are requested to mention this guidebook when seeking accommodation

---

•WALES

•ANGLESEY & GWYNEDD

Self-Catering / Caravan

Plas y Bryn Chalet Park, Bontnewydd, CAERNARFON, Gwynedd LL54 7YE
01786 672811
- e-mail: philplasybryn@aol.com
- website: www.plasybrynholidayscaernarfon.co.uk

Self-Catering

Anwen Jones, Betws Bach, Ynys, CRICCIETH, Gwynedd LL52 0PB
01758 720047
- e-mail: cottages@rhos.freeserve.co.uk
- website: www.rhos-cottages.co.uk

Farm B & B

Judy Hutchings, Tal y Foel, DWYRAN, Anglesey Gwynedd LL61 6LQ
01248 430377
- e-mail: riding@talyfoel.u-net.com
- website: www.tal-y-foel.co.uk

Self-Catering

Plas Cadnant Estate, MENAI BRIDGE Isle of Anglesey LL59 5NH
01248 717007
- e-mail: enquiries@plascadnantestate.co.uk
- website: www.plascadnantestate.co.uk

Farm Cottage Self-Catering

Mrs C.A. Jones, Rhedyn, MYNYTHO, Pwllheli, Gwynedd LL53 7PS
01758 740669
- e-mail: katie@rhedyn.freeserve.co.uk
- website: www.rhedyn.freeserve.co.uk

Caravan

Mrs C. Jones, Parc Wernol, Chwilog, PWLLHELI, Gwynedd LL53 6SW
01766 810506
- e-mail: catherine@wernol.com
- website: www.wernol.com

•NORTH WALES

Guest House / Self-Catering

Jim & Lilian Boughton, Bron Celyn Guest House, Lôn Muriau, Llanrwst Road, BETWS-Y-COED North Wales LL24 0HD
01690 710333
- e-mail: broncelyn@betws-y-coed.co.uk
- website: www.betws-y-coed.co.uk/broncelyn

WEBSITE DIRECTORY

Guest House
Mr & Mrs D. Pender, Bryn Bella Guest House, Llanrwst Road, BETWS-Y-COED, Gwynedd LL24 0HD
01690 710627
- e-mail: **brynbella@clara.net**
- website: **www.brynbella.co.uk**

Hotel
Fairy Glen Hotel, Dolwyddelan Road, BETWS-Y-COED, North Wales LL24 0SH
01690 710269
- e-mail: **fairyglen@amserve.net**
- website: **www.fairyglenhotel.co.uk**

Guest House
Mrs V.J. Watson-Jones, Glan Heulog Guest House, Llanrwst Road, CONWY, North Wales LL32 8LT
01492 593845
- e-mail: **glanheulog@no1guesthouse.freeserve.co.uk**
- website: **www.walesbandb.com**

Hotel
Caerlyr Hall Hotel, Conwy Old Road, Penmaenmawr, CONWY, North Wales LL34 6SW
01492 623518
- website: www.nwi.co.uk/snowdonia/caerlyrhall/in or: **www.caerlyrhallhotel.co.uk**

Hotel
Mrs B. Baldon, Tal y Bont, CONWY, Gwynedd LL32 8YX
01492 660766
- e-mail: **bbaldon@lodgehotel.co.uk**
- website: **www.lodgehotel.co.uk**

Hotel
Hafod Country Hotel, TREFRIW, North Wales LL27 0RQ
01492 640029
- e-mail: **hafod@breathemail.net**
- website: **www.hafodhouse.co.uk**

Caravans
Sun Valley Caravan Park, Marsh Road, Rhuddlan, North Wales LL18 5UD
01745 590269/07831 647568
website: **www.sunvalley.org.uk**

• CARDIGANSHIRE

Hotel
Highcliffe Hotel, School Road, ABERPORTH, Cardiganshire SA43 2DA
01239 810534
- e-mail: **ConwDJ@aol.com**
- website: **www.highcliffehotel.co.uk**

Self-Catering
Mr J.A. Tucker, Penffynnon, ABERPORTH, Cardiganshire SA43 2DA
01239 810387
- e-mail: **tt@lineone.net** or: **jann@aberporth.com**
- website:**www.aberporth.com**

Hotel
George Borrow Hotel, Ponterwyd, ABERYSTWYTH, Ceredigion, Cardiganshire SY23 3AD
01970 890230
- e-mail: **georgeborrow@clara.net**
- website: **www.george-borrow.co.uk**

Self-Catering
Anna & Graham Giles, Brongwyn Cottages, Brongwyn Mawr, Penparc, Cardigan SA43 1SA
01239 613644
- e-mail: **enquiries@cardiganholidays.co.uk**
- website: **www.cardiganholidays.co.uk**

Guest House
Bryn Berwyn, Tresaith, CARDIGAN, Cardiganshire SA43 2JG
01239 811126
- e-mail: **enq@brynberwyn.com**
- website: **www.brynberwyn.com**

Caravan Park
Manorafon Caravan Park, Sarnau, LLANDYSUL, Cardiganshire SA44 6QH
01239 810564
- e-mail: **manorafon@ukgateway.net**

Holiday Park
The Village Holiday Park, Cross Inn, NEW QUAY, Cardiganshire SA44 6LW
Tel: 01545 560624
- website: **www.oceanheights.co.uk**

• PEMBROKESHIRE

Self-Catering
John Lloyd, East Llanteg Farm Holiday Cottages, Llanteg, Near AMROTH, Pembrokeshire SA67 8QA
01834 831336
- e-mail: **john@pembrokeshireholiday.co.uk**
- website: **www.pembrokeshireholiday.co.uk**

Self-Catering
Quality Cottages, Cerbid, Solva, HAVERFORDWEST, Pembrokeshire SA62 6YE
01348 837871
- website: **www.qualitycottages.co.uk**

Farm B & B
Mrs Margaret Williams, Skerryback, Sandy Haven, St Ishmaels, HAVERFORDWEST, Pembrokeshire SA62 3DN
01646 636598
- e-mail: williams@farmersweekly.net
- website: www.pfh.co.uk/skerryback

Caravan - Static & Touring
Nolton Cross Caravan Park, Nolton, HAVERFORDWEST, Pembrokeshire SA62 3NP
01437 710701
- e-mail: noltoncross@nolton.fsnet.co.uk
- website: www.noltoncross-holidays.co.uk

Self-Catering
Mr Peter Davies, Character Cottages St Davids, Llaethdy, White Sands, ST DAVIDS, Pembrokeshire SA62 6PR
01437 721831
- website: www.stdavidsholidays.co.uk

Self-Catering
Steve & Sheila Craft, Felindre Cottages, Porthgain, ST DAVIDS, Pembrokeshire SA62 5BH
01348 831220
- e-mail: steve@felindrecottages.co.uk
- website: www.felindrecottages.co.uk

Self-Catering
Lower Moor Cottages, c/o Thelma M Hardman, High View, Catherine Street, ST DAVIDS, Pembrokeshire SA62 6RJ
01437 720616
- e-mail: enquiries@lowermoorcottages.co.uk
- website: www.lowermoorcottages.co.uk

Guest House
Mrs S.J. Thompson, Ramsey House, Lower Moor, ST DAVIDS, Pembrokeshire SA62 6RP
01437 720321
- e-mail: ramseyho.stdavids@btinternet.com
- website: www.SmoothHound.co.uk/hotels/ramsey.html

Farm Guest House
Mrs Morfydd Jones, Lochmeyler Farm Guest House, Llandeloy, Pen-y-Cwm, Nr SOLVA, St Davids, Pembs SA62 6LL
01348 837724
- e-mail: stay@lochmeyler.co.uk
- website: www.lochmeyler.co.uk

B & B
Mr & Mrs Narman, The Old Vicarage, Penally, TENBY, Pembrokeshire SA70 7PN
01834 842773
- e-mail: theoldvicarage@happy-holidays.co.uk
- website: www.happy-holidays.co.uk

Self-Catering Cottages
Mrs A. Colledge, Gwarmacwydd, Llanfallteg, WHITLAND, Pembrokeshire SA34 0XH
01437 563260
- e-mail: info@a-farm-holiday.org
- website: www.a-farm-holiday.org

•POWYS

B & B / Self-Catering
Laura Kostoris, Erw yr Danty, Talybont-on-Usk, BRECON, Powys LD3 7YN
01874 676498
- e-mail: kosto@ukonline.co.uk
- website: www.wi2.to/lifestyle/

Self-Catering
Julie Pugh, Crickie Farm, Llangorse, BRECON, Powys LD3 7TU
01874 658373
- e-mail: pughcrickie@aol.com
- website: www.crickiefarm.com

Guest House
Mr & Mrs Stephen & Melanie Dale, Beacons Guest House, BRECON, Powys LD3 8AH
01874 623339
- e-mail: beacons@brecon.co.uk
- website: www.beacons.brecon.co.uk

Guest House
Login House, Trecastle, BRECON, Powys LD3 8UP
01874 638030
- e-mail: charlotteroskill@btconnect.com
- website: www.loginhouse.co.uk

Motel / Caravans
The Park Motel, Crossgates, LLANDRINDOD WELLS, Powys LD1 6RF
01597 851201
- e-mail: lisa@theparkmotel.freeserve.co.uk
- website: www.theparkmotel.freeserve.co.uk

Caravan Park
Mr Golding, The Pines Caravan Park, Doldowlod, LLANDRINDOD WELLS, Powys LD1 6NN
01597 810068
- e-mail: info@pinescaravanpark.co.uk
- website: www.pinescaravanpark.co.uk

Farm / Board
Mrs C.E.A. Gilson, Pentre, Pontrobert, MEIFOD, Montgomeryshire SY22 6JL
01691 648348
- e-mail: pentre@btclick.com
- website: http://home.btclick.com/pentre

216 WEBSITE DIRECTORY

Farm B & B / Self-Catering
Lena Mary Powell, Gigrin Farm, South Street, RHAYADER, Powys LD6 5BL
01597 810243
• e-mail: accomm@gigrin.co.uk
• website: www.gigrin.co.uk

•SOUTH WALES

Narrowboat Holidays
Beacon Park Boats, The Boathouse, Llanfoist Wharf, ABERGAVENNY, Monmouthshire NP7 9NG
01873 858277
• e-mail: info@beaconparkboats.com
• website: www.beaconparkboats.com

Hotel / B & B
Owen Sims, Manager Customer Services, Welsh Institute of Sports, Sophia Gardens, CARDIFF, South Wales CF11 9SW
029 2030 0500
• e-mail: wis@scw.co.uk
• website: www.sports-council-wales.co.uk

Guest House / B & B
Mrs Sue Beer, Plas Llanmihangel, Llanmihangel, Near COWBRIDGE, South Wales CF71 7LQ
01446 774610
• e-mail: plasllanmihangel@ukonline.co.uk

Hotel
Mark Cottell, Culver House Hotel, Port Eynon, GOWER, Swansea, South Wales SA3 1NN
01792 390755
• e-mail: info@culverhousehotel.co.uk
• website: www.culverhousehotel.co.uk

Hotel
Hillcrest House Hotel, Higher Lane, MUMBLES, Swansea, South Wales SA3 4NS
01792 363700
• e-mail: stay@hillcresthousehotel.com
• website: www.hillcresthousehotel.com

Guest House
Chapel Guest House, Church Road, ST BRIDES WENTLOOG, Near Newport, Gwent, South Wales NP10 8SN
01633 681018
• e-mail: chapelguesthouse@hotmail.com
• website: www.SmoothHound.co.uk

B & B
Jan Murphy, Fairyland B&B, 91-93 Alexandra Road, Gorseinon, SWANSEA, South Wales SA4 4NU
01792 897940
• e-mail: fairyland@breakfasttime.co.uk
• website: www.ntl.com/~jmurphy/

Self-Catering
Mrs J.E. Phillips, 71 Tycoch Road, Tycoch, SWANSEA, South Wales SA2 9EG
01792 208658
• website: www.stay-at-oxwich.co.uk

Hotel
Worms Head Hotel, Rhossili, Gower, SWANSEA, South Wales SA3 1PP
01792 390512
• website: http://thewormshead.co.uk

•IRELAND

•Co CLARE

Self-Catering
George Quinn, Ballyvaughan Village & Country Holiday Homes, Frances Street, BALLYVAUGHAN, Kilrush, Co Clare
00353 659 051977
• e-mail: sales@ballyvaughan-cottages.com
• website: www.ballyvaughan-cottages.com

•Co MAYO

Caravan & Camping / Self-catering
Belleek Caravan & Camping Park, BALLINA, Co. Mayo
00353 9671533
• e-mail: lenahan@indigo.ie
• website: http://indigo.ie/~lenahan

•Co WATERFORD

B & B
Nora Harte, Cnoc-na-Ri, Nire Valley, BALLYMACARBRY, Co Waterford
0035352 36239
• e-mail: mharte@ireland.com
• website: http://homepage.eircom.net/~cnocnari/

Index of towns and counties.
Please also refer to Contents page 31

Aberdeen	ABERDEEN, BANFF & MORAY
Aberfeldy	PERTH & KINROSS
Alnwick	NORTHUMBERLAND
Alvechurch	WORCESTERSHIRE
Ambleside	CUMBRIA
Anstruther	FIFE
Appin	ARGYLL & BUTE
Arran	AYRSHIRE & ARRAN
Ashbourne	DERBYSHIRE
Ashburton	DEVON
Ashkirk	BORDERS
Ayr	AYRSHIRE & ARRAN
Barnstaple	DEVON
Bath	SOMERSET
Beaminster	DORSET
Berrynarbor	DEVON
Bideford	DEVON
Biggar	LANARKSHIRE
Bodmin	CORNWALL
Braunton	DEVON
Brecon	POWYS
Bridlington	EAST YORKSHIRE
Brighton	EAST SUSSEX
Brixham	DEVON
Bude	CORNWALL
Caernarfon	ANGLESEY & GWYNEDD
Callander	STIRLING & THE TROSSACHS
Cambridge	CAMBRIDGESHIRE
Cardigan	CARDIGANSHIRE
Carlisle	CUMBRIA
Castle Douglas	DUMFRIES & GALLOWAY
Cockermouth	CUMBRIA
Colchester	SUFFOLK
Criccieth	ANGLESEY & GWYNEDD
Crieff	PERTH & KINROSS
Croy	HIGHLANDS (SOUTH)
Culloden	HIGHLANDS (SOUTH)
Cupar	FIFE
Dalbeattie	DUMFRIES & GALLOWAY
Dalmally	ARGYLL & BUTE
Danby	NORTH YORKSHIRE
Dawlish Warren	DEVON
Dorchester	DORSET
Dunfermline	FIFE
Dunkeld	PERTH & KINROSS
Duns	BORDERS
Eastbourne	SUSSEX EAST
Edinburgh	EDINBURGH & LOTHIANS
Edzell	DUNDEE & ANGUS
Elgin	ABERDEEN, BANFF & MORAY
Exeter	DEVON
Exmoor	SOMERSET
Fairlight	EAST SUSSEX
Falkland	FIFE
Falmouth	CORNWALL
Faringdon	OXFORDSHIRE
Fordingbridge	HAMPSHIRE
Fort William	HIGHLANDS (SOUTH)
Gatehouse of Fleet	DUMFRIES & GALLOWAY
Gigha	ISLE OF GIGHA
Gloucester	GLOUCESTERSHIRE
Great Yarmouth	NORFOLK
Harrogate	NORTH YORKSHIRE
Hawkshead	CUMBRIA
Hayle	CORNWALL
Holsworthy	DEVON
Hope Cove	DEVON
Horning	NORFOLK
Ilfracombe	DEVON
Ilminster	SOMERSET
Invergarry	HIGHLANDS (SOUTH)
Inverurie	ABERDEEN, BANFF & MORAY
Isle of Gigha	ARGYLL & BUTE
Jedburgh	BORDERS
Kelso	BORDERS
Kennford	DEVON
Kessingland	SUFFOLK
Keswick	CUMBRIA
Kincraig	HIGHLANDS (SOUTH)
Kingussie	HIGHLANDS (SOUTH)
Kirkoswald	CUMBRIA
Kirriemuir	DUNDEE & ANGUS
Lairg	HIGHLANDS (NORTH)
Lake District	CUMBRIA
Lewes	EAST SUSSEX
Llandudno	NORTH WALES
Llanteg	PEMBROKESHIRE
Loch Earn	PERTH & KINROSS
Lochgilphead	ARGYLL & BUTE
Lochinver	HIGHLANDS (NORTH)
London	LONDON
Looe	CORNWALL
Lowestoft	SUFFOLK
Lydney	GLOUCESTERSHIRE
Lymington	HAMPSHIRE
Middlewich	CHESHIRE
Minehead	SOMERSET

INDEX OF TOWNS/COUNTIES

Newcastleton	BORDERS	St Keverne	CORNWALL
Newcastleton	CUMBRIA	Silloth-on-Solway	CUMBRIA
Newquay	CORNWALL	Slapton	DEVON
Newton Abbot	DEVON	Southport	LANCASHIRE
Newtonmore	HIGHLANDS (SOUTH)	Spean Bridge	HIGHLANDS (SOUTH)
Niton Undercliffe	ISLE OF WIGHT	Stanley	PERTH & KINROSS
North Cumbria	CUMBRIA	Stow-On-The-Wold	GLOUCESTERSHIRE
Oban	ARGYLL & BUTE	Studland Bay	DORSET
Odiham	HAMPSHIRE	Tarbert	ARGYLL & BUTE
Onich	HIGHLANDS (SOUTH)	Tewkesbury	GLOUCESTERSHIRE
Paignton	DEVON	Tintagel	CORNWALL
Perth	PERTH & KINROSS	Torpoint	CORNWALL
Polperro	CORNWALL	Torquay	DEVON
Poolewe	HIGHLANDS (MID)	Troon	AYRSHIRE & ARRAN
Pooley Bridge	CUMBRIA	Ullswater	CUMBRIA
Pooley Bridge/Lake Ullswater	CUMBRIA	Wadebridge	CORNWALL
Porlock	SOMERSET	Wareham	DORSET
Preston Brook	CHESHIRE	Wasdale	CUMBRIA
Pwllheli	ANGLESEY & GWYNEDD	Watchet	SOMERSET
Rugby	WARWICKSHIRE	Wells	SOMERSET
St Brides Wentloog	SOUTH WALES	Woolacombe	DEVON
St Ives	CORNWALL	York	NORTH YORKSHIRE

Other specialised

FHG PUBLICATIONS

Published annually: available in all good bookshops or direct from the publisher.

- Recommended COUNTRY HOTELS OF BRITAIN   £5.25
- Recommended WAYSIDE & COUNTRY INNS OF BRITAIN   £5.25
- Recommended SHORT BREAK HOLIDAYS IN BRITAIN   £5.25
- PETS WELCOME!   £6.75
- B&B IN BRITAIN   £4.25
- THE GOLF GUIDE Where to Play / Where to Stay   £9.99

FHG PUBLICATIONS LTD
Abbey Mill Business Centre,
Seedhill, Paisley, Renfrewshire PA1 ITJ

Tel: 0141-887 0428 • Fax: 0141-889 7204
e-mail: fhg@ipcmedia.com • website: www.holidayguides.com

OTHER FHG TITLES FOR 2002

FHG Publications have a large range of attractive holiday accommodation guides for all kinds of holiday opportunities throughout Britain. They also make useful gifts at any time of year. Our guides are available in most bookshops and larger newsagents but we will be happy to post you a copy direct if you have any difficulty. POST FREE for addresses in the UK. We will also post abroad but have to charge separately for post or freight.

The original
Farm Holiday Guide to COAST & COUNTRY HOLIDAYS
in England, Scotland, Wales and Channel Islands.
Board, Self-catering, Caravans/Camping, Activity Holidays.

BED AND BREAKFAST STOPS
Over 1000 friendly and comfortable overnight stops.
Non-smoking, Disabled and Special Diets Supplements.

SELF-CATERING HOLIDAYS in Britain
Over 1000 addresses throughout for self-catering and caravans in Britain.

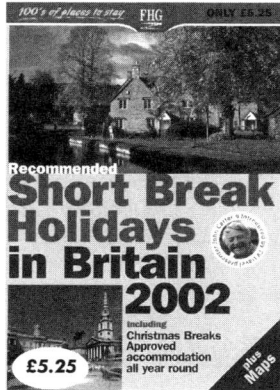

Recommended
WAYSIDE AND COUNTRY INNS of Britain
Pubs, Inns and small hotels.

Recommended
COUNTRY HOTELS OF BRITAIN
Including Country Houses, for the discriminating.

Recommended
SHORT BREAK HOLIDAYS IN BRITAIN
"Approved" accommodation for quality bargain breaks.

CHILDREN WELCOME! ☐
Family Holidays and Attractions guide.
Family holidays with details of amenities for children and babies.

**The GOLF GUIDE –
Where to play Where to stay** ☐
In association with GOLF MONTHLY. Over 2800 golf courses in Britain with convenient accommodation. Holiday Golf in France, Portugal, Spain, USA, South Africa and Thailand.

PETS WELCOME! ☐
The original and unique guide for holidays for pet owners and their pets.

The FHG Guide to **CARAVAN & CAMPING HOLIDAYS**, £4.25 ☐
Caravans for hire, sites and holiday parks and centres.

B&B IN BRITAIN, £4.25 ☐
100's of choices for touring and holidays in Britain. Airports, Ferries and Channel Tunnel Supplement.

Tick your choice and send your order and payment to ....

FHG PUBLICATIONS, ABBEY MILL BUSINESS CENTRE, SEEDHILL, PAISLEY PA1 1TJ
TEL: 0141- 887 0428; FAX: 0141- 889 7204
e-mail: fhg@ipcmedia.com
Deduct 10% for 2/3 titles or copies; 20% for 4 or more.

FHG

Send to: NAME...
          ADDRESS ....
          ....
          ....
          POST CODE ....
I enclose Cheque/Postal Order for £...
          SIGNATURE ....DATE ....

Please complete the following to help us improve the service we provide. How did you find out about our guides?:

☐ Press   ☐ Magazines   ☐ TV/Radio   ☐ Family/Friend   ☐ Other